St Antony's Series
Series Standing Order ISBN 0–333–71109–2
(*outside North America only*)

You can receive future titles in this series as they are published by placing a standing order. Please contact your bookseller or, in case of difficulty, write to us at the address below with your name and address, the title of the series and the ISBN quoted above.

Customer Services Department, Macmillan Distribution Ltd, Houndmills, Basingstoke, Hampshire RG21 6XS, England

Politics, the Military, and National Security in Jordan, 1955–1967

Lawrence Tal

First published 2002 by
PALGRAVE MACMILLAN
Houndmills, Basingstoke, Hampshire RG21 6XS and
175 Fifth Avenue, New York, N.Y. 10010
Companies and representatives throughout the world

PALGRAVE MACMILLAN is the global academic imprint of the Palgrave Macmillan division of St. Martin's Press, LLC and of Palgrave Macmillan Ltd. Macmillan® is a registered trademark in the United States, United Kingdom and other countries. Palgrave is a registered trademark in the European Union and other countries.

ISBN 0–333–96398–9

This book is printed on paper suitable for recycling and made from fully managed and sustained forest sources.

A catalogue record for this book is available from the British Library.

Library of Congress Cataloging-in-Publication Data
Tal, Lawrence, 1962–
        Politics, the military and national security in Jordan 1955–1967 /
        Lawrence Tal.
            p. cm. – (St. Antony's series)
        Includes bibliographical references and index.
        ISBN 0–333–96398–9
            1. Jordan – Politics and government – 1952–1999. 2. Jordan – Military policy. 3. National security – Jordan. I. Title. II. St. Antony's series (Palgrave (Firm))

        DS154.55 .T334 2002
        956.9504'3—dc21   2002072331

10   9   8   7   6   5   4   3   2   1
11   10   09   08   07   06   05   04   03   02

Printed and bound in Great Britain by
Antony Rowe Ltd, Chippenham and Eastbourne

Contents

List of Illustrations

Notes on Transliteration and Usage

The only diacriticals included in the Arabic transliteration are `ayns (`) and hamzas ('). Commonly accepted English forms, particularly those used in Foreign Office and Department of State diplomatic correspondence, are used for some personal and place names. For example, Hussein, Abdullah, Faisal, Abdel Nasser, Saud, and Amman are used throughout the text and notes.

Acknowledgements

This book could not have been completed without the assistance and advice of colleagues in Jordan, the United States, and Britain.

In Jordan, I thank: Yusef Abdel Qadir al-Tell, Moraiwid al-Tell, and Tariq al-Tell for their encouragement and help in arranging interviews; Majd al-Ma`ayta and other archivists at the Department of Libraries, Documentation, and National Archives, Ministry of Information; Aysa al-Juhmani at the Directorate of Press and Publications, Ministry of Information; the staff of the Hashemite Room, University Library, University of Jordan; and historian Suleiman Musa for his advice on archival sources on the kingdom.

In the United States and Britain, I am grateful for the kind assistance I received from the staffs of the National Archives in Washington, DC; the Public Record Office in Kew, London; the Bodleian Library at the University of Oxford; and the Private Papers Collection, Middle East Centre, St Antony's College, Oxford.

In Oxford, Avi Shlaim deserves a debt of gratitude for his constructive advice and challenge throughout this project. I also thank Roger Owen, Derek Hopwood, Eugene Rogan, and Philip Robins for their helpful comments on early drafts of this study. Last, but not least, I am grateful to Diane Ring, Elizabeth Anderson, and Angela Mills for creating a hospitable environment at the Middle East Centre at St Antony's College.

My thanks also to Associated Press, who supplied all the photographs, and to the University of Texas Library Online website at http://www.lib.utexas.edu/maps/faq.html#3.html for the map of Jordan.

Although all errors of fact or interpretation remain my own, several other scholars were kind enough to read drafts of this study. Charles Tripp, Professor P.J. Vatikiotis, Patrick Seale, Ambassador Richard Parker, Charles King, and Robert Satloff made invaluable suggestions on how to tighten my arguments.

On a personal note, I thank my parents, Frank Fathi Tal and Kathleen McGrath Tal, for their support and patience. Finally, I dedicate this book to my wife, Amy.

Introduction

This book is about the making of a modern Middle Eastern state, at a time when both its borders and its existence were under threat. How the Hashemite Kingdom of Jordan traversed the years 1955 to 1967 as a fairly stable country while instability was prevalent in neighbouring Arab states is a question which has perplexed analysts for years. The Hashemite state lacked economic, political, and military resources and was threatened by domestic and regional forces during the years between the signing of the Baghdad Pact and the outbreak of the June 1967 war. However, despite the challenges of radical pan-Arabism, the Arab–Israeli conflict, and the Cold War, Jordan successfully protected its national security and became one of the most stable polities in the region.

This study focuses on the most tumultuous period in Jordanian history, when the kingdom's political obituary was penned numerous times. During those years, border clashes, war, coup attempts, riots, and other forms of civil disorder seem to have been the defining features of Jordanian politics. Few Arab or Western commentators believed that the young, inexperienced Hussein would survive the 1950s. Very few thought he would outlast his Arab nationalist contemporaries in the 1960s, and virtually nobody guessed that he would live to become the world's longest serving head of state by the 1990s.

In addition to the perennial problems of resource scarcity and external dependence, the Hashemite state faced numerous foreign and domestic challenges between 1955 and 1967. The Baghdad Pact crisis of late 1955 ushered in an era of turmoil in the region as the pan-Arabist movement inspired by Egyptian President Gamal Abdel Nasser rose to challenge conservative Arab monarchies such as Jordan. Until the disastrous June 1967 war, Jordan was buffeted by the winds of radical pan-Arabism, an ideology that inspired most Jordanian domestic opposition groups. Indeed, the kingdom's confrontation with Nasserism is a major theme of this study. The Israeli military threat to Jordan was another distinctive feature of the 1955 to 1967 period. Finally, the foundations of the Palestinian resistance movement that would challenge the Hashemite state in 1970 were laid at the first Arab summit in 1964.

Much of the difficulty in explaining Jordanian stability during this period can be traced to the tendency of scholars and other commentators to focus on the personality of the late King Hussein. Indeed, more has been written about Hussein than about almost any other Middle Eastern politician. This focus on the king, however, has clouded out questions about why the Jordanian state has been relatively stable and about the nature of the Jordanian political system.

The chief shortcoming of the regi-centric argument is that no state, including Jordan, depends exclusively on the personality and guidance of an individual, no matter how strong he or she may be. The death of King Hussein in 1999 (after 46 years in power) and the smooth succession of his son, King Abdullah II, may have surprised those who argued for decades that 'Jordan is Hussein, and Hussein is Jordan.' However, the peaceful transition merely demonstrates the fact that every successful ruler governs with the support of a coterie of civil and military advisors, and Jordan is no exception. Even history's most authoritarian leaders – including Adolf Hitler, Josef Stalin, and Kim Il Sung – ruled with a base of support in the army and the political elite.

A second explanation sometimes advanced to explain Jordan's stability is that the Hashemite state used sheer coercion to overcome its domestic enemies. This interpretation emphasises the role of the military in imposing order on an otherwise unruly populace. One difficulty with the coercion argument is that there are numerous counter-examples of authoritarian states plagued by insecurity. The use of intimidation is no guarantee of order or permanence. The Shah of Iran ruled with an iron fist, but was overthrown in 1978–79. Ferdinand Marcos autocratically ran the Philippines for decades, but was felled in 1986. Nicolae Ceausescu governed Romania for years before being deposed by a popular revolution in 1989. Zaire's Mobutu Sese Seko was considered almost invincible, yet he was easily toppled in 1997.

Another problem with this argument is that it contradicts the historical evidence. If Jordan's stability was predicated primarily on the state's use of the instruments of coercion, why did the kingdom liberalise its political system in 1956 and in 1962? Or why did Jordan lift martial law in 1958? To be sure, civil dissidence was a feature of Jordanian politics in the 1950s and 1960s. But the kingdom also witnessed long periods of relative calm. Indeed, the army spent more time in the barracks than deployed on the streets.

A third explanation for Jordanian stability maintains that Jordan exists today primarily because the Western powers wanted it to survive. On this reading, Jordan is an 'artificial' entity manufactured and sponsored by Britain and the United States. When the chips were down, the West could be counted on to bail Jordan out of trouble. One difficulty with the Western powers argument is the assumption that Jordan was manipulated by Britain and America and had little leverage vis-à-vis the great powers. In fact, rather than being exploited by the West, Jordan adroitly used internal and regional crises to convince reluctant Western policymakers that it was worth supporting. Through brinkmanship and shrewd diplomacy, Jordan managed to ratchet up Western interest in its survival.

A fourth explanation for Jordan's stability focuses on the role of Israel in supporting the Hashemite kingdom. This view is predominant among Israeli and some American scholars. Despite the impression one gets from some of the available literature, Israel was not a major factor behind Jordan's survival between 1955 and 1967. While Israel aided Jordan in 1958, and various Labour administrations were committed in principle to the maintenance of the Hashemite monarchy, the Jewish state was often responsible for creating instability in Jordan. Israel's large-scale military raids against the West Bank in 1956 and 1966 contributed to opposition to the Hashemite state. Moreover, although Israeli leaders privately assured Hussein of their support for his position on several occasions after 1963, Israel seized the entire West Bank in 1967.

While the above arguments are often compelling, none of these interpretations fully explains Jordan's durability. Each is necessary, but not sufficient, to explain how the Hashemite state overcame the numerous challenges it faced during the most turbulent period in its history, 1955 and 1967.

The argument advanced in this book is that Jordan remained secure due primarily to the cohesion of what I call its 'national security establishment', a ruling coalition of security and foreign policy professionals that included the monarchy, the political elite, and the military. While national security establishment members often disagreed over the means of protecting Jordanian national security, they agreed on the ultimate end of security policy: the preservation of the Hashemite monarchy and the protection of the territorial integrity of Jordan. Those policymakers not wholly committed to the state were removed from the decisionmaking process and usually purged from the national security establishment. This broad consensus on the ultimate aim of security policy among Jordan's ruling elite largely accounts for the kingdom's relative stability.

This book hopes to move beyond the traditional explanations for Jordanian stability by concentrating on the national security establishment that ruled (and continues to rule) the Hashemite Kingdom of Jordan. The following chapters demonstrate that Jordanian stability depended on accommodating the interests of an entire class of individuals in the national security establishment and in security policymaking. When these interests were not accommodated, instability often followed.

The argument advanced is not merely a mechanistic one about the inherent power of bureaucrats or elites in security policymaking. The book also shows how conceptions of Jordanian national security shifted during the 1955 to 1967 period, and how the monarchy was able to redefine and 'reframe' security interests and policies in order to maintain cohesion in the national security establishment.

The study makes use of primary sources from the British, American, and Jordanian archives, and interviews with surviving Jordanian decisionmakers. In addition, the study builds on the work of previous scholars by making extensive use of the Arabic and English published literature on Jordan.

While the book is an analytic, historical study, it is a story with contemporary relevance. Post-Hussein Jordan and its particular challenges are beyond the scope of the study, but the basic explanation advanced here may contribute to an understanding of the mechanics of Jordanian national security policymaking in the reign of King Abdullah II. The circumstances confronting the young King Hussein in the mid-1950s were not identical to those of today, but Hussein's successful consolidation of power depended largely on the wise counsel of his advisors, a lesson not lost on the relatively inexperienced and untested King Abdullah II.

List of Abbreviations

AU	Arab Union
BBC	British Broadcasting Corporation
CIA	Central Intelligence Agency (US)
COS	Chiefs of Staff (UK)
DOS	Department of State (US)
FO	Foreign Office (UK)
FRUS	*Foreign Relations of the United States*
ILP	Islamic Liberation Party (Jordan)
JNA	Jordanian National Archives
NA	National Archives (US)
NSP	National Socialist Party (Jordan)
NATO	North Atlantic Treaty Organisation
NSC	National Security Council (US)
PRO	Public Record Office (UK)
RAF	Royal Air Force (UK)
RJAF	Royal Jordanian Air Force
UAR	United Arab Republic
UK	United Kingdom
UN	United Nations
UNRWA	United Nations Relief and Works Agency
US	United States
USSR	Union of Soviet Socialist Republics

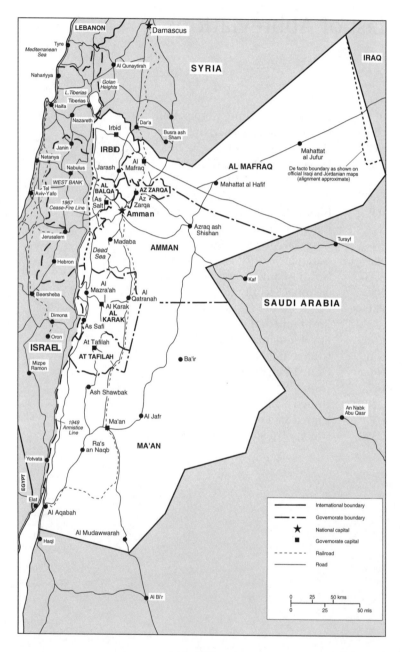

Map of Jordan

1
Jordan's National Security Establishment

Throughout its history, the Hashemite Kingdom of Jordan has faced significant internal and external challenges to its national security. A resource-poor country with a small population, Jordan has been subject to the push and pull of regional politics. Unlike richer, more powerful states, the Hashemite state has been limited in its ability to project its influence and has had to struggle to protect its very existence. Jordan's precarious position has led to national security concerns being at the core of its domestic and foreign policies since the state's inception.

The national security problem in Jordan

Although most scholars acknowledge the numerous threats to stability in Jordan, few have analysed the notion of national security in the kingdom.[1] This book suggests that Jordanian national security from 1955 to 1967 incorporated those variables which threatened the stability of the state and survival of the monarchy. War, riots, coup attempts, bombings, and other forms of disorder were all hazards to national security. But Jordanian security was about more than civil dissidence. National security encompassed economic variables (such as the vital need to secure foreign aid), political variables (for example, stifling parliamentary and media opposition), and ecological variables (such as crop failures and water shortages).

In other words, national security encompassed those factors perceived by decisionmakers to threaten either the survival of the monarchy or the territorial configuration of Jordan. In this sense, national security in Jordan between 1955 and 1967 comprised a far greater range of factors than national security did in, say, the US, where national security was primarily concerned with the 'Soviet nuclear threat' or the outbreak of war in western Europe. Given the dynamic and potentially destabilising national security environment, Jordanian decisionmakers constantly 'reinvented' their security policies as their perceptions and interests shifted over time.

Jordanian national security policy was flexible enough to accommodate many factors. The scope of security policy tended to narrow during crises threatening public order. At those junctures, restoring harmony to the political sphere became the top priority of decisionmakers. Conversely, the scope of security policy tended to widen during times of stability. Policymakers could then afford to pay more attention to economic development and ecological issues.

Despite this fluidity, Jordan's national security policy was always designed to alleviate three constraints on the kingdom: external dependence, a hostile regional environment, and internal fragility. Because Jordan lacked material resources, it constantly needed to diversify its sources of foreign aid by forming, breaking, and maintaining alliances with external actors. Jordan's position among hostile powers affected the kingdom's foreign policies and limited King Hussein's regional influence. The kingdom's domestic predicament meant that the state had to devote many of its scarce assets to controlling its population through coercion and cajolery.

The setting for national security policy

Since its creation in 1921, Jordan has remained reliant on foreign actors. The durability of the Hashemite state derives, in part, from the infusions of external aid which primed Jordan's economy. Despite its dependency, though, Jordan is no more 'artificial' than any other state, insofar as states are 'artifices', or artificial creations of individuals or groups pursuing political ends. Every state in the Levant was created by the imperial administrations of Britain and France. Many Latin American, African, and Asian states, too, were 'invented' by colonial powers.

However, when Jordan (then Transjordan) was created by British Colonial Secretary Winston Churchill 'on a Sunday afternoon' in 1921, its chances of survival appeared slim. Jordan had a total area of 91 880 square kilometres, of which 72 000 square kilometres were desert, and lacked natural resources. Jordan possessed no oil and was dependent on outside powers for its energy needs. Jordan also lacked sufficient water supplies to meet its long-term needs. The only resources the country had in abundance were potash and phosphates.

Another impediment to state-building was Jordan's tiny, heterogeneous population which owed no allegiance to the Hashemites. Fewer than 250 000 people, including a Sunni Muslim majority and Christian, Circassian, and Chechen minorities, inhabited the territory.[2] The Hashemites succeeded in integrating disparate ethno-religious groupings into its political system with the help of foreign aid. External rents allowed the monarchy to build a base of support and co-opt potential opponents. Amir Abdullah (who became king at independence in 1946) overcame Jordan's geographical, economic, and demographic handicaps by creating a 'neo-patrimonial', rentier state. The phenomenon of 'rentierism', whereby external sources of state revenue are utilised to 'buy' support from the governed, is an important factor in explaining the Hashemite monarchy's longevity.[3]

Infusions of foreign aid allowed the state to expand its economic role. The result was to make even more Jordanians dependent on government largesse. The monarchy neutralised potential opponents with state jobs and special privileges. Political crosscurrents emerged, whereby different factions negated each other in competing for bigger shares of the state-controlled dole. Rent-seeking and the selective use of patronage thus characterised political association in Jordan and cannot be divorced from any analysis of national security policy.

From 1921 to 1957, Jordan's chief patron was Great Britain, which initially paid King Abdullah I a monthly subsidy of £5000. Annual British aid reached £100 000 by the mid-1920s, £2 million by the mid-1940s, and £12.5 million by 1957.[4] Although British aid to Jordan was small when compared to Whitehall's aid to, say, India – where annual British military expenditure reached £287 million in 1944[5] – it furnished Abdullah with a solid economic base. Abdullah, in effect, 'occupied a median position between a European power, that held ultimate control, and a local social structure.'[6]

A major shift in the pattern of Jordan's external dependence came in 1957. Under the terms of the Eisenhower Doctrine – which promised American aid to any Middle Eastern state threatened by 'International Communism' – the United States replaced Britain as Jordan's principal foreign sponsor. Annual American aid to Jordan rose from $1.4 million in 1951 to $34 million in 1958.[7] By 1970, Jordan had received over $700 million in US assistance. Jordan ranked second only to Israel in terms of per capita American aid.[8]

To put the impact of external funding on Jordan's economy in perspective, aid accounted for up to one-third of Gross Domestic Product (GDP) between 1952 and 1966.[9] Annual economic growth rates of nearly 10 per cent during the 1960s were largely the result of foreign aid.[10] Jordan diversified its sources of external support when it joined the World Bank and International Monetary Fund in 1955.

Jordan's demographic and economic difficulties were compounded by the 1948 Palestine war. The fighting, coupled with Abdullah's annexation of the West Bank in 1950, increased Jordan's population three-fold. The population of the capital, Amman, grew from 30 000 in 1948, to 250 000 in 1961, to 350 000 in 1967.[11] The newly-arrived Palestinian refugees remained potential sources of trouble for the Hashemite monarchy. The war, moreover, left Jordan with a 650-kilometre frontier with Israel, forcing the kingdom to divert scarce resources from economic development to national defence.[12]

The war also made Jordan dependent on the Arab powers for trade. By 1964, Jordan depended on intra-regional sources for 61 per cent of its trade, the highest figure in the Middle East.[13] In 1948, Jordan had lost the use of port facilities in Haifa, the main outlet to the Mediterranean, and became dependent on the seaports of al-Aqaba and Beirut. Al-Aqaba was underdeveloped and too small to provide docking facilities for large ships. Using al-Aqaba, moreover, forced Jordan to pay high tolls for transit through the Suez Canal. Shipping and receiving goods through Beirut necessitated maintaining close ties with Syria, a problem during times of inter-Arab tension. Further, Jordan was forced to pay land transit fees to the Syrian and Lebanese governments. Jordan's problems were exacerbated by its poor infrastructure. One highway connected the East and West Banks. Most villages were not linked by paved roads or telephone lines. One railroad functioned in the kingdom, and the motorway from Amman to al-Aqaba was poor.

The war had an indirect impact on Jordan's economy. The Arab loss of Palestine provided the catalyst for the rise of the radical pan-Arab movement and ensuing Arab cold war. The export of phosphates, potash, and agricultural products required good relations with neighbouring states. During crises – for example, when Syria closed its border with Jordan in 1959 – the kingdom was essentially landlocked and suffered economically. Tourism revenues were also crisis-dependent. Tourism provided $7 million in 1951 and almost $93 million in 1966. However, during the Suez crisis, Jordan experienced a 27 per cent decrease in tourism. The 1957 disturbances contributed to a 20 per cent drop in tourism.[14]

Another ramification of the 1948 war was the emergence of conflict over the scarce water resources of the Jordan river basin. The river supplied the bulk of Jordan's water needs by the 1960s. The country had few other reliable sources of water. Rainfall was irregular, and groundwater stored in aquifers was expensive to extract. There were sundry plans for the integrated development of the Jordan river basin, but none were found satisfactory by all riparian states. Israel's exploitation of the river depleted Jordan's water base and increased the possibilities of inter-state conflict.[15]

Jordan's regional predicament: a tough neighbourhood

A second security constraint on Jordan was its position in a hostile regional environment. The national boundaries created by colonial administrators were contested by various Levantine states, and cross-border conflict was a regular feature of regional politics in the 1950s and 1960s. The period was marked by a high degree of inter-state tension. Consequently, Jordan's foreign relations seldom remained static. Alliances were formed, readjusted, and broken as Amman jockeyed to secure a firm footing during crises and play off adversaries against each other. In 1957, for example, Jordan used Saudi Arabia and Hashemite Iraq as a counter-weight to Egypt and Syria. In 1958, Israel and Britain aided Jordan against Iraq, Egypt, Syria, and Saudi Arabia. In 1961, Jordan improved relations with Damascus to undercut Cairo. In 1962, Jordan repaired ties with Saudi Arabia and formed an alliance against Egypt. In 1967, Syria became hostile to Jordan, so Hussein buttressed his relations with Egypt.

The Soviet Union never enjoyed decisive influence in Jordan.[16] While the USSR was popular among leftist circles in the kingdom, Moscow never controlled local political parties. Nor did it exercise anything other than ideological leverage over indigenous leaders. One reason was, quite simply, that Moscow never had substantial interests in the Hashemite Kingdom. Unlike Egypt, Syria, or Iraq – the ideological poles of the Arab world – Jordan was viewed by the Soviets as a bastion of Western imperialism, a reactionary state.[17] The Soviets claimed that Hussein's 'throne rests on foreign bayonets.'[18]

Another reason for the lack of Soviet influence in Jordan sprang from the philosophy and ambitions of the Hashemite dynasty. As descendants of the Prophet Muhammad, neither Abdullah I nor Hussein would have any truck with Communism. They believed, as did many Muslims, that Communism was an anti-Islamic creed. Hussein's address before the United Nations (UN) in 1960 was an example of his unequivocal rejection of Communism: 'I wanted to be sure that there is no mistake about where Jordan stands in the conflict of ideologies that is endangering the peace of the world.... In the great struggle between Communism and freedom, there can be no neutrality.'[19]

While Hussein inherited his grandfather's (King Abdullah I) policy of moderation toward Israel – establishing secret ties with Israeli leaders in 1963 – Israel remained a threat to Jordanian national security. In October 1953, for instance, a force led by Ariel Sharon devastated the village of Qibya, killing 66 villagers, most of them women and children.[20] In October 1956, Israel launched a reprisal raid against the West Bank village of Qalqilya, forcing Jordan to ask Britain for military assistance. In November 1966, Israel assaulted the village of al-Samu`, killing 21 Jordanian soldiers during an ambush.

Another security threat came in the form of radical pan-Arabism. Beginning with Husni al-Za`im's military coup in Syria in 1949, and closely followed by the Egyptian Free Officers' successful revolution of 1952, 'Arab radicalism' emerged as a potent political force in the Middle East. What these new political actors shared in common was a desire to transform the prevailing social, economic, and political status quo in the post-colonial Arab world. An intrinsic element of the nascent radical movement was the widespread belief that all vestiges of Western economic and military control over the Arab world had to be removed before the Arabs could once again prosper as they had during the early days of Islam.

At the forefront of the Arab radical movement was Egypt's Gamal Abdel Nasser. After he consolidated his regime in Egypt, Nasser sought to extend his influence to the rest of the Arab world. His first targets were the 'moderate', or pro-Western, monarchies of Jordan, Iraq, and Saudi Arabia. Because of the tremendous popularity of Nasser, Egypt was able to arouse oppositional sentiments in Jordan, where the young Hussein was perceived by many Arabs to be an 'imperialist stooge and lackey'. In the pan-Arabist atmosphere of the 1950s, the Hashemite monarchy in Jordan seemed archaic. While other Arab countries severed their ties with the West, Jordan retained its dependence on Britain and America. Far from being an autonomous, sovereign nation, Jordan seemed a satellite of the West.

Nasser scored a series of political victories which strengthened his leverage in Jordan. In 1954, he negotiated a treaty calling for Britain's evacuation from the Suez base; in 1955, he broke the Western monopoly on arms sales to the Middle East with his Czech arms deal; in 1956, Nasser soared to popularity with his defiance of the Western powers during the Suez affair; in 1957, he used the UN to compel Israel to disgorge Egyptian territory captured during the Sinai invasion; in 1958, Nasser formed the United Arab Republic (UAR) with Syria; and in 1964, Nasser convened the first Arab summit, which led to the formation of the Palestine Liberation Organisation (PLO).

Because of these actions, Jordanian opposition groups, especially those on the West Bank, 'united under the symbol of Nasser's leadership.'[21] The growth in popularity of the transistor radio gave the Egyptian leader a large audience for his speeches. Further, Nasser's use of colloquial Arabic expressions and his ability to deploy symbols and themes in Arab history made his speeches easily accessible to the largely illiterate masses across the Arab world. British diplomat Sir Anthony Parsons describes the impact Nasser's visits to Syria and associated speeches had on Jordan's population during the 1950s and 1960s: 'It was as though a powerful electric current had been passed through the country. Such was his power over people's minds in those days.'[22]

The domestic environment

A third constraint on Jordanian security was the fragility of its domestic political scene. The Hashemite family from Arabia was widely viewed by Jordanian inhabitants as the collaborator with a foreign power. After the Arab loss of Palestine and the onset of the Cold War, local opposition groups coalesced to oppose the Hashemite monarchy. Rural–urban migration increased the pool of potential recruits to opposition groups, which attracted the bulk of their rank-and-file support from the mass of unemployed and underemployed labour in the major cities. Political opposition leaders often offered employment and other economic benefits to lure potential constituents to Amman.[23]

The years from 1955 to 1967 witnessed the crystallisation and, in many cases, the virtual extinction of four broad strands of opposition within Jordan. The first comprised groups opposed to the existence of an independent Jordanian state. One example was the *hizb al-tahrir al-islami*, or Islamic Liberation Party (ILP), a group of 'Islamic Trotskyists' calling for the establishment of a Caliphate in Jordan.[24] The ILP had one elected member of the lower house, Sheikh Ahmad al-Da'ur, who regularly opposed government policy. The party claimed it eschewed violence, but was believed responsible for mounting largely ineffectual bombing attacks against the Hashemite state. The ILP was probably penetrated by the intelligence services at an early stage and never seriously threatened security. Others opposed to the state included radical pan-Arabists. Some members of the *hizb al-qawmiyyeen al-'arab*, or Arab Nationalist Party, advocated Jordan becoming part of a larger Arab union. The Hashemites, they believed, were bent on preserving the 'artificial' division of the Arab world.

The second strand of opposition encompassed those who accepted the notion of a territorial Jordanian state, but opposed the Hashemite monarchy. Examples included radical members of *hizb al-watani al-ishtiraki*, the National Socialist Party, *hizb al-ba`thi al-urdunni*, the Jordanian Ba`th Party, and *hizb al-shuyu`i al-urdunni*, the Jordanian Communist Party, an offshoot of the Palestine Communist Party. Many party activists of this ilk, be they pan-Arabist or leftist in political orientation, supported Nasserism.

The third opposition grouping included the 'constitutional opposition', such as the Muslim Brotherhood, which accepted the legitimacy of the state under the terms of the 1952 Constitution. The Brotherhood came to a *modus vivendi* with the Hashemites at an early stage and agreed to support the monarchy in return for freedom to operate charitable and educational foundations.[25] A key factor behind the organisation's support for the Hashemites was Nasser's suppression of the Muslim Brethren in Egypt in 1954–55. 'The Brotherhood was not as much pro-Hussein as it was anti-Nasser.'[26] The Brotherhood became a valuable ally of the monarchy in its struggle against leftists. Consequently, when the government banned political parties in 1957, the Brotherhood was allowed to continue operating.

The fourth source of opposition came from the Palestinians. The Palestinians, however, were not a monolithic community with unified aims; many were active in the pan-Arabist, leftist, and Islamist movements. When Abdullah incorporated the West Bank into his kingdom after 1948, he co-opted Palestinian notables into his governments.[27] Refugees, for their part, were often more concerned with their economic position than opposing the Hashemite state.[28] Others, however, denounced Hussein and tried to topple the Hashemites: Abdullah was assassinated by a disgruntled Palestinian, and Hussein was challenged by Palestinian guerrillas after the birth of the PLO in 1964.

Nevertheless, the integration of Palestinians into East Bank social and political structures continued apace throughout the 1950s and 1960s. Indeed, Palestinians became 'indispensable to the functioning of the monarchy.'[29] With inter-marriage and migration between the East and West Banks, 'it would be hard to say exactly where Jordanians leave off and Palestinians begin.'[30] Because Jordanian census data do not classify citizens on the basis of ethnic origin, precise estimates of Jordan's Palestinian population are not available.

While inter-communal tensions did not become pronounced until the birth of the Palestinian liberation movement in the mid-1960s, Transjordanians and Palestinians often viewed each other with mutual suspicion. Palestinians resented Transjordanian control over the levers of power in the government and security services. Transjordanians, for their part, often considered the Palestinians a disloyal group opposed to the state.

However, the contention that Palestinians were the radicals in Jordanian politics during the 1950s and 1960s, while Transjordanians remained quiescent supporters of the monarchy, is untenable. First, every military coup attempt in Jordan (discussed in subsequent chapters) was launched primarily by Transjordanians. This partly reflected Transjordanian primacy in the armed forces. But it also reflected the fact that Transjordanian ancestry did not automatically translate into support for the Hashemites. In fact, some of the monarchy's staunchest critics were Transjordanian.

Second, during crises the West Bank often remained fairly calm, while the East Bank erupted. Despite its reputation as a flashpoint for tensions, the West Bank had more to lose from an Israeli intervention due to its proximity to the Jewish state. Hence, one cannot pinpoint with precision a geographic centre of gravity for Jordan's opposition movements.

Third, the leadership of Jordan's extremist fringe included many Transjordanians. For example, the Communist Party's Ya`qub Ziyadin was an East Banker, as was Arab Nationalist Hamad Farhan. The leader of the militant Democratic Front for the Liberation of Palestine (formed in the post-1967 era), Nayif Hawatmah, was a Transjordanian from al-Salt. Even General Mashour al-Haditha, the military commander who defected to the PLO in 1970, was a Transjordanian from the Huwaytat tribe. In sum, members of all the prominent Transjordanian clans and tribes could be found in Jordan's opposition groups.

A further point to emphasise on Transjordanian–Palestinian relations concerns the 'Jordan first' or 'East Bank first' school of thought sometimes discussed by 'Jordanists' and other commentators.[31] The idea of Transjordanian nationalism first emerged in response to the inception of the Hashemite state and had its origins in a series of 'national congresses' held on the East Bank during the 1920s. East Bank particularism gradually coalesced into an inchoate Transjordanian nationalism after the 1948 war, when some East Bankers began to worry that the Palestine problem would be resolved at their expense by granting political and economic privilege to Palestinian refugees living in Jordan.

However, the notion of an independent East Bank-centred Transjordanian identity was not a significant political factor in the 1955 to 1967 period. Transjordanian–Palestinian tensions in Jordan did not become destabilising until after the June 1967 war. These tensions erupted into violence during the bloody 'Black September' civil war in

1970, which resulted in the Palestinian guerrilla movement's elimination from Jordan in 1971.

Jordan's national security establishment

Given Jordan's precarious external and internal security situation, the Hashemite monarchy has never been able to govern Jordan unaided. King Abdullah I was the first to understand that the Hashemites required the support of a broad-based political coalition to aid them in building a modern state on the East Bank of the Jordan River. Since Abdullah's time, the Hashemites have proven adept in aligning their dynastic interests with those of the Transjordanian and Palestinian urban and tribal notable classes. The key, of course, was to ensure that the ruling coalition was strong enough to safeguard the Hashemite state, but not powerful enough to challenge the Hashemite monarchy's predominance.

What I have termed the 'national security establishment' was the principal policymaking body in Jordan from 1955 to 1967. (The national security establishment remains, albeit in different form, the backbone of the Hashemite state today.) The group – a ruling coalition of foreign policy and security professionals from the monarchy, the political elite, and the military – was not a formal institution like America's National Security Council or the United Kingdom's Chiefs of Staff Committee. Indeed, one did not necessarily have to hold formal office to be a member of the security ruling elite. Rather, the security establishment comprised those members of the ruling elite who were united by their commitment to maintaining the Hashemite monarchy and protecting the territorial integrity of Jordan. While decisionmakers often formed political alliances with each other, they owed supreme allegiance to the throne.

Because national security was, and remains, the fundamental concern of the Hashemite state, the national security establishment constituted the primary arena for political competition in Jordan. Inclusion in security policymaking was essential for political and economic empowerment. Exclusion closed off the major gateway to upward mobility in Jordan. Accordingly, security policies reflected the outcomes of political struggles among the elite. What constituted security policy at any given moment could often be traced to the influence of certain actors or factions.

Each of the national security establishment's institutions functioned in concert with the others. No single institution, however powerful, could govern Jordan unaided. The monarchy was the ultimate source of authority in the kingdom, but the king needed the support of the political elite and the military. The throne required political leaders to run the day-to-day affairs of state – such as cabinet formation, election management, economic reform, and diplomacy – and military leaders to protect the kingdom from foreign and domestic threats. The political elite tended to be more influential with the king during times of calm than during times of crisis, when the army had more leverage in policymaking. However, each member of the monarchy, the political elite, and the military recognised that he was part of a team whose paramount loyalty was to the Hashemite state.

The monarchy

The position of the monarchy in Jordan between 1955 and 1967 is best described as that of principal arbiter between rival factions in the national security establishment. The palace has traditionally been the centre of political interaction in Jordan. Unlike democratic systems, where political actors – at least ostensibly – succeed on merit, Jordanian politicians knew their fortunes depended on access to the monarchy. For its part, the Hashemite monarchy understood (and continues to understand) that Jordanian stability depended on its ability to accommodate the interests of a wide range of individuals in the ruling coalition.

The monarchy had a religious and historical pedigree that few could match. As descendants of the Prophet Muhammad and former custodians of the holy places in Arabia, the Meccan Hashemites were able to mobilise Islamic themes and symbols to legitimise their reign. The Hashemite role in the 'Great Arab Revolt' against the Ottoman Empire strengthened its claim to legitimacy. Republican regimes, on the other hand, had to appeal to notions of popular sovereignty to justify their governance.[32]

The monarchy's dominant position was enshrined in Jordan's Constitution (1952).[33] The Constitution granted far-ranging powers to the executive branch. The king, for example, was declared immune from legal responsibility for his actions. The document also appointed the king supreme commander of the armed forces, allowed him to declare war and sign international treaties or agreements, and to convene, adjourn, suspend, or dissolve parliament.

Despite the powers vested in the executive, governing Jordan was not a one-man show from 1955 to 1967. While King Hussein later ruled in an autocratic manner, during the years covered by this study he was in a much weaker position. As one former advisor commented in the mid-1990s, 'the king used to be a boy surrounded by men. Now he's a man surrounded by boys.'[34] Ali Hillal Dessouki and Karen Aboul Kheir write: 'During the early years of his reign, Hussein was not the uncontested decision-maker in foreign, or domestic, policy. His powers were constrained by the presence of a number of strong figures with independent bases of support.'[35]

While Hussein was overshadowed in the early days of his reign, this book chronicles how the inexperienced monarch gradually gained confidence and maturity and became the undisputed decisionmaker in Jordan. The atmosphere of constant crisis in the early days of the king's reign did much to transform him from a youth into an adult. As one foreign ambassador to Amman remarked after the 1957 crisis, Hussein seemed to age 'about three years' each week.[36] Two factors were vital to Hussein's successful consolidation of his power. King Hussein created vested interests in the survival of his rule by first, co-opting potential rivals and second, circulating the elite through the ruling establishment.

Co-optation has historically been an important part of the Hashemite system of rule. Indeed, 'no regime rules through coercion alone.'[37] The monarchy's monopoly of control over Jordan's resource base and its ability to attract foreign aid allowed it to incorporate potentially disobedient tribal and clan notables into the Hashemite state. Early in his reign, Hussein recognised that reward-patronage was a better method of rule than coercion. He understood the need to include a broad range of individuals and social classes in the ruling establishment. To be sure, the king was willing to employ coercion to protect the security of the Hashemite state. However, Hussein's success between 1955 and 1967 owed more to his ability to create and maintain vested interests in his rule than to his use of violence. In sum, 'the selective distribution of economic awards' was a 'cornerstone' of the king's pattern of rule.[38]

Elite circulation was another aspect of Hussein's method of rule. One of the greatest strengths the king developed over the years was an ability to remove potential rivals from the ruling establishment. Soon after coming to power in 1953, Hussein ensured that elites were regularly rotated through the security establishment in order to keep potential opponents weak. It was not uncommon for ministers to hear of their resignations, retirement, or transfers on the radio. Moving someone from the palace to, say, the Senate signalled he had fallen from favour. Conversely, keeping a sacked prime minister on as court adviser meant he still had the king's ear.

King Hussein – like his father, King Talal, and grandfather, King Abdullah I, before him – began acting as mediator between competing groups in the national security establishment by the early 1960s. That is, Hussein relied on others in the decisionmaking process, but took ultimate responsibility for policy decisions. He usually tilted toward one faction at the expense of others. Those closest to the palace had the most impact on policymaking. Other members of the elite waited in the wings – that is, unless purged from the establishment by Hussein or other factions – until they were tapped by the king and returned to power.

Although he gradually became the central figure in Jordan, Hussein resisted the temptation to appear overly authoritarian. Hussein's accessibility to his people and his casual aura won him many supporters in a region where rulers often made no bones about their contempt for their subjects. As Shah Reza Pahlavi memorably put it when asked why Iran did not become a constitutional monarchy: 'When the Iranians learn to behave like Swedes, I will behave like the King of Sweden.'[39]

To shore up his reign, Hussein made numerous personal visits. Army bases, government offices, refugee camps, schools, factories, farms, and shops furnished the king with opportunities for face-to-face contact with his constituents. Such visits boosted the monarch's credibility and narrowed the gap between ruler and ruled. Not one to cower in his palace, Hussein sought occasions to use his charisma to its fullest.

Hussein's communication skills were important assets for him. In the 1960s, for instance, the king made an average of 25 speeches per year.[40] The growth of the transistor radio and the advent of television provided new fora for bridging the gap between palace and people. By late 1961, there were 64 699 licensed radio sets in Jordan and, presumably, many unlicensed sets.[41] Egyptian President Gamal Abdel Nasser's rousing speeches proved the efficacy of wireless communications, a lesson not lost on Hussein.[42] Accordingly, the monarchy spared little expense building Jordan's fledgling broadcast service into a radio network capable of competing with Egypt, Syria, and Iraq on the propaganda front.

Hussein's leadership qualities included personal bravery. As he put it in 1967: 'When your time comes to die, you die.'[43] His ability to remain calm during emergencies earned him the moniker of 'brave young king' (or BYK, as Hussein was known in US diplomatic circles). Even Hussein's enemies never questioned his courage. During crises, Hussein showed pluck by confronting rebellious leaders and mutinous troops. He sometimes piloted his helicopter over public disturbances, monitoring the army's handling of rioters. He was quick to visit the scene of border clashes with Israel. Hussein's daring went a long way toward bracing his popularity among Jordanians.

The political elite

The Jordanian political elite occupies an important position in the king-dom's history, despite its relative neglect in the available literature. Between 1955 and 1967, the primary function of Jordan's political elite was to assist (and periodically guide) the monarch in governing the kingdom. As the British ambassador to Jordan remarked in 1963: 'Per head of population Jordan is probably the most advised country in the world.'[44] Some of Jordan's political leaders were empowered solely through their affiliation with the palace, while others derived their powers from family or tribal bases of support.

Many Transjordanian political leaders who served the Hashemite state had strong clan bases in the towns and villages of the East Bank. (See Appendix for short biographies of key members of the Jordanian politi-cal elite in the 1950s and 1960s.) Membership of a family or tribe that cast its lot with King Abdullah after state formation in 1921 made one part of *al-ibna'a al-balad*, or 'the sons of the country'. While some Trans-jordanian leaders had resisted the centralising impetus of the Hashemite state, the monarchy adeptly incorporated tribal and settled populations into the state structure through co-optation. The Hashemites, in effect, created vested interests in Jordan's survival by persuading local leaders to maintain stability by acting as intermediaries between the state and its citizens.

Most Palestinians who were co-opted into the political elite lacked local roots and depended on their association with the Hashemite state to build networks on the East Bank. For example, Samir al-Rifa`i, Ibrahim Hashim, and Suleiman Tuqan had familial links to Palestine, but used their ties with the state to construct alliances in Jordan. King Abdullah's granting of patronage to prominent Palestinian families after the annexation of the West Bank in 1950 ensured that the Palestinian notable classes became as dependent on the monarchy as their East Bank counterparts.

Jordan's minority communities were also assimilated into the Hashemite system of rule. Co-opted by Abdullah at state formation, Circassians, Chechens, and Christians stocked the elite units of the armed forces and furnished policymakers who prospered in the upper echelons of the ruling coalition. Minorities were rewarded for their fealty with prestigious jobs and over-represented in the Lower House of parliament.

The monarchy constantly sought to maintain a balance among its var-ious constituencies. Transjordanian leaders could deliver the support of a large tribal or family grouping, whereas those of Palestinian origin were of limited value to the monarchy in this regard. However, Palestinian leaders – precisely because they lacked a powerful local base – tended to be loyal to the monarchy because they depended primarily on the state for their wherewithal. Someone like Beni Sakhir chieftain `Akif al-Fayiz, for example, presented a greater potential threat to the monarchy than someone like Fakhri al-Khalidi, a doctor from the West Bank. Similarly, Jordan's ethnic and religious minorities had a small domestic power base and did not threaten the monarchy per se. However, minority leaders were useful to the monarchy because they were relatively immune to the communal tensions which began to strain Transjordanian–Palestinian relations by the mid-1960s.

Regardless of their geographical and confessional differences, Jordan's political elite were a fairly cohesive group in terms of social origin. Most came from urban backgrounds – only 12 per cent of those in cabinet positions in the 1960s hailed from villages.[45] Most had secondary schooling, and many were university educated. Given Jordan's fairly egalitarian land tenure system and the relative lack of economic-based class conflict in the kingdom, the political elite generally enjoyed the support of their communities. Once in power, the elite ensured that their supporters received tangible economic rewards in the way of price subsidies and employment opportunities.

The political elite were also cohesive in terms of their ideological belief in the legitimacy of the Hashemite state. The monarchy drew on its religious and political claims to leadership to construct a ruling ethos based on the notion that Jordan was an Arab state with a destiny that transcended its borders. As one member of the elite puts it, 'the monarchy convinced its supporters that Jordan was both a Jordanian *and* an Arab state.'[46] For example, King Abdullah's 'Greater Syria' ambitions were not considered illegitimate or immoral by members of the elite. In their estimation, the Hashemites' claim to Arab leadership was as good, if not better, than any other Arab regime's.

Despite their cohesiveness, Jordan's political elite often disagreed over policy formulation and formed factions, or informal alliances, with other actors between 1955 and 1967. Perceptions of mutual advantage led political leaders to band together with each other, with military leaders, and even with non-establishment figures. Geographic alliances were formed among northern and southern elements; tribal alliances were formed among and between certain tribes; and policy alliances were formed among those who supported a particular foreign or domestic programme. Factions were not immutable and they shifted as circumstances changed. Policymakers who were allies in 1955 were not necessarily united in 1967, and policies advocated during one crisis were not necessarily the same as those advocated during others.

Affiliation with a faction did not signify a rejection of the ruling establishment nor did it necessarily symbolise hostility toward other decision-makers. Members of Jordan's political elite – regardless of disagreements over policy and personal differences – understood that they owed supreme loyalty to the Hashemite state. Forming factions was merely a means of influencing national security policy. A faction's success depended on its proximity to the king and its ability to sway him. Those in the inner circle were the most influential, while those in the wings were less so.

Two formal positions were especially coveted by members of the political elite: prime minister and chief of court. On the one hand, prime minister – who often doubled as defence minister – was not always the best position to hold given the fact that premiers were forced to take public responsibility for all government policies. On the other, the prime minister could have a substantive policymaking impact if he had King Hussein's backing. Wasfi al-Tell, for example, was an extremely influential prime minister whose advice was highly valued by the king. Chief of court, similar to the post of White House chief of staff in the US, allowed a decisionmaker access to the inner circle without the risk of public backlash. Bahjat al-Talhuni, for instance, exerted more influence on policy when he was chief of court than when he was prime minister.

In the national security establishment, however, there existed a tenuous link between formal office and political influence.[47] As Bahgat Korany notes, informal groups 'based on marriage, kinship, religion, ethnicity, and socioeconomic factors' have been very influential in the politics of the developing world.[48] Informal actors had a substantive, and often decisive, input in the Jordanian policymaking process between 1955 and 1967. For example, Queen Zein, Hussein's mother, was extremely influential, despite her limited official role. Queen Zein – whom British Foreign Minister Selwyn Lloyd once dubbed 'the Metternich of the Arab world' – restrained her son from taking rash decisions on several occasions and ensured that Hussein always kept the monarchy's interests at the heart of his policies.[49]

The military

Jordan's military was created before the birth of the Hashemite state and has always been the paramount guarantor of stability in the kingdom. Writing in 1948, *New York Times* correspondent Dana Adams Schmidt claimed, 'there wasn't much of note in the desert kingdom of Transjordan except the king and his army.'[50] P.J. Vatikiotis writes that the military formed the state in Jordan, rather than the other way around.[51] Since 1948, the Jordanian military has fought in three Arab–Israeli wars and in one civil war, quelled numerous public disturbances by using deadly force, was involved in several coup attempts, unseated a prime minister, and planned offensives against Syria and Iraq.

Given the salience of the military in Jordan, however, there exist few studies on the subject. Many commentators rely on outdated data and stereotypes ascribing the military's fidelity to 'beduin culture'. The fact is that the loyalty of the Jordanian military can be accounted for in terms of vested interests. Soldiers were well-paid, received excellent benefits, and occupied prestigious positions in society. From its inception, the army served both as a security force and as a way of subsidising tribes that were settling on farms and in towns.

Economic dependence bound the military to the state. By 1965, Jordan had the highest force levels in the Arab world. About 23 of every 1000 Jordanians served in the military, while only 14 were employed in manufacturing.[52] In a society where males comprised about 90 per cent of the labour force, the army was a principal employer.[53] In 1963, for example, Western officials calculated that one Jordanian soldier's pay contributed to the upkeep of seven to ten other individuals.[54] Jordan's military, then, was more than a fighting force. It was also a social welfare system providing economic advantage to those from impoverished rural and urban areas.

From the beginning of his reign, King Hussein understood that the military was the ultimate protector of the Hashemite state. As one American diplomat stated bluntly during the turbulent 1950s: 'No government is likely to remain in power without army support. The allegiance of the army to the Throne is the major source of royal power in the real sense.'[55] When Hussein wanted to replace the linchpin of Jordan's national security system, Britain, in 1956, the first step he took was to Arabise the military. Controlling the army was the most effective way of controlling Jordan. The military attracted the bulk of Jordan's external aid and was the sole institution with the powers of direct coercion.

Consequently, the Hashemites actively sought the wherewithal to transform the army from a Praetorian guard into a national establishment. From a force of five officers, 75 riflemen, and 25 machinegunners in 1920, the Arab Legion, as it was known in British times, reached a strength of 25 000 by 1956, 50 000 by 1965, and 65 000 by 1967. Hussein also directed his efforts toward building a modern, albeit small, air force and a fledgling navy.[56] Annual defence expenditures jumped from \$29.4 million in 1955 to \$58.8 million in 1965. In 1967, for example, Jordan dedicated nearly 14 per cent of its GNP to military spending; the only countries spending more on defence at the time were Laos (17.8%), Saudi Arabia (17.1%), and South Vietnam (14.1%).[57]

Although the Jordanian military was the site of several coup attempts – discussed in subsequent chapters – it never experienced the disunity and turmoil that characterised the military in Egypt, Syria, and Iraq. Haim Gerber suggests that the social composition and structure of Jordan's military partly accounts for the absence of a successful coup d'état. The personal supervision and training of the Arab Legion by British officers promoted the development of a relatively egalitarian, non-class based force. Unlike countries like Iraq – where the 'British authorities were not selective in their choice of candidates for the officer corps' and recruited mainly from the lower classes – Jordan's military was not plagued by tensions generated by disparities in income or education. This, when placed within the context of Jordan's balanced agrarian and urban class structures, is why 'the army did not become a mirror of the class struggle as in other Arab countries.'[58]

Another factor contributing to the army's cohesiveness was the absence of an independent political ethos among Jordan's officer corps. Unlike Turkey's officer class, which regards itself as the paramount guardian of Turkish secular democracy, or the Egyptian Free Officers, which viewed themselves as social and political reformers, Jordan's officers generally identified with the philosophy and ambitions of the Hashemite state. As Eliezer Be`eri notes, 'they neither regard themselves nor are they regarded by others as "intelligentsia in uniform"'.[59]

Finally, the military was not blighted by significant Transjordanian–Palestinian tensions before 1967. To be sure, Transjordanians dominated the officer corps and the non-commissioned ranks. But both Transjordanians and Palestinians shared the national defence burden. For example, of the 355 Jordanian soldiers killed in action in 1948, 151 were from Transjordanian tribal backgrounds – including 55 from the Sirhan tribe, 21 from the Huwaytat, 14 from the Banu Sakhr, and 11 from the Shamar – while others hailed from Transjordanian urban backgrounds.[60] In short, Transjordanian and Palestinian soldiers both had common economic and social interests in the maintenance of the Hashemite state.

Conclusion

This chapter has argued that Jordan's precarious security environment necessitated the creation of a cohesive ruling establishment to safeguard the Hashemite state. As a 'foreign' entity, the Hashemite family from Arabia understood that the preservation of the state would depend on the inclusion of a broad range of domestic interests in national security policymaking. The monarchy's ability to redefine security policies and threat perceptions to accommodate the interests of the tribal and urban notable classes would be key to its survival and to Jordanian stability in the 1955 to 1967 period.

2
Between Imperialism and Arabism

The period between December 1955 and October 1956 witnessed Jordan loosening the grip of British control and donning the mantle of Arabism. King Hussein used the Baghdad Pact crisis as a pretext for Arabising the national security establishment. Arabisation bolstered national security by blunting regional and domestic criticism that Jordan was merely a British puppet. However, Arabisation produced insecurity by encouraging actors not wholly committed to the Hashemite state to expand their space in security policymaking. Uncertainty in the domestic political arena coincided with turmoil on the external front. The Suez affair highlighted the ever-present Israeli threat and the necessity of finding a new foreign patron to replace Britain.

The Baghdad Pact

The Baghdad Pact was a Western defence scheme designed to protect the Northern Tier – Turkey, Iraq, Iran, and Pakistan – against Soviet encroachment. Neutrality in the Cold War would no longer be an option for the Arab states. Under the prodding of Egyptian President Gamal Abdel Nasser, Jordan was forced to choose sides in the East–West conflict.

To Britain, Jordan was 'the most reliable link in the chain of British bases between Suez and the Persian Gulf.'[1] Britain had moved its Middle East headquarters from Egypt to Cyprus in December 1952. Although Britain was in the process of dismantling its bases and extricating its forces from the Middle East, London planned to retain a foothold in the region. Cyprus provided an excellent 'jumping off' point from which Britain could conduct a limited military operation in the Levant.[2] After the October 1954 Suez base disengagement agreement capped the decline of British influence in Egypt, Jordan (and Iraq) assumed greater importance to Whitehall. Jordanian accession to the Pact could thereby buttress Britain's position in the region.

The most important Arab power in deciding the fate of the Pact was Egypt. Nasser perceived the Pact to be a Western scheme designed to perpetuate colonial control over the Arab world and divide the Arab peoples. Nasser's vision, to be sure, was predicated on the notion that Egypt was the undisputed leader of the Arab states. Cairo and Baghdad had long vied for leadership of the Arab world, and Nasser and Iraqi Prime Minister Nuri al-Sa`id were rivals. Hence, Nasser rejected any agreement which fortified his enemies and challenged Egypt's bid for regional dominance.

Nasser fortified his anti-Western position by arranging a Soviet–Egyptian arms deal (the so-called 'Czech arms deal') in September 1955. The arms deal did much to turn Jordanian public opinion firmly against the Baghdad Pact.[3] Politicians from all sides of the spectrum roundly praised Nasser's move and denounced the Pact. Radio Cairo and Radio Damascus broadcast anti-Western tirades. Egyptian and Syrian intelligence agents stepped up their support for Jordanian opposition groups, and Saudi Arabia funded Jordanian dissidents.[4] By October 1955, tensions were brewing in the kingdom. As one American diplomat noted: 'British influence, long a stabilizing force in Jordan, is steadily declining and if tested might be found insufficient. The Throne, formally [the] source of real strength has become virtually impotent.'[5] Jordan, in effect, had become the first battleground in the wider struggle between the Arab radicals and the Arab moderates.

Jordan's 'British ruler'

Among Jordan's most powerful decisionmakers was British General John Bagot Glubb – popularly known as 'Glubb Pasha' or 'Abu Hunayk' (referring to a battle wound on Glubb's jaw from the First World War) – commander of the Arab Legion. Glubb's power derived from his monopoly of control over the military. After Glubb took over the Legion in 1939 (the army was founded in 1921), he enlarged the officer corps and enlisted ranks. By the time of Jordan's independence in 1946, the strength of the army was approximately 8000, up from 1300 in 1941.[6]

After the 1948 war in Palestine, in which Glubb's troops on the West Bank performed better than any other Arab army, the Legion was rapidly expanded. What P.J. Vatikiotis calls the army's 'transformation from a corps d'elite to a national military establishment'[7] occurred between 1948 and 1956. Glubb, who believed the new Israeli state threatened

Jordan, wanted to develop an efficient, well-trained force capable of defending the West Bank.[8] He formed a national guard for local defence in the early 1950s and began a recruitment drive, importing more British officers to fill command billets. With the expansion of the number of combat manoeuvre units came the need to establish a technical corps and a training wing. Glubb used the British model to organise formally the artillery and combat engineering units. By 1953, the Jordanian army had grown to approximately 20000 men with 18 regiments. Despite the rapid enlargement of the armed forces, Glubb took pride in knowing the names and personal backgrounds of most of his soldiers.[9]

Although Glubb technically served under contract to the Jordanian government, many Jordanians considered him the de facto ruler of Jordan. So powerful was Glubb's influence that he 'ran the Arab Legion as if it [were] a British division, and was very good at extorting from Whitehall whatever he thought it ought to have in terms of money and equipment.'[10] Since the military was the backbone of the Hashemite state, by controlling the training, funding, and organisation of the armed forces, a British officer, in effect, dominated the security establishment.

Glubb's conception of national security was based on his belief that Britain and its allies were the best guarantors of Jordanian stability. Although Whitehall was in the process of redefining its relations with its imperial dominions, its treaty relationship with Jordan – in Glubb's estimation – should remain solid. Glubb fervently supported the Baghdad Pact. He believed the agreement would bolster Jordan against the radical Arab states and help the kingdom defend its Western border against Israel.[11]

Glubb's views were shared by some decisionmakers, but opposed by others. Hazza` al-Majali (from the southern town of al-Karak) thought the Pact would buttress security by creating an alliance against Nasserism. Although not yet in a powerful position, Wasfi al-Tell (from the northern town of Irbid), believed 'the Arab world did not possess the intrinsic power to sustain a neutralist posture' and advocated cooperation with the West against Arab radicalism.[12] Tawfiq Abul Huda (from Acre, Palestine) adopted a neutral stance publicly, but privately supported the Pact. The Circassian Prime Minister Sa`id al-Mufti was suspicious of Soviet intentions in the Middle East, but refused to countenance an unpopular agreement. A member of an ethnic minority, al-Mufti would not risk endorsing the Pact for fear of retribution against his supporters. Na`im Abdel Hadi from Nablus and `Azmi al-Nashishibi – both members of the cabinet, but not members of the ruling establishment in the sense that they were firmly committed to the Hashemite state – from Jerusalem denounced the Pact as an anti-Arab union.

Because Jordanian security policy was traditionally made by those closest to the monarch, Glubb and the pro-Pact camp were influential in persuading the 20-year-old Hussein that Jordan's interests were best served by signing the agreement. Hussein clearly understood the economic constraints on Jordan's national security and was convinced that the Baghdad Pact would bring the kingdom much-needed military and economic resources.[13] Specifically, he calculated the Pact could provide the wherewithal to create a modern air force.

After Turkey declined a Jordanian request for military aid, Amman turned to its patron, Britain. Whitehall – which had long been keen to enlarge the British military presence in Jordan – quickly offered Jordan ten Vampire jets and even toyed with the idea of appealing to Hussein's vanity by making him an honourary field marshal in the British army. Most important for Jordanian security, the Cabinet Defence Committee agreed to increase Britain's subsidy to Jordan. In return for joining the Pact, Jordan would receive £16.5 million in 1956 (up from £10 million in 1955) and £12.5 million per annum thereafter.[14]

To demonstrate its seriousness, Britain dispatched the chief of the Imperial General Staff, General Sir Gerald Templer to Amman on 6 December. Templer's task, in effect, was to close the deal with Jordan. The general, however, was 'no diplomat by divine call'.[15] Templer wrongly assumed Hussein was the chief powerbroker in Jordan and failed to lobby other policymakers. As the British general proudly reported, 'his first visits [had] been encouraging and the British promises of additional aid to the Arab Legion and a revision of the Anglo-Jordanian Treaty have been quite effective.'[16]

Templer's assessment could not have been more off the mark. Jordan's increasingly politicised population – stirred up by Egyptian radio broadcasts and intelligence agents – widely opposed the Baghdad Pact.[17] Thousands of anti-Pact leaflets were distributed throughout the kingdom – everyone from the Communists to the Muslim Brotherhood denounced the alliance. Egyptian Colonel Anwar al-Sadat even offered Palestinian ministers Na`im Abdel Hadi, `Azmi al-Nashishibi, and `Ali Hasna £9000 each for their resignations.[18]

The anti-British atmosphere persuaded Prime Minister al-Mufti to steer clear of the Pact. Although Hussein, al-Majali, and Court Chief Fawzi al-Mulqi urged the cautious al-Mufti to sign the Pact agreement, the premier refused to budge, and the Templer mission collapsed.

Templer ended his less-than-successful visit by denouncing al-Mufti as 'a jelly who is frightened of his own shadow.'[19]

The king and his coterie remained determined to bring Jordan into the Pact and appointed a hardline government led by Hazza` al-Majali. Al-Majali, described by one journalist as 'a gentleman of exception with wit and charm' and limited English language skills, was widely perceived as being pro-British.[20] Opposition groups, buoyed by the disintegration of the Templer talks, mobilised against the al-Majali government, and demonstrations were duly held on 17 December in Amman, Hebron, Jericho, al-Aqaba, Nablus, Irbid, al-Salt, and Bethlehem. Policymakers debated whether to disperse the crowds. Glubb advocated deploying the army, while policymakers such as Samir al-Rifa`i felt it would be a mistake to provoke the demonstrators and, in so doing, play into the opposition's hands.

The impressionable Hussein wavered until the crowds grew unruly and began stoning Western diplomatic missions and companies based in Amman. In response, Glubb unleashed the Arab Legion, which used automatic weapons and whips to disperse the demonstrators.[21] At least 15 protesters were killed, and scores wounded during the street fighting. However, these draconian measures only inflamed the opposition and delivered little more than a modicum of stability.[22] Like its predecessor, the al-Majali government crumbled – this time after a mere five days. As American diplomat Richard Parker noted on 31 December, the West's 'dreams' that Jordan would join the Pact 'have been rudely interrupted.'[23]

Remembering the backlash when the army fired on protestors in October 1954, Hussein decided to adopt a different tack. He reasoned that he could broaden his narrowing popular base by dissolving the current parliament and holding new elections. The Lower House had been elected in the gerrymandered 1954 polls and lacked credibility. Limited pluralism, Hussein conjectured, might create stability and restore the throne's reputation and boost his own tarnished image.

Hussein asked Ibrahim Hashim, a perennial caretaker prime minister, to form a government to supervise the elections. However, outcry by a group of parliamentarians protesting the legality of the dissolution decree persuaded Hussein to reverse his decision to hold elections. Opposition groups seized upon this as evidence of the cleavages within the security establishment and announced that further anti-government demonstrations would be held.[24]

The December riots had been a bellwether of things to come. The age of 'street politics' had arrived in the Hashemite kingdom with a vengeance. No longer content to accept the status quo, many Jordanians believed mass protests could bring them what a restrictive political system could not. As American Ambassador Lester Mallory concluded: 'The man of the street and the refugees for the first time flexed their political muscles and found them strong.'[25]

The dawning of a new era

The riots which erupted in Jordan in January 1956 set the stage for a period of great upheaval in Middle Eastern politics. As Elizabeth Monroe wrote in 1963: 'Seen through Western eyes, the tale of events in 1956 is like the narrative in a Greek myth; disaster follows disaster.'[26] From the Baghdad Pact crisis in Jordan to the Suez war, events seemed to confirm the emergence of a new Arab order.

On 7 January, crowds in Amman stoned the prime minister's office, set fire to the Department of Forestry, and destroyed a number of automobiles (including those belonging to opposition leaders Suleiman al-Nabulsi and `Azmi al-Nashishibi). Mobs attacked the UNRWA building, the American Point IV development office, and the British Bank of the Middle East.[27] In Jerusalem, 300 rioters charged the American consulate, where US Marines used tear gas to disperse the crowds. In al-Zarqa, Colonel Patrick Lloyd, a British officer serving with the Royal Artillery, was killed by rioters after becoming isolated leading a charge against protesters; Lloyd was stoned and shot at point-blank range.[28]

The riots were the most severe in Jordanian history and confirmed the ascendancy of Arab radicalism in the kingdom. '[T]he crowd had complete run of the streets; no attempt was made either by the Police or by the Army to interfere with them.'[29] The reason the security services did not immediately respond was due to disagreement in the national security establishment over the merits of using force. In particular, Prime Minister Ibrahim Hashim felt that the demonstrations could be stopped without calling in the army. According to Glubb, after the mobs began attacking, looting, and burning government buildings – especially the Ministry of Agriculture, where some 7000 rioters had gathered – Hashim reversed his stance: 'Disperse them at once! Open fire! They will burn down the city.'[30] Glubb's troops used tear gas and gunfire to stop the rioters from committing further acts of violence.

Recognising that the current policy of confrontation was not working, Hussein appointed the pragmatic, but forceful, Samir al-Rifa`i to form a government on 8 January. Al-Rifa`i's policies were instrumental in checking Jordan's descent into lawlessness. 'Al-Rifa`i's approach to politics was to avoid confrontation when circumnavigation was possible and to view adversaries as potential allies, not inevitable enemies.'[31] Al-Rifa`i foreswore the Baghdad Pact, lifted the military curfew, and extracted a commitment from Egypt to cease its propaganda offensive.[32]

Once in power, al-Rifa`i undercut his main political rivals and solidified his position in the inner circle of decisionmaking. In particular, he sought to undermine Hazza` al-Majali by forming a close association with the latter's nemesis, Bahjat al-Talhuni (from Ma`an). A marriage between al-Rifa`i's son, Zaid, and al-Talhuni's daughter cemented the alliance. Prime Minister al-Rifa`i also transferred al-Majali's ally, Wasfi al-Tell, from the Press Bureau to the Taxation Department.[33] Al-Rifa`i's actions showed how decisionmakers could use security-related crises for their own political (or economic) ends.

In addition to highlighting the decline of British influence in Jordan, the crisis led to tensions in the Jordanian army and strengthened the Free Officers (*dubat al-ahrar*) movement in the Arab Legion. Robert Satloff writes that the Free Officers were probably formed in 1952.[34] James Lunt, on the other hand, writes that the group appeared in 1954,[35] while declassified American diplomatic reports suggest the organisation dated from 1951.[36]

What is certain is that, influenced by military coups in Syria and Egypt, a cluster of pan-Arabist and leftist officers formed a political organisation in the Legion in the early 1950s. The group's structure was relatively amorphous, and operational planning was confined to a small clique.[37] While details on the composition of the movement are sketchy, its objectives were clear-cut: to sack Glubb and Arabise the Legion.[38] Wider goals – such as overthrowing the monarchy and installing a republican government – may have existed in inchoate form, but were not the movement's founding goals.

A 'Glubbless' Jordan

Hussein's dismissal of Glubb on 1 March was a milestone in Jordanian history. In a stroke, Hussein eliminated his main domestic rival and Arabised the institution governing Jordan. Given the turbulent political climate, it could have been politically self-destructive for the Hashemites to retain a British-controlled security system. Glubb was widely considered 'the power behind the throne in Jordan.'[39] In short, 'Glubb was the symbol of the foreign power which dominated the Legion and Jordan's entire economic and political life.'[40] Indeed, the Legion itself was becoming dangerously unpopular – the municipal government in

Jerusalem went as far as naming a street after a girl student who had been killed by Arab Legion gunfire in the December riots.[41] Hussein claimed he dismissed Glubb for failing to devise adequate security plans for the West Bank. Jordanian historians Munib al-Madi and Suleiman Musa echo the king's criticism and also censure Glubb for insisting that Jordan's army would not be ready for Arabisation until 1985.[42] To be sure, Glubb and Hussein disagreed over the former's 'defence in depth' concept, which involved defending key points on the armistice line rather than policing the entire frontier. But it is unfair to reproach Glubb for his defensive plans. In fact, as argued later in this book, Glubb's strategy might well have saved the West Bank in 1967 had it been implemented.

There were actually deeper motivations behind Glubb's sacking. First, Hussein hoped to check his internal and external foes by taking an anti-imperialist stance against Britain. By removing Glubb, Hussein would demonstrate he was breaking the fetters of imperialism and distancing his country from London. Throughout Jordan and the Arab world, the Legion 'seemed an alien force, run by British officers, taking orders not from Jordan, but from their British commander, General Glubb.'[43]

Second, Hussein wanted to wrest control of the army from the British and undercut Glubb's base of support in Jordan. In some regiments, Glubb was as popular, if not more, than the young king. To consolidate his rule, Hussein had to remove Glubb from the political equation. By controlling the Legion, Hussein could control the national security establishment. The throne, ostensibly the exclusive source of authority in Jordan, did not monopolise the levers of power. For example, Hussein had wanted to transfer control of the police force from the Legion, a British-run institution, to the Ministry of Interior, a Jordanian-run institution. Such was Hussein's limited prerogative that his prime minister replied, 'the British would not approve.'[44]

Finally, Hussein wanted to gain control of the £12 million annual subsidy to Jordan, which Britain deposited in a special account at the Ottoman Bank in London rather than placing it in the Hashemite treasury in Amman.[45] If Hussein controlled the purse strings, he would augment his power base in Jordan and tighten his grip on the national security establishment. Managing the state's resources would allow Hussein to co-opt recalcitrant urban and tribal notables and create vested interests in the preservation of his reign.

All available evidence indicates that Hussein took the final decision to sack Glubb, but was influenced by the Free Officers. As Ambassador Mallory reported, the termination was 'Hussein's own doing but with considerable assistance, prompting and nudging.'[46] The Free Officers also persuaded Hussein to remove Brigadier W.M. Hutton, the chief of staff, Colonel Sir Patrick Coghill, the director of the general intelligence service, and eight other British officers.

Shahir Yusef Abu Shahut, a member of the Free Officers' executive committee, suggests that Ali Abu Nuwar (from al-Salt) established close links with Hussein while the former was posted to France and the latter studied at Sandhurst.[47] Ba'thist Free Officer Mahmud al-Ma'ayta insists that Hussein was well aware of the Jordanian Free Officers.[48] In his memoirs, Hussein admits Abu Nuwar was a close friend, 'in whom [he] had placed great hopes – faith and trust too.'[49] James Morris writes: Abu Nuwar 'was always with the King, always whispering in his ear, always pressing upon his susceptibilities, always prodding his pride.'[50] Thus, claims that Hussein and Abu Nuwar were confederates in the plan to sack Glubb and Arabise the army are not improbable.

Other key players backed Hussein's decision. Hussein's uncle, Sharif Nasser, knew that Glubb's departure would remove a competing influence on Hussein.[51] Sharif Nasser understood that constricting the inner circle surrounding the malleable Hussein was essential for input in security policymaking. Samir al-Rifa'i also backed Glubb's sacking. Where he differed from Hussein, though, was 'on form, not fundamentals'.[52] Al-Rifa'i felt Hussein was acting impetuously in the way he planned to fire Glubb, a move sure to antagonise Whitehall; better to wait and dismiss him on 31 March (when Glubb's contract with the Jordanian government expired). But, as Malcolm Yapp correctly divines, Hussein 'wanted to make a splash over the affair in order to prove to his subjects that he was no less a nationalist than his Egyptian critics.'[53]

Although Hussein chose the timing of the anti-Glubb coup, the Free Officers orchestrated the putsch. On the night of 28 February, Hussein ordered Abu Nuwar to set in motion plans for Glubb's ouster. According to Hussein: 'It was a surgical operation which had to be done brutally.'[54] Codenamed Operation Dunlop (prosaically named after the British manufacturer of the tyres fitted on Arab Legion vehicles), the plan involved surrounding Glubb's house with armoured cars, cutting his telephone lines, and encircling the airport with troops.[55] The lines to the residences of other British officers were also severed, and British advisors to the air force were confined to quarters.[56] Operation Dunlop ensured that Glubb, had he so desired, could not rally his supporters and stage a counter-coup. The script was played out as written, and Glubb quietly departed Jordan (never to return) on 2 March. Figure 2.1 shows the Arab Legion Household Cavalry in Nablus following Glubb's dismissal.

There are two surprising features about the Glubb affair. The first is how shocked the British government was when it heard of Glubb's

Figure 2.1 The Arab Legion Household Cavalry rides into Nablus during King Hussein's triumphant visit following the dismissal of General Glubb, 7 March 1956.

dismissal. Whitehall had ample time to fathom how far Hussein and Glubb's relations had deteriorated. Glubb himself believed plans were afoot to unseat him and had exiled Mahmud al-Rusan (from Irbid) to the Jordanian embassy in Washington in 1953 and Ali Abu Nuwar to the embassy in Paris in 1952.[57] By May 1955, Sam Cooke, Glubb's senior British officer, admitted, Glubb 'is having a very rough ride with the King and seems to be heading for a fall.'[58] The same month, Prime Minister Tawfiq Abul Huda told the British ambassador that 'a situation [is] arising that might lead to [Glubb's] resignation.'[59]

The second feature is how cordial Anglo-Jordanian relations remained after the crisis. Prime Minister Anthony Eden, in particular, was outraged by Glubb's dismissal and blamed Nasser for influencing Hussein. Anthony Nutting, a former cabinet minister, maintains that Glubb's termination was an important factor causing Eden to develop his visceral distaste for Nasser and, in part, led to the Suez invasion.[60] Foreign Secretary Selwyn Lloyd, in Cairo to visit Nasser, also seemed to think Egypt was responsible. 'It's absurd,' Nasser chuckled to his advisors, 'he thinks we engineered the Glubb business.'[61]

The general feeling within the Eden government was that the British subsidy to Jordan would 'undoubtedly ultimately be withdrawn.'[62] British officials increasingly considered the subsidy 'a waste of money' and began encouraging the US and Iraq to back Jordan.[63]

Jordanian diplomacy and the power of a 'Jordan lobby' in Britain accounted, in large part, for the resilience in Anglo-Jordanian relations. Hussein assured Eden that his dismissal of Glubb was not meant to reflect Jordanian dissatisfaction with London. Jordanian diplomatic representatives reiterated that Glubb's sacking had been a domestic political issue. Glubb's behaviour upon returning to London went a long way toward convincing Britain that Jordan should not be punished. Glubb reassured Foreign Office officials that Jordan was still a friend of the West. Glubb wrote a pro-Jordanian letter to the editor of the *Daily Telegraph*. Sir Alec Kirkbride, another central figure in Jordanian history, was assured by Hussein and al-Rifa`i that Jordan would honour the Anglo-Jordanian treaty. Accordingly, Kirkbride 'begged' the British government 'not to overreact'.[64]

While Glubb's expulsion created a hiccup in Anglo-Jordanian relations, it boosted Hussein's popularity in Jordan and the Arab world. Glubb – widely regarded as 'the ultimate source of power in Jordan' – would no longer play a role in governing the kingdom.[65] Local opposition groups and the radical Arab states felt Hussein had finally realised the futility of his dependence on the West and responded to the cry of Arabism. 'Glubb's dismissal is not an unmitigated evil', Ambassador Mallory argued. 'The action has gone far toward removing Jordan's defensive position and inferiority complex vis-à-vis other Arab states.'[66] Hussein basked in the aftermath of Glubb's ouster and displayed a new-found confidence. He boasted that 'Jordan now feels that its army is an Arab army, which will protect the country and repel any aggression and which receives and obeys orders from its supreme Arab commander.'[67]

Cohesion lost: Arabisation

The period following Glubb's departure was among the most precarious in Jordanian history. Whereas the military – the paramount guarantor of the Hashemite state – had been tightly controlled by the British in earlier years and did not interfere in national politics, it became politically active after Glubb's departure. The opportunities for activism came with the *ta`rib*, or Arabisation, of the Legion, which was renamed the Jordan Arab Army. Hussein filled the positions vacated by the British with Jordanian officers, and young officers, many with little military experience, were promoted almost overnight. One American report noted: 'Jockeying for position among Arab officers in the Arab Legion began as soon as General Glubb departed Jordan on March 2.'[68] Communities of interest formed in the army, in particular, and in the national security establishment, in general, as newly promoted officers sought to fill the vacuum created by the British exodus.

The first, and dominant, grouping in the complex web of army politics was the Ali Abu Nuwar faction (which probably included, among others, Ali Abu Nuwar, his cousin Ma`an Abu Nuwar, Shahir Yusef Abu Shahut, Adib Abu Nuwar, Mahmud al-Ma`ayta, Muhammad al-Ma`ayta, Turki Hindawi, Mazin `Ajluni, Dhafi Juma`an, and `Azmi Mihyar). Ali Abu Nuwar was appointed commander of the 1st Brigade on the West Bank and subsequently became assistant chief of staff to Chief of Staff Radi al-`Ennab. Acting on a tip from Mahmud al-Ma`ayta (from al-Karak), Abu Nuwar ordered the arrests of Mahmud al-Rusan, Radi Abdullah (from Irbid), Abdullah Majeli (from the Bani Sakhr tribe), Muhammad Amin Barakat, Abdullah al-`Ayyid, and Qassim al-`Abd.[69] The arrests served as a warning to rival officers that Abu Nuwar was consolidating his authority.

As early as 4 March, the US Army attaché in Amman, Lieutenant Colonel James Sweeney, identified the Abu Nuwar faction as holding the keys to Jordan's future. 'Only time', he wrote, 'will tell if Hussein will be the [deposed Egyptian King] Farouk of Jordan.'[70] Abu Nuwar's politics were considered decisive in determining the political direction of the army. As one US official noted at the time: Abu Nuwar's 'appointment would increase political instability and would widen dissension in the Legion.'[71] Abu Nuwar, in short, now held veto power over Hussein. As Israeli military intelligence noted, 'Hussein [is] no longer [the] master of his own fate and will retain [the] throne only if he accommodates himself to the views and plans of Nuwar.'[72]

A second faction was the Ali al-Hiyari group. Al-Hiyari (from Irbid) assumed the assistant chief of staff position vacated by Brigadier James Hutton, but was edged out by Ali Abu Nuwar. He then took command of the 1st Division in al-Zarqa, relieving Major-General Sam Cooke. The US embassy reported that al-Hiyari was 'considered the most ruthless Arab officer in the Legion and one of the most able.'[73] He played competing factions off each other and established links with Radi Hindawi and `Akash al-Zabn (a Bani Sakhr).

A third group was the Sadiq al-Shar`a faction. Al-Shar`a, from Irbid, was supported by his brother, Salih, and Mustapha Khasawneh. Sadiq al-Shar`a was considered by the US to be one of the best officers in the Jordanian military and eventually developed a reputation as being 'America's man' in the army. Although the al-Shar`a contingent would figure prominently in Jordanian politics in 1959, in 1956 the group was of indeterminate political direction and had few coherent objectives other than to derail the Abu Nuwar faction's bid for authority.

A fourth faction, which would not become predominant until 1958, was the Sharif Nasser group. As Hussein's uncle, Sharif Nasser had direct access to the king and was a long-time powerbroker. He had lobbied against Glubb and was ensconced in the palace inner circle, despite his 'hashish smuggling activities'.[74] In a vivid example of how the military provided patronage, Sharif Nasser used rents from smuggling activities and commissions from arms sales to create his own private welfare system. Retired soldiers were given sinecure and employment opportunities by Sharif Nasser. The Sharif persuaded Hussein to let him form a Royal Guards contingent to safeguard the royal family. Sharif Nasser handpicked the unit's soldiers and, in effect, created his own private force. Sharif Nasser resented Abu Nuwar for vetoing his efforts to secure a command position in the army. One of Sharif Nasser's closest allies was Habis al-Majali (a cousin of Hazza`).[75]

Although faction-building characterised military politics during this period, many officers were not committed to any particular group. Older officers were generally more concerned with maintaining pension rights and benefits than with the army's political direction. Younger officers were often more receptive to the ideals of radical pan-Arabism and tended to be more ambitious politically. Moreover, they wished to secure greater economic reward and military power. Of the anti-Abu Nuwar groups, most lacked the organisational capability for serious political action.

Abu Nuwar's power was confirmed on 26 May, when Hussein issued a royal decree naming him chief of staff. He was promoted from lieutenant-colonel to major-general and managed to secure promotions for many of his supporters and for officers whose support he hoped to win. Promotions included Ali al-Hiyari, Habis al-Majali, Muhammad al-Ma`ayta, Radi Hindawi, Fawaz Maher (a Circassian), and Sadiq al-Shar`a (all promoted from colonel to brigadier).[76] `Izzat Hassan, Mahmud Musa, Karim Ohan, Adib Qassim, and `Akash al-Zabn were promoted to colonel. Shahir Yusef Abu Shahut was made a lieutenant-colonel.

Arabisation also provided an unprecedented opportunity to reorganise the security apparatus. Division Headquarters was abolished and separate brigade headquarters were formed.[77] The police forces were separated from the army and rechristened the Public Security Department (*al-amn al-'amm*).[78] This move gave the Interior Ministry control of the police apparatus and allowed the army to devote its attentions to broader security concerns.[79] On the one hand, decentralising command and control functions could lead to greater tactical fluidity and responsiveness in the army. On the other, the new structure created opportunities for independent political action as army factions carved out relatively autonomous centres of power.

In the end, Abu Nuwar's decision to reorganise the military would contribute to his undoing. While undeniably providing patronage to his cronies, Arabisation also undercut Abu Nuwar by ceding power to his political enemies. It did not seem to occur to Abu Nuwar to retain as much power as possible, particularly in the armour and infantry units so critical to any plan to alter Jordan's political system.

Abu Nuwar's first move was to undercut Prime Minister Samir al-Rifa'i, who was increasingly clashing with Hussein over foreign policy. Whereas al-Rifa'i advocated compromise with Cairo, Hussein believed Jordan should pursue its own brand of Hashemite-led Arabism. The premier and the monarch also disagreed on whether Jordan should openly confront Egypt over the Algerian issue. Encouraged by Abu Nuwar, Hussein demanded al-Rifa'i's resignation in late May. Israeli intelligence sources commented, this is 'another step in [Abu] Nuwar's consolidation of power.' The US agreed that any new cabinet would 'be vetted by Ali Abu Nuwar and colleagues.'[80]

The Abu Nuwar camp approved Hussein's choice for prime minister, Sa'id al-Mufti. British Ambassador Charles Johnston reported that al-Mufti's 'chief attribute was a desire to avoid responsibility and who was thus well fitted to occupy the role of non-governing Prime Minister.'[81] The Circassian's popularity had risen with his refusal to join the Baghdad Pact, and his distaste for bucking popular opinion endeared him to opposition groups. Al-Mufti's middle-of-the-road policies encouraged opposition elements to renew their call for parliamentary elections.

The Abu Nuwar faction's rapid rise to predominance was widely unpopular among the old guard in the national security establishment. While most members of Jordan's ruling elite supported the notion of Arabisation in principle, they were far less happy with it in practice. For example, senior military figures such as Habis al-Majali had been bypassed in favour of inexperienced officers with no proven record of service to the Hashemite state. Similarly, veteran politicians such as Samir al-Rifa'i resented having to share with men far junior to him decisionmaking power and influence with the king. The old guard tried to persuade Hussein that he was endangering Jordanian national security by relying on unproven – and possibly untrustworthy – individuals.

King Hussein, however, was confident that he was on the right course and he ignored the advice of some of his advisors that he was moving ahead too quickly with his plans to Arabise the national security establishment. Backed by members of the Abu Nuwar faction, Hussein decided to give elections another try. He calculated that limited political pluralism would brace Jordan against foreign and domestic threats by bringing more opposition elements into parliament. In accordance with constitutional procedure, al-Mufti resigned and was replaced by Ibrahim Hashim, described by British Ambassador Johnston as 'an elderly and enfeebled gentleman, who considered his only function to be to act strictly as a caretaker.'[82]

Members of the old guard again cautioned Hussein about the dangers inherent in permitting opposition groups increased political space. While some decisionmakers favoured the idea of holding elections, many believed that radical elements opposed to King Hussein would triumph and, in so doing, create instability for the Hashemite state. Coupled with the rapid pace of Arabisation, liberalising Jordan's political system too quickly could be disastrous for the monarchy.

The king's tilt toward domestic opposition groups also alarmed British and American policymakers. Britain thought 'there was a real danger in Jordan of civil war or a pro-Egyptian Government through a coup d'état.'[83] American Secretary of State John Foster Dulles correctly divined that Hussein was so desperate to improve his own political standing that he was in danger of undermining the very foundations of the Hashemite state.[84] Washington was particularly opposed to Jordan's apparent appeasement of Egypt's Nasser, whom Dulles considered 'an extremely dangerous individual.'[85]

The Suez affair

Gamal Abdel Nasser's nationalisation of the Suez Canal Company on 26 July stunned the Arab world and sent shock waves rippling through Jordan. Hussein immediately transmitted his congratulations to Nasser. Opposition groups were ebullient and issued proclamations declaring their unequivocal support for Nasser's move. On the West Bank, committees of 'guidance and defence' were formed to defend towns and villages against Israeli encroachment. The Muslim Brotherhood reportedly organised 5000 men from Jerusalem, and more from Jericho, for military training. Another 2000 Palestinians volunteered to defend Egypt against any attack by the imperial powers.[86] While the kingdom's direct involvement in the ensuing crisis was negligible, the affair radicalised even further Jordan's opposition groups and forced the kingdom into adopting a militant Arabist stance. The only immediate security threat posed by the Suez crisis came from Israel. Policymakers, despite their factionalism, believed that Israel would use the imbroglio as a pretext for striking the West Bank. Moshe Dayan later confirmed the national security establishment's fears and said that Jordan was, indeed, a target for Israeli military planners under certain circumstances.[87]

In July, British and Jordanian officials discussed plans for defending Jordan against Israel. The British Chiefs of Staff gave Jordan details of Operation Cordage, a plan to shield the kingdom from an Israeli attack.[88] Cordage envisaged British airstrikes against Israeli airfields and radar sites. British bombers based in Cyprus and on aircraft carriers would launch the raids. The Royal Navy would impose a naval blockade on Israeli shipping in the Red Sea, and the Royal Marines would attack Israeli coastal cities (such as the port of Eliat). Britain's plans were for defensive purposes and were in keeping with the security guarantees outlined in the Anglo-Jordanian Treaty (Glubb's expulsion did not affect the terms of the treaty, although opposition groups were increasingly calling for Jordan to abrogate its agreement with Britain).

Although Operation Cordage furnished a sense of security in the national security establishment, policymakers felt Jordan required further safeguards. In June, Ali Abu Nuwar lobbied Iraq for military assistance. In August, Hussein went to Damascus to discuss a 'Northern Defence Alliance'.[89] In September, Abu Nuwar pressed the Saudis for economic and military assistance. In October, Jordan went as far as signing a defence agreement with Egypt and Syria.[90] Under the terms of the pact, Egyptian General Abdel Hakim ʿAmer would command the joint Arab forces. 'On the eve of the Suez war, Jordan found itself in the anomalous position of being formally bound to both Britain and Egypt.'[91]

Within the newly Arabised security establishment, the decision to join forces with Egypt and Syria was not a contentious proposition. Despite the vocal opposition to radical Arabism from many decision-makers, most believed that strength in unity was the kingdom's best hope of fending off an Israeli threat. Even members of the old guard who were losing power to the Abu Nuwar faction recognised that their paramount task was to defend the Hashemite state at any cost.

Accordingly, they temporarily shelved their political differences to face the common threat, Israel.

Events seemed to confirm that Israel wanted war. According to Moshe Dayan, the Ben-Gurion government approved 'vigorous military steps against Jordan.'[92] On 11 September, Israel attacked the police station at Khirbat al-Rahwa on the West Bank, killing 15 Jordanian soldiers.[93] Israeli troops killed another five Jordanians near Hebron-Beersheba in retaliation for an Arab attack on Israel. On 13 September, Israel launched a raid which killed 11 Jordanians. Two weeks later, an Israeli assault on the Sharafi police post left 29 Jordanians dead. These attacks, coupled with the devastating Qalqilya raid in early October – which resulted in over 70 Jordanian deaths – united the national security establishment.[94]

Israel's raids were ostensibly in response to guerrilla raids being launched from the Arab states. Jordanian decisionmakers were well aware of Israel's superior military capability and took steps to remove any pretext for an assault against Jordan. In fact, in July the army had been ordered 'to shoot infiltrators entering or coming from Israeli territory.'[95]

Western policymakers agreed that Jordan had legitimate cause for concern. Ambassador Mallory reported, 'Israel by her own actions has rendered [the Jordan–Israel] armistice agreement and UNTSO [United Nations Treaty Supervision Organisation] virtually useless.'[96] Dulles warned Israeli Ambassador Abba Eban that Israel's recent 'massive retaliatory raids against posts in Jordan ... partook of the nature of acts of war.' Further, '[t]hese heavy blows by Israel were having the effect of weakening the Government of Jordan and hastening the fragmentation of that country.'[97] Britain warned Israeli Foreign Minister Golda Meir it would protect Jordan against any Israeli aggression. 'On hearing this, Meir burst with rage, denouncing [this] statement as nothing short of an "ultimatum".'[98]

Israel insisted that its policy toward Jordan was designed to protect the security of the Jewish state. In particular, Israeli leaders were alarmed by Jordan's quest for Iraqi military support.[99] Because Baghdad had not signed an armistice agreement with Israel, Israeli leaders considered any deployment of Iraqi troops to Jordan a threat. Thus, when Baghdad agreed to dispatch troops to Jordan after the Qalqilya raid, Nuri al-Sa`id reassured Israel through diplomatic channels that Iraqi troops would be used only for defensive purposes.[100] The Jordanians, however, believed that Iraqi troops would only provoke Israel and wisely declined Baghdad's offer. Iraq kept its troops on the border, but Jordan permitted Syrian forces to enter the Ajlun area on 1 November and Saudi troops to deploy to the Ma`an vicinity on 15 November.[101]

The Anglo-French-Israeli invasion of Egypt – commonly referred to in Arab political discourse as *al-`adwan al-thulathi*, or the 'Tripartite Aggression' – on 29–31 October stirred passions in Jordan and resulted in direct policy clashes in the national security establishment. Egyptian General Abdel Hakim `Amer, under the provisions of the joint defence agreement, ordered Syria and Jordan to mobilise against Israel as part of Operation Beisan, a plan envisioning an Arab armoured thrust to alleviate Israeli pressure on the Egyptian front.[102]

Paradoxically, it was the group of Jordanian policymakers who would later be denounced as 'radicals' who opposed Jordan entering the war on Egypt's behalf. Hussein personally wanted Jordan to fight, but was overridden by Prime Minister Suleiman al-Nabulsi (who had formed a leftist government after the 21 October parliamentary elections, discussed in the next chapter) and Abu Nuwar. Al-Nabulsi – although sympathetic to the radical pan-Arabist cause – actually refused a direct order from Hussein to launch an offensive against Israel. (According to Lunt, the assault was to be initiated from the West Bank town of Jenin.[103]) 'The idea was ridiculous,' al-Nabulsi argued. 'We were no match for the Israelis, particularly with the British and the French involved on their side.'[104] Abu Nuwar, despite his alliance with leftist officers in the army, also behaved pragmatically and opposed Hussein's plan to send Jordanian troops to war.[105] Al-Nabulsi and Abu Nuwar's successful efforts to dissuade Hussein from embroiling Jordan in a war with Israel suggest that neither was quite as radical as many historians have claimed.

Conclusion

The year 1956 ended with Jordan unsure of its future political course. The Baghdad Pact crisis and the Suez affair signalled the emergence of radical pan-Arabism as a threat to the Hashemite state. The Suez affair also highlighted the ever-present Israeli threat to Jordanian national security. Even more worrying, for the first time since Hussein came to power in 1953, visible cleavages began to appear in Jordan's national security establishment. Arabisation had bolstered the power of potentially destabilising elements in the army and in the political elite. The victors of the forthcoming struggle would gain control of the kingdom's ruling coalition and, in so doing, gain control of Jordan.

3
Radicals versus Royalists

Never in Jordan's history did rival security policies polarise the national security establishment as they did in 1956–57. The confidence King Hussein gained by expelling General Glubb and his growing belief that Jordan could reach an accommodation with Arab radicalism caused him to take a more active role in policymaking. Hussein's Arabisation programme and his decision to hold free parliamentary elections brought to power factions that challenged the primacy of the monarchy in Jordan.

Jordan's first free parliamentary elections

The decision to hold elections on 21 October 1956 was embraced by most sectors of Jordanian political life. The opposition welcomed the opportunity to expand its political space. The Free Officers favoured elections which might empower leftists and pan-Arabists. The only reservations came from the old guard, which cautioned the king that free elections could create instability by bringing extremist elements into power. Hussein, however, hoped to exploit the popularity he had gained by dismissing Glubb and disregarded the counsel of the veteran advisors who had served his father and grandfather.

The relatively unfettered polls 'produced the first genuinely free election in Jordan's history.'[1] While voter turnout was low (50–60 per cent of eligible voters outside Amman and 20–30 per cent in the capital), opposition parties not surprisingly swept the polls.[2] Of the 142 candidates competing for 40 seats (20 from each Bank) in the Lower House, the National Socialist Party (NSP) won 12 seats, independents won ten, the Arab Constitutional Party won eight, the Muslim Brotherhood won four, the National Front (Communists) won three, the Ba`thists won two, and the Islamic Liberation Party (ILP) took one seat.[3]

The Suez crisis contributed to leftist and pan-Arabist victories by stoking the fires of anti-Westernism and pro-Nasserism. Campaign literature denounced imperialism, and the media gave extensive, and highly laudatory, coverage to Gamal Abdel Nasser's recent trips to Saudi Arabia and Syria. Opposition parties unanimously called for abrogating the Anglo-Jordanian Treaty. Even conservatives 'were forced by public opinion either to vie with their radical opponents for the most extreme nationalist position or to drop out of the election altogether.'[4] Another factor aiding militant parties was the outcry over recent Israeli raids on the West Bank, particularly the devastating Qalqilya assault.

The election results set alarm bells ringing in London. One official noted: 'Extremists of both wings [left and right] have been strengthened as a result of the October elections.' Moreover, 'neither development bodes well for what remains of British influence in Jordan.'[5] Whitehall knew that treaty revision would be the first task of the new parliament. Jordan had offered Britain a foothold in the Levant and a reliable ally amid hostile powers.[6] Arabisation, coupled with the Suez fiasco, led Britain to the conclusion that the time had come to extricate itself from Jordan. Foreign Secretary Selwyn Lloyd, among others, felt that British aid represented 'wasted' money.[7]

Suleiman al-Nabulsi: Jordan's Kerensky?

In keeping with the free atmosphere of the elections, King Hussein asked NSP leader Suleiman al-Nabulsi (from al-Salt) to form the new government. While al-Nabulsi had failed to win a seat in the Lower House, his party dominated the new chamber. 'To this day, the legacy of al-Nabulsi and the government he headed remain a symbol for both the best and the worst of Jordanian political life.'[8] His supporters maintain he presided over the only popularly elected government in Jordan's history. His detractors view him as a leader who led the Hashemite state to the brink of oblivion.

Al-Nabulsi seems to have been all things to all people. Sir Alec Kirkbride, for example, considered him 'a staunch conservative.'[9] Others recalled that al-Nabulsi had supported Transjordanian nationalist Subhi Abu Ghanima.[10] British Ambassador Charles Johnston found al-Nabulsi 'terrifyingly reminiscent of Kerensky.'[11] Hussein claimed al-Nabulsi was committed to Cairo and Moscow. Al-Nabulsi figured himself a political reformer who wanted to hold free elections and reduce corruption.[12] Kamal al-Sha`ir said that 'al-Nabulsi was pro-Nasser, but not a Nasserite.'[13] What is clear is that al-Nabulsi's tenure in the security establishment was remarkably short. He never held another government post after 1957.

The faction al-Nabulsi assembled comprised both moderates and radicals. The NSP itself was a middling coalition of middle-class political figures who banded together for electoral convenience. As Robert Satloff notes: 'What political philosophy the party espoused was nationalist but mildly so, unionist but in moderation, reformist but not revolutionary, royalist but within constitutional limits.'[14] Prominent members of the NSP included Hashemite stalwart Hazza` al-Majali, Abdel Halim al-Nimr (a former King Abdullah I supporter from al-Salt), and the affluent Hikmat al-Masri (from Nablus). Radicals included Ba`thist Abdullah al-Rimawi and Communist Abdel Qadir Salih.[15] There might have been more militants in the al-Nabulsi faction had not other parties formed a tactical alliance against the radicals before the polls.[16]

The chief weaknesses of the al-Nabulsi faction and its government were its heterogeneity and lack of coherent policy objectives. The radicals wanted to unseat Hussein and declare Jordan a republic, while the moderates merely wanted to align Jordan with the pan-Arab states and the USSR. Although the faction eventually cobbled together an anti-Western security policy, it failed to develop a cohesive programme for dominating the national security establishment. Nevertheless, the *leitmotif* of the al-Nabulsi era was distinctly anti-royalist. As Uriel Dann writes of the al-Nabulsi camp: 'The Hashemite tradition was nothing to them; the king, if permitted to reign, should certainly not rule.'[17]

The foreign aid controversy

A major issue concerning policymakers after the elections was foreign aid. Jordan could only survive 'for about one year [after 1956] without any foreign aid', but required external support thereafter to maintain living standards at their current levels.[18] With British influence in Jordan waning, the Jordanians turned to the US to lobby for foreign aid.

Hussein hoped to play to the Eisenhower administration's fear of Communism. The US, however, was unwilling to offer Jordan a full commitment of support. First, virtually every significant American policymaker considered Jordan an unviable entity. Britain concurred with the US assessment. In December, Secretary of State John Foster Dulles asked his British counterpart, Selwyn Lloyd, '[w]hat is the future of Jordan?' Lloyd replied, 'I don't think it's got one.'[19] Second, Jordan was only important to Washington as part of the geopolitical equation. Maintaining a stable, pro-Western government in Jordan was a prerequisite to resolving the Palestinian problem and undermining Soviet influence in the Middle East.[20] Jordan, however, was not considered important for its own sake.

The promulgation of the Eisenhower Doctrine in January 1957 was the issue on which the foreign aid question would hinge in the coming months. The Doctrine proclaimed America's readiness to provide economic, political, and military support to Middle Eastern states threatened by 'International Communism'. Guided by the philosophy of the Doctrine, the American government authorised the use of $200 million for assistance to those Middle Eastern countries facing Communist 'aggression'.

The doctrine was not popular in the Arab world and was widely viewed in Jordan as a form of 'economic imperialism'. Suleiman al-Nabulsi pressured Hussein to sign the so-called Arab Solidarity Agreement (ASA) in Cairo on 19 January 1957. In exchange for Jordan forsaking the British subsidy, Egypt, Syria, and Saudi Arabia would provide Jordan with an annual income of 12.5 Egyptian Pounds for ten years. The royalists had not secured an alternative to the Arab offer and reluctantly accepted al-Nabulsi's *fait accompli*.[21]

The ASA was a watershed insofar as Jordan was on the brink of trading the linchpin of its security system, Britain, for a precarious alliance with the radical Arab states. For the first time since 1921, Jordan would have no formal security association with a major Western power. While the ASA was popular in Jordan and the Arab world, it underscored the gradual power shift which was taking place in the national security establishment. The monarchy's prominence in national security policymaking could no longer be taken for granted, a fact illustrated by some of al-Nabulsi's recent policies.

In December, the cabinet had liberalised censorship restrictions and encouraged opposition groups to publish literature. The Muslim Brotherhood began producing 'The Islamic Struggle' (*al-kifah al-islami*), the NSP published 'The Charter' (*al-mithaq*), and the Communists distributed 'The Masses' (*al-jamahir*).[22] A burgeoning pamphlet literature championing anti-Western, anti-Zionist, and pro-Arabist themes appeared on the streets.[23]

In January 1957, Al-Nabulsi empowered the hitherto ineffectual Lower House Committee on Foreign Relations by asking it for policy recommendations.[24] The Committee, dominated by radicals, asked the government 'to observe carefully the followers and agents of the Baghdad Pact', blasted the Eisenhower Doctrine, and advocated establishing relations with the USSR. The Lower House endorsed the Committee's findings.

In addition, Abdullah al-Rimawi and Abdel Qadir al-Salih persuaded al-Nabulsi to purge pro-British officials from the government.

The royalists retaliate

Al-Nabulsi's tilt toward the militants alarmed old guard royalists. Sharif Nasser urged Hussein to clip al-Nabulsi's wings before it was too late. Court Chief Bahjat al-Talhuni and Samir al-Rifa`i warned Hussein that his prerogative was diminishing with each passing day. Thus persuaded, the king began 'looking for a pretext to dismiss Nabulsi' and replace him with al-Rifa`i.[25]

Al-Rifa`i was also suspicious of Ali Abu Nuwar and resented the latter's close relationship with Hussein. He accused Abu Nuwar of 'playing a double game' by befriending both Hussein and the al-Nabulsi faction.[26] Al-Rifa`i reckoned, however, that Abu Nuwar could be ousted with no great difficulty: 'Abu Nuwar's great failure had been his inability to eradicate the various factions and to unite the Army behind him.'[27] Hussein maintained ties with his friend, Abu Nuwar, but agreed that al-Nabulsi's conception of Jordanian national security was inimical to the monarchy's interests.[28]

On 2 February, Hussein sent al-Nabulsi a public message outlining the throne's opposition to Communism: 'We perceive the danger of Communist infiltration within our Arab home as well as the danger of those who pretend to be Arab nationalists while they have nothing to do with Arabism.'[29] Hussein's oblique attack on Egypt's Nasser and veiled warning to his premier was 'the most important Jordanian political event' to date establishing the young king as an enemy of the radicals.[30]

Hussein's statement was worded to attract the interest of the United States. Dulles responded that 'we [are] highly gratified at [Hussein's] recent public action in pointing out [the] Communist menace.'[31] American Ambassador Lester Mallory, who had previously opposed granting additional aid to Jordan, recommended supporting the kingdom if Hussein accepted the Eisenhower Doctrine.[32] British Ambassador Charles Johnston praised Hussein's message as 'both opportune and courageous.'[33]

The royalists, who had coalesced into a faction with the objective of undercutting the al-Nabulsi faction, translated words into action and adopted a more restrictive media policy. The royalists' ability to do so stemmed from their continued control of the state's coercive powers. While the Free Officers and other potentially disloyal groups machinated in the army, they had not yet established a significant degree of control over the security apparatus.

The Communist magazine, *al-jamahir*, and other leftist publications (including the Soviet daily, *Tass*) were banned as security threats.[34] When the Communists tried to defy the ban in late February, the security services destroyed 5000 copies of *al-jamahir*.[35] Hussein personally cautioned the al-Nabulsi government and the press about attacking the Eisenhower Doctrine. The royalists also backed pro-monarchy and anti-leftist publications such as 'Around the World' (*hawl al-`alam*), which published attacks against the Communist Agriculture Minister Abdel Qadir al-Salih.[36]

The palace believed al-Nabulsi's faction was dominated by militant Ba`thists and Communists and moved to eliminate them from government. As Snow writes, Hussein realised that the 'government and the monarchy as he understood it were simply not compatible. Each was manoeuvring to exclude the power of the other, and the government was quite patently winning the contest.'[37] Hussein, under the prodding of his advisors, ordered his premier to fire Abdullah al-Rimawi and Abdel Qadir al-Salih. Al-Nabulsi, however, refused to obey Hussein's order.[38] A British official predicted, 'there will be a bust-up in Jordan fairly soon.'[39]

Al-Nabulsi counterattacks

The al-Nabulsi faction debated how best to prevent the royalists from steering Jordan toward alignment with America. Some argued that al-Nabulsi should resign over the palace's anti-democratic practices. Al-Rimawi, however, persuaded them that resignation would be tantamount to approving royalist control over policymaking. The government had a popular mandate over its policies and should remain in office. If forced out, the faction could take to the streets and mobilise the population. Al-Rimawi believed the Free Officers would rally the army to al-Nabulsi's side. Moreover, Egypt and Syria would probably back the al-Nabulsi faction.[40]

Al-Rimawi's entreaties convinced al-Nabulsi to remain in power and continue orienting Jordanian national security policy toward alignment with Cairo and Damascus. On 13 March, the al-Nabulsi government announced it had negotiated the termination of the Anglo-Jordanian Treaty.[41] Jordan had renounced its major source of foreign support in favour of aid from the radical Arab states.[42] The al-Nabulsi government declared 14–16 March a national holiday. The minister of education ordered teachers to bring students to anti-British rallies. Communist banners were displayed on the streets, and National Front leaders Ya`qub Zayadin and Abdel Rahman Shuqayr harangued the crowds, who chanted 'long live Bulganin and Khrushchev.'[43] In a speech at the largest Palestinian refugee camp in Jericho, al-Nabulsi proclaimed that Jordan should draw closer to Egypt and Syria. In late March, Ambassador Mallory reported that al-Nabulsi seemed 'intent on destroying Jordan as presently constituted' and predicted that a 'coup de palais' was in the offing.[44]

The al-Nabulsi camp – particularly al-Rimawi and Justice Minister Shafiq Irsheidat – decided it should force a showdown with King Hussein. On 7 April and 10 April, the prime minister presented Hussein with lists of royalists to be retired from government. One of those royalist stalwart Bahjat Tabbara, the director of public security. Eliminating Tabbara would tighten al-Nabulsi's grip on the security apparatus. Hussein reluctantly agreed to replace Tabbara with Muhammad al-Ma`ayta, a Free Officer. When al-Nabulsi attempted to sack Bahjat al-Talhuni, however, Hussein demanded al-Nabulsi's resignation. On 11 April, Hussein asked Fakhri al-Khalidi, a Palestinian doctor who had served with the Ottoman army, to form a loyalist government. Ambassador Johnston reported: 'It is clear that the long postponed trial of strength is now approaching.'[45]

Showdown at al-Zarqa

Like many crises in Jordanian history, the origins of the April affair remain hazy. The official version is that Ali Abu Nuwar and the Free Officers – supported by the al-Nabulsi faction – planned a coup against the monarchy, but Hussein was tipped off by loyalists and stopped the rebels before they could translate their plan into action.[46] The plot allegedly began with Operation Hashim on 8 April, when Captain Nadhir Rashid ordered elements of the First Armoured Car Regiment to surround Amman. Deployed in four locations, the troops took a census of cars entering and leaving the capital before Hussein ordered them back to their barracks.

According to the official version, the next stage of the plot unfolded when Ali Abu Nuwar, Ali al-Hiyari, and Muhammad al-Ma`ayta delivered an ultimatum to Hussein through Sa`id al-Mufti: Either appoint an acceptable government, or the army would rebel.[47] Lieutenant-Colonel Ma`an Abu Nuwar, a cousin of Ali's, then ordered the Princess Alia Brigade to conduct Operation Thabit, a desert exercise requiring the troops to leave their weapons in the barracks. The purpose of Operation Thabit was ostensibly to remove units which might rally to Hussein's side.

The last stage of the conspiracy supposedly unfolded in al-Zarqa on the night of 13 April, when Hussein confronted rebellious elements of the army. Along with Sharif Nasser and other advisors, Hussein proved his mettle by wading into crowds of armed, angry troops and convincing them to remain loyal. The evening ended with Ali Abu Nuwar cringing before Hussein and begging for his life. Hussein allowed Abu Nuwar to depart for Syria. The monarchy was forced to declare martial law, ban all political parties (parties did not reappear until the 1993 elections), and accept American support under the Eisenhower Doctrine.

There are several weaknesses with the official account of the crisis. First, nearly every English and Arabic discussion of the imbroglio relies on the royalist faction's version of events. Most authors merely repeat what Hussein and his advisors told them without investigating other possibilities. Second, recently declassified British and American documents indicate a substantial degree of careful planning for a royalist coup against the radicals in the months before the April showdown. Third, the military trials conducted later in the year failed to establish satisfactorily the guilt of the alleged plotters. One assessment considered the evidence 'totally inconclusive'. No link was established between Abu Nuwar and al-Nabulsi.[48] Fourth, the plotters received light sentences for their alleged crimes.[49] Had the conspiracy cut as deep as Hussein claimed, surely the plotters would have been dealt with harshly. Every major figure convicted by the military courts was rehabilitated, and some were returned to power. Finally, few former Jordanian officials (including royalists) interviewed for this book believe the official version.

Another interpretation of the crisis – which has yet to gain credibility – is that the coup was engineered by the royalist faction and the Americans, who agreed to replace the British subsidy to Jordan after the crisis.[50] Purging the leftists was the price Hussein paid for US support. The Free Officers, who had been instrumental in organising the coup against Glubb in 1956, had served their purpose, were no longer useful to Hussein, and were thus expendable.[51]

This view received its first public airing on 11 April, when Abdullah al-Rimawi told a journalist the crisis between the al-Nabulsi government and the palace was 'the result of an American plot.'[52] The story acquired significance on 20 April, when Ali al-Hiyari (who replaced Abu Nuwar as chief of staff on 14 April) defected to Damascus and denounced Hussein for intriguing with the US and loyalist officers. Al-Hiyari denied that he and Abu Nuwar had conspired and claimed they had been framed by the royalists, who concocted a fake military coup in order to purge their competitors from power.[53]

Abu Nuwar backed al-Hiyari's account and, from exile in Damascus, accused American Ambassador Mallory and Military Attaché

Lieutenant-Colonel James Sweeney of bringing down the al-Nabulsi government. In late April, *Time* magazine reported the crisis had been manufactured. 'In actual fact, the young King had carefully planned it.'[54] Writing in 1959, Benjamin Shwadran says: 'While no United States representative may have gone to the King and told him outright to oust Nabulsi and Washington would help him, this might have been indicated to him.'[55]

In subsequent years, every alleged plotter denied there was a coup d'état planned against Hussein. For example, in an interview in 1971, Suleiman al-Nabulsi insisted all plots 'were deliberately generated by the Palace and by the West in order to create an atmosphere of siege' and maintain Western hegemony over Jordan.[56] Ali Abu Nuwar (until his death) maintained he had been wrongly implicated on trumped up charges by his rivals.[57] Ma`an Abu Nuwar, too, insisted he was wrongly implicated as did virtually every former Free Officer.[58]

Like its official counterpart, the alternative version has several defects. First, despite their protestations to the contrary, the actions and statements of some of the alleged plotters in 1956–57 raise suspicions about their political intentions. A revolutionary impetus clearly existed in sectors of the army and the political elite, although there was no well-laid plot against Hussein. Second, the evidence repudiates the accused plotters' claims that the US was anxious to gain a permanent foothold in Jordan. On the contrary, few American policymakers considered Jordan worth supporting, and most thought Hussein's throne would collapse. That the US decided to back Jordan was the result of adept royalist diplomacy, not Washington's desire to acquire a satellite state. As Satloff accurately argues, the strategic relationship between Jordan and the US 'was far from assured.'[59]

Was there a coup planned?

There is no incontrovertible evidence of a well-planned coup attempt against the throne, although many leftist and pan-Arabist elements sympathised with the notion of toppling the Hashemites. Free Officer Nadhir Rashid says that 'things were moving' toward a coup. Sharif Zaid bin Shakir, who later became chief of staff and prime minister, says that Nadhir Rashid's Operation Hashim 'was the closest that the conspirators came to effecting a coup.'[60] In October 1957, Ambassador Johnston noted:

It seems clear that the conspiracy was an amateurish performance of disparate and ill-coordinated elements, rather than, as in today's official Jordanian version, part of a diabolical master-plan which was only foiled by the vigilance and loyalty of Bedouin elements in the Army and the determination of the King himself.[61]

Satloff concludes that Johnston's assessment is accurate insofar as there may have been a scheme among junior officers and another among the army's senior leadership. Neither, however, was well-coordinated.[62] As former CIA official Miles Copeland writes, Abu Nuwar 'planned and actually attempted a coup which held the prize for the clumsiest in modern history until the cup was passed on to King Constantine of Greece in 1968.'[63]

While there was enough disloyal talk among the Free Officers to raise royalist suspicions that a coup was being planned, there was scant proof of any real coordination between al-Nabulsi and Abu Nuwar. Al-Nabulsi was a politician who let his radical colleagues prod him into confronting the royalists. Abu Nuwar, similarly, sought self-aggrandisement and allowed himself to be influenced by more militant members of the Free Officers.[64] As Shwadran puts it, 'Abu Nuwar was primarily interested in Abu Nuwar.'[65]

Thus, while there are elements of truth in both the official and the unofficial versions, neither fully explains what transpired. The 'third version' advanced here is most consistent with the available evidence. The April crisis is best viewed as the culmination of a power struggle between competing factions with rival conceptions of national security. Put simply, the al-Nabulsi faction's security conception was one which challenged the primacy of the monarchy. The royalists had two choices: either accept the radical, and possibly republican, leadership of the al-Nabulsi faction and its backers in Cairo and Damascus; or reassert the prerogative of the throne. To continue along the path charted by al-Nabulsi could mean the end of Hashemite rule – and maybe an end to the Hashemites – so there was really very little choice for Hussein.

The royalists first secured US backing for their coup. In February, Hussein told Ambassador Johnston 'he was working on a "master plan" for combating Communism in Jordan which would cover not only publicity and internal security but also education.'[66] Hussein 'emphasized he was fighting on two fronts, the Israel one and the Communist one.'[67] Britain believed there was 'an immediate prospect' of trouble in Amman and encouraged America to share the economic burden for Jordan.[68] On 5 March, Hussein told Ambassador Johnston that he 'proposed very early action against Communism in Jordan.'[69] On 12 April, a British dispatch noted that the US embassy in Amman 'had advance knowledge of

[Hussein's] intentions [to undercut his rivals]. They say that from April 5 onwards it was clear that anti-Hussein forces were getting the upper hand, and that he must act before April 14 if he was not to lose all power of initiative.'[70] A British official commented on this assessment: 'The Americans seem to have been more closely in touch with King Hussein over all this than we have been.'

Having secured US backing, the royalists needed a pretext for launching their coup. On the one hand, the Free Officers had no coherent political programme other than a general belief in pan-Arabism and an opposition to royalists such as Bahjat al-Talhuni, Samir al-Rifa`i, Sa`ad Jum`a, Midhat Jum`a, and Sharif Nasser (among others).[71] On the other, there was enough conjectural evidence of perfidy to support the royalist putsch. Nadhir Rashid's mysterious Operation Hashim, in particular, provided justification for the royalist coup against the radicals. As Munib al-Madi and Suleiman Musa note, a mere traffic census does 'not require' using armoured vehicles.[72]

A link between Abu Nuwar and al-Nabulsi was easily established. 'General Abu Nuwar in fact was in the habit of spending long hours with Abdullah Rimawi which can certainly not have been required simply for the conduct of government business.'[73] Confirmation of the relationship between the Free Officers and the al-Nabulsi faction came in early April, when al-Nabulsi, al-Rimawi, Ali Abu Nuwar, and other officials held a late-night meeting at an Amman nightclub called the Gardenia. Further, on 13 April a German diplomat observed a meeting of al-Nabulsi's ministers at Salah al-Tuqan's house. Al-Nabulsi himself was seen pacing nervously. 'The conversation was animated and excited, until in the evening an officer arrived, presumably with news from Zerqa, when the animation subsided into silence and gloom.'[74]

Once the royalists marshalled enough evidence against Abu Nuwar and al-Nabulsi – which was not particularly difficult – they set their plans in motion. Sharif Nasser ensured they had the support of the tribes that formed the basis of the loyal units in the army. `Akif al-Fayiz (son of the paramount sheikh of the Bani Sakhir) deployed 2000 tribal irregulars in Amman to support Hussein.[75] The royalists also made sure they had the backing of the Muslim Brotherhood. The fiercely anti-leftist and anti-Nasserite Brotherhood had a strong organisational base in al-Zarqa, where the major army garrisons were located. According to one report, '[o]ften the young King drove out for secret, late-night meetings with chosen leaders on lonely roads outside Amman.'[76]

To precipitate the showdown, royalist intelligence operatives, backed by a CIA covert operations specialist, 'spread word' that a plot was afoot to unseat the king.[77] The Brotherhood took to the streets, while loyal units attacked known Abu Nuwar supporters. During several exchanges of small-arms fire, three soldiers were killed and several wounded in al-Zarqa on the night of 13 April.[78] Only Hussein's arrival calmed the troops. The young monarch demonstrated personal courage as he waded among his confused troops, shouting, 'I am your king. If you don't want me, I will go!'

That Abu Nuwar was not guilty of the black deeds of which he was accused is supported by the fact that Hussein allowed him (and other suspects) to leave Jordan unharmed. Indeed, the king may have sent 'a message' (the contents of which remain unknown) to Abu Nuwar in Syria.[79] Abu Nuwar was eventually pardoned and appointed Jordan's ambassador to Paris. Ma`an Abu Nuwar, not convicted, but often suspected, became ambassador to London and minister of information.[80] Nadhir Rashid was appointed head of the General Intelligence Directorate (*mudiriyyat al-mukhabarat al-`amma*).

The left's golden moment

After the collapse of the al-Nabulsi government and the drama at al-Zarqa, opposition groups convened a 'national conference' in Nablus. On 22 April, 23 Lower House deputies and over 200 opposition delegates – 'the makings of a separatist government' – attended the conference.[81] In solidarity with the gathering, shopkeepers closed for business, and activists organised street demonstrations in Amman and on the West Bank. Public transport ground to a halt.

If ever there was a 'golden moment' for Jordan's opposition, it was then. Never before or since have opposition groups explicated such a coherent anti-monarchial policy. The delegates demanded: (1) that the al-Khalidi government be replaced by a 'popular government'; (2) that Sharif Nasser and Bahjat al-Talhuni be dismissed, and US Ambassador Mallory and Military Attaché Sweeney be expelled; (3) that all 'nationalist officers' arrested in al-Zarqa be reinstated; (4) that Jordan unite with Egypt and Syria; and (5) that Jordan reject the Eisenhower Doctrine.[82]

Hussein sent urgent messages to Washington that he needed explicit assurances of complete US backing. On 24 April, Dulles told Eisenhower that Hussein 'has a program which is a good tough program and if it works it will be wonderful for us.'[83] Through 'intelligence channels', Hussein said he planned to introduce martial law and suspend the constitution.[84] Eisenhower told Dulles to give Hussein 'anything he needs in the way of encouragement', including a 'temporary pact', arms, or a military training mission. Eisenhower, moreover, 'said that the young King was certainly showing spunk and he admired him for it'. He told Dulles, 'let's invite him over one of these days'.[85] Whitehall noted, '[t]he Americans clearly attach the greatest importance to what is going on in Jordan.'[86]

The Eisenhower administration translated words into actions with an unequivocal declaration of support for Hussein, whom *US News and World Report* argued had 'become a main pillar of US policy in the seething Middle East.'[87] First, America applauded '[the] courage and determination [Hussein] is showing in efforts [to] resist [the] machinations [of] those who would destroy Jordan.'[88] On 24 April, the US Joint Chiefs of Staff informed its commanders: 'The maintenance of a government in Jordan favorably disposed to the West now depends upon the life and continuing resolution of the King.'[89] Most significant was Eisenhower's Press Secretary James Hagerty's statement at a press conference on 24 April. Hagerty announced that America regarded 'the independence and integrity of Jordan as vital' to its interests.[90]

Second, Washington granted Jordan $10 million in 'mutual security' funds on 29 April. This grant was approved within a few hours and was the quickest negotiated aid package in US history. Benjamin Shwadran wrote: 'The extraordinary speed with which the $10,000,000 grant was made indicated that the plan had been very carefully and methodically worked out.'[91] In late June, it was announced that the US would provide Jordan with another $10 million in military aid and $10 million in economic assistance. After the crisis, the Central Intelligence Agency began paying Hussein 'millions of dollars' under a covert programme named 'No Beef'.[92] Queen Zein, a powerful actor behind the scenes in the national security establishment, also reportedly began receiving payments from the CIA.[93]

Third, the Eisenhower administration ordered the Sixth Fleet Amphibious Task Group into the Mediterranean as a show of force for Hussein. On 25 April, the battleship *Wisconsin*, the aircraft carrier *Lake Champlain*, and 12 support ships were deployed as 'a precautionary measure'. The US also considered airlifting paratroopers to Amman and al-Mafraq. Britain, which had nearly 900 troops in al-Mafraq and believed '[i]t is obviously in our interest to sustain King Hussein against the Syro-Egyptian plot', cooperated with the US.[94]

Fourth, Washington warned Israel against making any aggressive moves toward the West Bank in order to exploit the instability in Jordan. Israel insisted that it was worried that Syria or Egypt would take advantage of the unstable situation and endanger the Jewish state. Secretary Dulles said 'the US would respond very strongly' if another Arab state attacked Jordan and that the US supported the maintenance of the status quo in the kingdom.[95] On 25 April, Dulles informed Eisenhower: 'The Government of Israel has been told of our firm view that Israel should exercise the greatest restraint in the present crisis in Jordan.'[96] Britain assured Hussein that it was 'doing everything [it] could to restrain the Israelis from any intervention' in Jordan.[97]

Fifth, the US actively worked to enlist Saudi support for Hussein. Dulles told Saudi Arabia he had 'irrefutable evidence' that Syria and Egypt were 'carrying out widespread covert operations' against Jordan 'in collaboration with Communists'.[98] He said the US had evidence of an 'Egyptian sponsored plot' to assassinate Hussein and urged Saud to protect his own 'personal security'. More than 7000 Saudi troops – in Jordan since the Suez crisis – were seconded to Hussein. The Saudis also began 'bribing' local leaders to support Hussein.[99] As Fawaz Gerges writes: 'The Jordanian crisis ushered in a regional realignment of forces: Nasser and [Syrian President Shukri] Quwatli attacked Hussein and accused him of suppressing Arab nationalists at home.' King Saud, however, 'refused to go along with his two former allies and instead switched camps.'[100]

Cohesion restored: the royalist consolidation

With the backing of a critical mass in the national security establishment, King Hussein banned all political parties and declared martial law. The martial law regulations provided the army with virtually unchecked power and strengthened the hand of the military vis-à-vis others in the ruling elite. Martial Law Administration Number One of 1957[101] provided for the appointment of military governors and permitted authorities to arrest, search, and detain any 'suspicious' person. The security forces could search any business or residence at any hour, and there were no appeals against the judgements of military courts and military commanders. Military tribunals were set up, one in Amman and one in Jerusalem. The tribunals were not to be bound by standard legal procedures or by the rules of evidence. Martial law, in effect, 'was truly the momentous step that changed everything' in Jordan.[102]

The security apparatus began crushing the opposition with a vengeance. Armoured cars and tanks filled the streets of Amman, and trucks with loudspeakers blared warnings to Jordanians to stay off the streets. Posters of King Hussein were pasted over pictures of Gamal Abdel Nasser. The atmosphere in the capital was captured by Ambassador Johnston on 25 April:

> The streets of Amman this morning are deserted except for troops and police. Some of the Bedouin soldiers have their faces blackened,

a traditional measure designed to prevent recognition and family feuds in the event of bloodshed. This disturbing spectacle had a healthy effect in the streets of Amman in the crisis of ten days ago.[103]

The BBC reported that as many as 964 persons had been arrested in Amman alone by 27 April.[104] Among those arrested were Ba`thist Munif al-Razzaz, and Communist activist Muhammad Bajis al-Majali. National Front leader Abdel Rahman Shuqayr initially hid in Nablus before fleeing the country. George Habash was arrested, as were numerous other pan-Arabists and Nasserites.[105] Saudi troops stationed on the West Bank reinforced Jordanian troops in keeping the curfew. Trade unions were disbanded, and the licenses withdrawn from all leftist publications. Defence orders proscribed books, magazines, and newspapers written by leftists, radical Islamists, pan-Arabists, and even Jehovah's Witnesses.[106]

Ibrahim Hashim was appointed premier in the wake of the April crisis, but Samir al-Rifa`i as foreign minister was the motor driving the new administration. Al-Rifa`i ensured his brother, Abdel Mun`im, was reappointed ambassador to the US. Hashim used his position to undercut his Nablus rival, Hikmat al-Masri. He charged al-Masri with developing a plan to spend £50000 bribing deputies to ensure his election as the first president of the 'Jordanian Republic'.[107] Old scores were also settled in the military as officers scrambled to fill the positions vacated by the Free Officers.

Another group which benefitted was the Muslim Brotherhood, which supported the royalist coup. Because of its support for King Hussein during the crisis, the Muslim Brotherhood was allowed to remain registered as a charitable organisation. The Brotherhood's support would be translated into an enduring, if mutually suspicious, affiliation with the national security establishment.

Hussein and his advisors recognised the role broadcasts had played in the crisis – Cairo and Damascus had harangued Hussein on a daily basis – and expanded the Hashemite Broadcasting Service (HBS). The trials of the conspirators were given prominent coverage in the media and signalled 'the reasserted dominance of the Throne in Jordanian affairs.'[108] In April, the HBS suspended broadcasting from Jerusalem and Ramallah, and transferred its programming to the medium and short waves broadcasting from Amman. This measure was taken 'to ensure full control by the Palace of the National Radio.'[109] Old equipment was replaced with new, powerful transmitters, and radio jamming equipment was installed to block broadcasts from Cairo and Damascus.[110]

The central position of the army in Jordan had been demonstrated during the crisis. Accordingly, the US deemed it important that the military 'remain an effective force for the maintenance of internal security in the country' and approved an arms package for Jordan.[111] In September, Jordan received 40 jeeps with 106 mm recoilless rifles, .30 and .40 calibre machine-guns, and other military hardware. In October, army commanders abolished the current headquarters structure and brought the independent brigades under the command of the supreme headquarters. The reorganisation reduced the dangers of independent political action on the part of subordinate commanders.

Conclusion

Although the royalist faction's handling of the April crisis bolstered internal security by reasserting the monarchy's primacy in policymaking and restoring cohesion to the national security establishment, Jordan's tilt toward the US angered the radical Arab states. Syria denounced the US arms shipment as a threat. Radio Cairo provoked demonstrations at refugee camps in Jericho and Ramallah by condemning Hussein, Queen Zein, Sharif Nasser, and Samir al-Rifa`i as a 'gang of assassins whose hands are still smeared with blood.' The seeds of the next crisis had been sown.

4
The July Crisis

The July 1958 crisis in Jordan had its roots in external events. The Iraqi revolution and the threat of the radical pan-Arabists led Jordan's national security establishment to invite British troops back to Jordan to bolster domestic security. British military support – coupled with American economic aid – allowed King Hussein and his advisors to complete the process of domestic consolidation that had begun in April 1957.[1]

The Arab Cold War

Although Jordan remained under martial law, local opposition forces, supported by Egypt and the Syrian intelligence services, remained active in late 1957.[2] In September, for example, bombs exploded outside the United States Information Service offices and Turkish embassy in Amman.[3] In December, the authorities in Nablus arrested five persons for 'communist activities' and found a large cache of weapons and explosives. Police in Jerusalem arrested five members of the Islamic Tahrir, or 'Liberation', party for anti-royalist activities.[4] The month of December ended with several more bomb explosions, one of which inflicted heavy damage to the offices of an American oil prospecting company in Jordan.

This period witnessed the emergence of what Malcolm Kerr calls the 'Arab Cold War'.[5] The Arab Cold War splintered the Arab world into two camps. One was the 'revolutionary', pro-Soviet camp of radical Arab states such as Egypt and Syria. The other was the 'reactionary', pro-Western camp of conservative Arab states such as Hashemite Iraq and Jordan (and later Saudi Arabia).

At the end of 1957, Egypt and Syria began discussions aimed at setting up a union between the two countries.[6] Jordan decisionmakers feared the merger would give Nasser a foothold in the Fertile Crescent, and shift the locus of the pan-Arabist movement to Damascus – a mere two-hour drive from Amman. Jordanian policymakers crafted a security policy designed to resist Egypt's attempts to bring Jordan under its aegis and to form a rival union of conservative Arab states.[7] A Jordanian union with Hashemite Iraq was particularly desirable from Amman's perspective. First, Iraq could bolster Jordan's economy and offer employment opportunities to Jordanians. Second, Iraq's military could deter the Syrians or the Israelis from attacking Jordan.[8] Finally, Iraq could help settle Jordan's 500 000 disenfranchised Palestinians.

Iraqi King Faisal II favoured union, but other Iraqi leaders had reservations.[9] The real decisionmaking power in Baghdad lay in the hands of two powerful men: Nuri al-Sa`id and Crown Prince Abdel Illah.[10] Although a long-time proponent of Hashemite unity, al-Sa`id argued that Jordan was an economic burden and had troubles with Israel. Abdel Illah considered Jordan's large Palestinian population a threat to stability. He said that 'Hussein's trouble stemmed from the fact that 70 per cent of his subjects were Palestinians with no loyalty to the throne; the balance of 30 per cent were tribesmen who would sell their swords to the highest bidder.'[11]

On 1 February 1958, Nasser and Syrian president Shukri al-Quwatli announced the formation of the United Arab Republic (UAR).[12] Despite their misgivings, Nuri al-Sa`id and Abdel Illah agreed to unite with Amman.[13] Hussein and Faisal agreed on the basic structure of the federation and decided they would rotate leadership duties. On the morning of 14 February, the Hashemite cousins announced the formation of the Arab Union (AU).[14] Hussein emotionally declared that '[t]his is the happiest day of my life, a great day in Arab history.'[15]

The union agreement contained several clauses which the national security establishment hoped would fortify security.[16] First, Jordanian and Iraqi foreign policy efforts would be united. Second, the armies of each state would be coupled under joint command, and mutual defence plans devised. Third, the economies of the two countries would be united. Iraq would contribute 80 per cent of the union budget, and Jordan would contribute 20 per cent – these figures reflected the relative size of each country's population. All trade and customs barriers would be removed, and mutual development plans prepared.

Although the UAR was the impetus for the formation of the AU, the Jordanian–Iraqi federation was a more practicable proposition than the Egyptian–Syrian merger. The UAR united two geographically distant territories; the only lines of direct communication between Damascus and Cairo were the Mediterranean sea and air lanes. Moreover, Egypt, previously under British occupation, had a different administrative structure to Syria, where the legacy of the French Mandate remained. On the other hand, the AU united two contiguous territories. Jordan and Iraq had been linked to Britain, the Jordanian and Iraqi legal and military systems were markedly similar, and both countries' currencies were tied to the British pound sterling. Most important, both were Hashemite-led, and there was a history of proposed unity schemes between Jordan and Iraq.[17]

Reactions to the AU

The UAR's reaction to the AU was favourable, at least in public. Nasser sent Faisal an effusive telegram in which he described the AU as a 'blessed step' on the road to Arab unity. From Syria, however, came signs that the UAR would not allow the rival union to go unchallenged. Damascus sent no message to the AU other than to say that it had just uncovered a Hashemite-supported plot to undermine the government. 'Imperialist and Zionist agents' had allegedly infiltrated Syria from Jordan. In addition, the US had supposedly given $1 million to royalist hardliner Sharif Nasser to arm and equip beduin tribes in southern Syria.[18]

On 27 February, Nasser signalled that the propaganda battle between the UAR and the AU had begun. During a speech in Damascus, Nasser harshly attacked the AU and, in particular, singled out Samir al-Rifa`i for his efforts 'to please his imperialist masters and the dollar.'[19] Jordan struck back at Nasser by accusing the latter of 'secretly carrying on negotiations with the Jews in the corridors of the UN.'[20] Jordan also issued orders making it illegal to listen to Radio Cairo's Voice of the Arabs (*sawt al-`arab*) or Radio Damascus. Authorities also began jamming Radio Cairo on the medium wave, particularly around news time.[21]

Convinced that Iraqi backing made the AU an even match for the UAR, Jordan escalated the propaganda war with Cairo. Hussein sent Midhat Jum`a, the undersecretary for propaganda and publicity for the foreign ministry, to Baghdad to help coordinate a joint radio campaign against the UAR. Jum`a, 'a master of the vituperative style of Arabic' and the 'brains behind the Jordanian broadcasts to Cairo', instructed the Iraqis on how to bring their broadcasting policy in line with Amman's.[22]

The Jordanian transmitter in Ramallah was too weak to be widely received in Cairo, but Nasser was worried that 'the outspoken and hard-hitting commentaries' from Jordan would have an effect in Damascus.[23] To regain the political initiative, Nasser directed his propaganda attacks against a soft spot in the Hashemite armour. He charged Jordan with leaving the Palestinian towns of Lydda and Ramle to the Zionists during the 1948 war on 'orders from London, the orders of Imperialism.' Nasser said Jordan had conspired with 'Imperialism and world Zionism' to betray the Palestinians.[24]

The AU was almost as unpopular in Jordan as it was in the UAR. Many West Bankers were especially opposed to the AU. On 20 February, a large hoard of arms, which included 90 landmines, was discovered in Nablus. Two days later, opposition elements in Nablus tried to declare an unofficial public holiday to celebrate the election of Nasser as the president of the UAR. The security forces blocked the move and arrested 19 persons, which included ex-army officers, parliamentary deputy Fa'iq Anabtawi, and ex-deputies Na`im Abdel Hadi, Hikmat al-Masri, and Walid Shak`a.

Plans for a coup d'état

Months of civil violence led to the discovery of a plot against Hussein. Uriel Dann suggests that the plot was unearthed by Israeli intelligence, which passed the information to the CIA station in Amman.[25] Dan Raviv and Yossi Melman confirm Dann's claim, but maintain Colonel Yuval Ne`eman, military attaché at the Israeli embassy in London, received a coded message from Tel Aviv which he, in turn, relayed to the Foreign Office.[26] This view is echoed by Andrew Tully, who writes that the CIA uncovered the plot by noticing that 'certain Jordanian Army officers were spending money with considerable abandon in Amman night clubs.'[27] The funds allegedly came from Jordanian exiles in Cairo and Damascus. The CIA, Tully claims, reported to Hussein that plans were afoot to assassinate him while he was flying one of his helicopters. American diplomatic records, on the other hand, suggest it was the Jordanians who ferreted out the conspiracy.[28] CIA involvement is confirmed by Douglas Little, who relies on declassified American intelligence reports.[29]

Where the information came from remains a subject of historical debate. What we do know is that the conspiracy was supposedly conceived by Lieutenant-Colonel Mahmud al-Rusan, who collaborated with his brother, Muhammad, and Sadiq and Salih al-Shar`a.[30] Today, Sadiq and Salih al-Shar`a deny their involvement in the coup attempt, and no conclusive evidence was ever brought against them.[31] Al-Rusan's contact in Damascus was supposedly Colonel Mahmud al-Musa, who liaised with Abdel Hamid Sarraj, the Syrian interior minister.

While all evidence points to the existence of machinations in the army in late June and early July, it is by no means clear that Nasser or the Syrians were responsible. It is more likely that one military faction used the murmurs of dissatisfaction from some members of the officer corps and rumours of an attempted coup to undermine a second faction. The command structure of the army had split between a group led by Chief of Staff Habis al-Majali and another linked to Major General Sadiq al-Shar`a, who was temporarily in Baghdad on AU military business.[32] The al-Majali contingent sought to undercut the al-Shar`a faction – which had 'a formidable concentration of power in their hands'[33] – by demonstrating the latter's lack of allegiance to king and country. Although the al-Rusan plot was probably better organised than the Free Officers' abortive attempt in 1957, it was far from a well-coordinated plan and, consequently, was foiled quite easily.

Although Sadiq al-Shar`a himself was not involved in any outright coup attempt, he may have been aware of the plot hatched by Mahmud al-Rusan and his small cabal of followers. When asked if there was contact between the Jordanian and Iraqi plotters, al-Shar`a says today: 'These are dangerous questions', but admits that it was 'possible' that there were links between the two sides.[34] Others doubt any involvement whatsoever of the al-Shar`a faction. One retired non-commissioned officer asks, 'what kind of coup is it when the main organiser [Sadiq al-Shar`a] is off in Baghdad?'[35] (Al-Shar`a was visiting Baghdad on AU military business when the revolution erupted.)

Ironically, the actual opportunity for toppling the Iraqi monarchy partly came from the royalists themselves. During the first few days of July – probably right after he heard about the coup plans – Hussein requested additional military support from Baghdad. Nuri al-Sa`id decided to send the Iraqi 20th Infantry Brigade, stationed outside of Baghdad, to join the Iraqi forces at al-Mafraq.[36] At five o'clock in the morning of 14 July, on its way to Jordan, the brigade overthrew the monarchy and seized control of Iraq.

The Iraqi revolution

Hussein was awakened at 7:00 AM with the news from Baghdad. He immediately contacted his closest advisors who told him that Faisal, Abdel Illah, and Nuri al-Sa`id may have been killed. In addition, Ibrahim Hashim, Suleiman Tuqan, Sadiq al-Shar`a, and Khalusi al-Khayri were all trapped in Baghdad along with other Jordanians.[37] Hussein – no doubt remembering the successful Jordanian military role in suppressing Rashid Ali's 1941 coup – ordered Sharif Nasser to lead an expeditionary brigade across the Iraqi frontier to launch a counterattack against the rebels.[38]

Within the national security establishment, there were differing views on the merits of a Jordanian military intervention in Iraq. Many military commanders, including Habis al-Majali and Sharif Nasser, favoured intervention in Iraq.[39] Such views were echoed by figures such as Wasfi al-Tell, then serving in the Jordanian embassy in Tehran. Samir al-Rifa`i and Bahjat al-Talhuni, on the other hand, preferred a more cautious approach.

In his memoirs, Hussein claimed it was his cabinet members who wanted Jordan to intervene in Iraq and that he was personally against military action.[40] There are two reasons to doubt the veracity of Hussein's story. First, Sharif Nasser maintained that Hussein was entirely in favour of taking military action and had issued the orders personally. Given Hussein's own admission that he was shocked by the coup, and his desire to avenge the overthrow of his cousin, there is no reason to question Sharif Nasser's version of events. Sharif Nasser said that Hussein called off the military operation only when he 'yielded to the persistent advice of Samir Rifai and Bahjat Talhouni.'[41]

The second reason to question Hussein's story is that it is inconsistent with available declassified diplomatic documents. In a meeting with Western diplomats following the coup, Hussein was adamant that action be taken against the new Iraqi regime. He explicitly cited 'Glubb's exploit in 1941' as the basis for marching on Baghdad.[42] Both the British and American representatives in Amman warned Hussein that the Jordanian assault could end in disaster.

In return for calling off the attack, Hussein asked the West for economic, and possible military, support to prevent the revolution from 'spreading'. Given the UAR-imposed blockade of the Syrian border and a newly hostile regime in Iraq, Jordan was growing desperately short of petroleum products – petrol, oil, and kerosene. The US agreed to begin emergency resupply operations.[43] More important for security, however, were American and British assurances of support for the Hashemite monarchy. The US also ordered the Sixth Fleet to prepare several aircraft to evacuate Hussein from Amman.[44]

Next, decisionmakers took concrete steps to protect Jordan's domestic security. First, Hussein made a radio broadcast urging Jordanians to believe only official communiqués. He announced that he had assumed power as the head of the AU and had appointed Habis al-Majali as commander of the union army.[45] Second, Hussein appointed the reliable Sharif Nasser as military commander of Amman. Sharif Nasser quickly posted guards at all British and American diplomatic buildings and residences. He ordered his troops 'to suppress any hostile demonstrations ruthlessly.'[46]

Popular support for the Iraqi revolution was fairly muted. First, the security forces kept things quiet. In Jerusalem, the governor put special detachments on alert to protect foreign consulates and prepared plans to cordon off the old city at the first sign of trouble.[47] A few demonstrations and strikes took place in Nablus, but these were easily controlled by the army, which sealed off all entrances and exits to the city. Second, fears – particularly on the West Bank – of an Israeli intervention in Jordan helped bolster support for the king. Hussein may have been unpopular, but he was preferable to the Israelis.

Requesting Western assistance

Anglo-American military contingency planning for Jordan began soon after the promulgation of the Eisenhower Doctrine. Jordan gained significance in the military equation when planners realised that Hussein was determined to stay in power, despite Egyptian and Syrian efforts to unseat him.[48] A former assistant secretary of state for the Eisenhower administration, William M. Rountree, said that a 'division of labour' for the Levant – that is, American forces to deploy to Lebanon, British forces to deploy to Jordan – was decided at the very beginning of the planning stages.[49]

The details of the Anglo-American plans, however, were not finalised until the situation in the Middle East started to deteriorate in the spring of 1958. A British official commented:

> We are getting into a very dangerous phase in the Middle East. Nasser is like a tightrope walker who must go on or fall off. If he does go on, he is bound to bump into some major Western interests ... we shall be heading for some rather considerable disasters in the area.[50]

Alarmed by the diplomatic reports coming from Amman, Baghdad, and Beirut, British Prime Minister Harold Macmillan visited US President Dwight D. Eisenhower in Washington.[51] The two leaders agreed to 'translate the military plans into action' when 'the need was about as dire as one could imagine.'[52] In June, Britain's Chiefs of Staff Committee met and discussed the final details of the contingency operation in Jordan. The British operation called for the deployment of one parachute battalion from Cyprus.[53] The task of the battalion was to secure the Amman airfield and the residency compound at the king's palace. Evacuation plans were prepared for airlifting 1300 British and 'other friendly nationals', including Hussein and the royal family. The operation was codenamed 'Broil', and made no provision for the use of force to restore Hussein to power.

On 16 July, British and American diplomatic representatives were urgently summoned to the palace. Hussein told them that he had intelligence information about a coup planned for 17 July. He made a formal request for British and American forces. British representative Heath Mason promised that he would immediately forward Hussein's request to London, but wanted to make a few things clear. First, British troops would not be deployed to release Jordanian forces for a military attack upon Iraq. Second, British forces would not be involved in putting down domestic unrest; their operations would be limited to protecting the airfield and the palace.[54] Finally, due to Jordan's isolation, the forces deployed would probably have to overfly Israel, contingent upon permission from the Ben-Gurion government.[55] Hussein and Samir al-Rifa`i said they would prefer a British overflight of Syria, but would accept Israel if there were no other option.[56]

The explicit reason for the decision to request outside assistance was the confirmation of a UAR plot to unseat Hussein on 17 July. Both Dulles and British Prime Minister Harold Macmillan claimed to have independent confirmation of the plot and used such information to mobilise support for Jordan within their respective governments.[57] The idea that Nasser had ordered his agents to assassinate Hussein, however, seems unrealistic given what we know of the Egyptian leader's reluctance to provoke an Israeli seizure of the West Bank. American Ambassador Thomas Wright, at the king's side during much of the crisis, doubted the reliability of the information uncovered by Jordanian intelligence sources.[58] Charles Johnston, the British ambassador, although a fervent supporter of the king, admitted the crisis was primarily one of nerves.

The national security establishment was largely united in its decision to invite Western forces into Jordan. Cabinet and parliamentary leaders 'unanimously approved' a British presence on Jordanian soil; every ex-prime minister (except Suleiman al-Nabulsi, who remained under house arrest) supported the decision.[59] Even army leaders backed the decision. Hawks hoped the presence of Western troops would relieve them of their internal security duties and allow them to launch a countercoup in Iraq. Others merely desired the breathing space Western troops would provide to crush domestic opposition.

The British military intervention was a double-edge sword for the national security establishment. On the one hand, the crisis stoked Western interest in supporting Jordan as an ally against radical Arabism and Soviet-backed leftism. By tying British troops to a local crisis, decisionmakers gained insurance against external subversion. On the other, the presence of foreign troops on Jordanian soil eroded the state's sovereignty and played into the hands of the opposition.[60]

Operation Fortitude

Operation Fortitude, as the British military operation was renamed, began early on the morning of 17 July. The first British aircraft carrying the paratroops were over Israel when they were ordered to land immediately because permission had not been granted for overflight. Israeli anti-aircraft guns fired on the aircraft and forced them to return to Cyprus.[61] Other aircraft – under the orders of the parachute brigade commander, Brigadier Tom Pearson – continued on to Amman.[62]

The overflight problem was resolved once the Ben-Gurion government extracted an American promise to aid Israel in the event of 'retaliatory action from any quarter.'[63] As Moshe Zak notes, Israel's assistance to Jordan was in keeping with a strategic shift that had recently occurred in Prime Minister David Ben-Gurion's thinking. Whereas the Israeli leader had previously sought to exploit domestic problems in Jordan, he now believed the Hashemite state should be maintained as a bulwark against Nasserism.[64]

Jordanian decisionmakers understood that Operation Fortitude was as much a psychological as a military operation and wanted details of the British military build-up kept a secret.[65] 'Jordanian opinion believed the whole exercise was on a far larger scale than it really was; it seemed wholesome that this belief should continue.'[66] The sound of British aircraft flying over Amman made a vivid impact on the population and demonstrated to Jordanians that Hussein was backed by the West.[67]

Although Operation Fortitude temporarily lifted spirits, details of the Baghdad revolution shocked policymakers, particularly Hussein. Writing in 1959, Jordanian historians Munib al-Madi and Suleiman Musa called the revolt one of the 'most disgusting crimes in the history of the Arab world.'[68] The impact of the Baghdad atrocities, which included mutilation and cannibalism, upon the national security establishment cannot be underestimated.[69]

Ibrahim Hashim and Suleiman Tuqan had been taken from their hotel by the Iraqi army and turned over to mobs who 'instantly killed' them. Two other Jordanians were also murdered; 'frenzied crowds' then dragged all four bodies through Baghdad with ropes around their necks.[70] In particular, Hussein and al-Rifa`i were stunned by what happened to Iraqi strongmen Abdel Illah and Nuri al-Sa`id: 'The Crown

Prince's body was turned over to the mob at once. The hands and feet were hacked off and carried through the streets on spikes.' As for Nuri al-Sa`id's body, 'a car was driven backwards and forwards over it until it was flattened into the ground.'[71] This was the same man who once told Glubb that 'a dog could not bark in Baghdad without his hearing of it.'[72]

Interviewed in 1993, Sadiq al-Shar`a vividly recalled the violence. From his hotel room window, al-Shar`a witnessed a tank firing on Nuri al-Sa`id's residence. He, Suleiman Tuqan, and Ibrahim Hashim were arrested by Iraqi soldiers and first taken to the broadcasting station and then by truck to the Ministry of Defence, where an angry mob had gathered. When they arrived, Iraqi soldiers told the crowd: 'Hadol min jam`at Nuri al-Sa`id!' ('These people are supporters of Nuri al-Sa`id!') Hashim, Tuqan, and four others were beaten, stabbed, and stoned to death by the mob. Al-Shar`a, although he suffered a beating, saved himself by staying on the truck before being rescued by an Iraqi officer who fired his pistol at the mob. Al-Shar`a also witnessed Jordanian `Adnan al-Husseini having his throat slit 'like a sheep.'[73]

Jordanian despair was compounded by several bombings in Amman. On 29 July, a bomb exploded in the British Council library in Amman; there were no serious injuries, but the building was damaged.[74] On 2 August, a bomb exploded at the Jordanian Development Board in Amman.[75] Two suspects were arrested soon after the blast. They admitted that they worked for Syrian intelligence and also claimed responsibility for the British Council bombing. During interrogation, they gave information which led to the discovery of a large explosives cache and the arrest of a Lebanese photographer working for UNRWA who had smuggled explosives into Jordan on UN aircraft.[76] Writing in the *New York Herald Tribune* on 31 July, Anthony Nutting summed up the feelings of many: 'However much one may admire the courage of this lonely young king, it is difficult to avoid the conclusion his days are numbered.'[77]

The royalists strike back

Rather than turning inward or disintegrating as its enemies hoped, the national security establishment was spurred into action and began consolidating its power. Taking advantage of the security provided by the British presence, the king and his advisors decided to make a declaration to their opposition: far from being finished, they intended to use all necessary means to retain their grip on power. Hussein ordered that the perpetrators of the recent bombings be put to death in a public execution. In addition, the death sentence would also apply to smugglers who had recently been caught near Irbid and to five beduin who had been involved in bringing arms from Egypt through the Wadi `Araba (the sentences were later commuted under pressure from Britain).

Hussein restored confidence in his rule by re-establishing personal contact with his army (see, for example, Figure 4.1).[78] In August, Hussein approved the redeployment of two infantry battalions from southern Jordan to replace units of the Second Infantry Regiment and an artillery regiment on the West Bank; these units would be redeployed at strategic locations around Amman. Sharif Nasser supervised a purge of the army, which still contained a small minority of opposition elements. (For instance, pamphlets distributed by 'the free soldiers of the Jordanian Arab Army' called for Jordanians to oppose the government.[79]) 'Suspect Palestinians' were transferred from central Jordan to the 4th Brigade at Ma`an, a brigade redesignated an 'engineer labor force.'[80] Loyal units, such as the Guards Regiment, the 1st Armoured Car Regiment, and the 9th Infantry Regiment were placed on alert, while questionable units – such as the brigade at al-Zarqa commanded by Brigadier General Salih al-Shar`a and the 2nd Infantry Brigade at Khaw – were closely monitored.[81] During July alone, more than 150 officers and

Figure 4.1   King Hussein receives pledges of loyalty at the height of the crisis from the Jordanian Army in al-Zarqa on 9 August 1958.

top non-commissioned officers were arrested for alleged plotting against the government.[82] According to al-Rifa`i, Jordan's jails were not 'big enough to hold all those we suspect.'[83]

UN intervention

On 21 August, the UN General Assembly unanimously accepted an Arab League sponsored resolution calling for all Arab states to respect the 'territorial integrity and sovereignty' of other states, and to observe 'strict non-interference in each other's internal affairs'. Directed specifically at Nasser and the UAR, the resolution called upon the Secretary General to facilitate the withdrawal of foreign troops from Jordan and Lebanon.[84]

The UN presence vindicated the decision to accept British help by implying that there had been a significant external threat to Jordan's security. Hussein's opponents had charged that he was being protected from his people by Britain; he could now point to the UN as proof that there had been a real danger. Moreover, the UN mission was less of a political liability than the British presence. On 2 November, Britain completed its withdrawal from Jordan.[85] Brigadier Mike Strickland would serve as advisor to the army, and Wing Commander Jock Dalgleish would advise the RJAF.[86]

The day after the British withdrawal, Ambassador Johnston reported that Hussein's 'standing in the country has never been higher.'[87] During the height of tensions, Hussein travelled with a large armed contingent – ten motorcycles, 14 jeep-loads of troops, and two radio cars.[88] Now Hussein got enthusiastic welcomes on the West Bank. One diplomat's conclusion was that 'the King's behaviour throughout the crisis has caught the imagination of the younger generation even in centres normally opposed to him.'[89] Hussein also received a rousing welcome in Irbid, a hub of anti-Hashemite dissidence on the East Bank.

On 10 November, the famous Syrian MIG attack on Hussein occurred.[90] While flying over Syria en route to Switzerland for a holiday, Hussein's private jet was attacked by two Syrian MIG-17 fighters. Hussein and his co-pilot, Jock Dalgleish, managed to evade the interceptors and returned to a tumultuous welcome in Amman.[91] Throughout the kingdom, too, other Jordanians heard about the incident. Hussein responded to his people's concerns and broadcast a speech a few hours after his return. He thanked Jordanians for their 'enthusiastic welcome' and announced that he would not go on vacation after all: 'the best holiday and the best place is here with you.'[92] British Ambassador Charles Johnston noted: 'The episode has strengthened the already potent "Hussein Legend"'.[93]

Foreign policy successes

Jordan's relations with the Arab world changed significantly as a result of the crisis. The major threat to Jordan's continued existence as an independent entity – the expansionist tendencies of the UAR – was checked. Jordan succeeded in attracting international interest in a local crisis and, with Anglo-American assistance, used the UN's political machinery to defeat Nasser in the diplomatic arena. Once the Egyptian leader understood the depth of the Western commitment to Jordan, he de-escalated the conflict from a 'cold war' to a 'cold peace'. On 1 November, all air, road, and telephone communications between Jordan and the UAR were restored after an interruption of over three months. Even more indicative of the improved relations between the UAR and Jordan was Cairo's decision to allow new fighter aircraft ordered by Hussein to overfly Egypt.[94]

The security establishment's greatest success, though, was using the crisis to extract an additional US commitment to Jordan. American President Dwight Eisenhower and his cabinet were impressed at Hussein's determination to remain in power. Once again, Jordan had successfully played the Cold War card and convinced a hesitant US that, in Hussein's words, 'Jordan had become the only barrier against communism.'[95] Accordingly, Washington granted Jordan $56.1 million in aid in 1959. (Annual US assistance to Jordan in 1953, when Hussein came to power, had been a mere $1.3 million.[96])

Conclusion

The national security establishment's unity and shared threat perception in 1958 allowed Jordan to weather a potentially destabilising crisis. Continued dominance of the state's economic and coercive powers gave policymakers an edge over their domestic and regional adversaries. But as the national security establishment grew stronger, so, too, did the civil–military factions which formulated national security policy. By late 1958, latent tensions remained in the national security establishment as rivals once again began competing for dominance.

5
Confronting the United Arab Republic

The three years following the 1958 crisis witnessed the emergence of a proactive, more assertive Jordanian national security policy designed to undermine the United Arab Republic. National security establishment hardliners were able to convince King Hussein to expand Jordan's role in regional politics by convincing the monarch that Jordanian security could best be protected through external means. The hardliners comprised key elements of the royalist faction which had supported the young king during the 1957 and 1958 crises.

'Marketing' Jordan in Washington

Although the United States had been hesitant to grant Jordan security and economic guarantees, the kingdom's successful handling of the 1957 and 1958 crises and forthright stand against Communism finally won Hussein an invitation to visit Washington.[1] The Washington trip provided the Jordanians with a golden opportunity to make a face-to-face sales pitch to the Eisenhower administration. King Hussein, Sharif Nasser, Bahjat al-Talhuni, Abdel Mun`im al-Rifa`i, Ahmad al-Lawzi, Anastas Hanania, and Sadiq al-Shar`a, among others, knew their cause lacked 'sex appeal' in America.[2] They agreed, therefore, to shelve their political quarrels and make a collective effort to lobby US decisionmakers. After all, as British Ambassador Charles Johnston observed, 'the main object of the trip was to get more money from the United States Government.'[3] Jordanian policymakers had long been 'adept at inflating their [financial] figures by accounting devices in order to bolster up their appeals for help', but they now had an unprecedented opportunity to market Jordan as a strategic asset for the US.[4]

And market they did. In a series of meetings between the Jordanian delegation and US officials, the Jordanian line was essentially 'that you don't count dollars and cents when your security is at stake.'[5] Hussein made an impressive plea for continued US aid, outlining his vision of a stable Middle Eastern order and hoping to win a $100 million aid package.[6] First, he condemned Egypt's Gamal Abdel Nasser for 'helping to bring the Soviets' into the Middle East.[7] He restated Jordan's unequivocal refusal to bow to Nasserism. Second, Hussein rejected the notion that the Arab world could be neutral in the Cold War. The Arab states should choose between the US and the USSR. (This was the view of Jordanian politicians such as Wasfi al-Tell, who insisted that the Arab states could not afford to remain neutral.)

Eisenhower was profoundly impressed by the 'brave young king', as Hussein was increasingly known in Washington circles. Eisenhower 'made complimentary remarks concerning King Hussein's courageous attitude and leadership.'[8] Moreover, he noted the American and Jordanian positions regarding the Middle East dovetailed neatly. 'He realized that the Arabs were concerned also with Israel, but the real danger to the Middle East was communist imperialism.' Further, Eisenhower 'said he had always felt that the Arabs' religion was so incompatible with atheistic communism' that the USSR could not make inroads among 'the common people in Arab lands.' Hussein agreed ardently with Eisenhower and argued that Jordan was desperately in need of more arms to safeguard its national security. The other states 'against us', Hussein said, were armed with 'Joseph Stalin tanks'. Eisenhower privately expressed to other US policymakers the possibility of providing M-47 tanks to Jordan.

Hussein also put in a stellar performance on the public relations front. Cold War America was searching for heroes and found one in the young monarch. Hussein – who had made the cover of *Time* magazine in 1957 and who was being interviewed frequently by the American press – became the darling of the conservative media and won many friends in Congress with his dogged anti-Soviet stance. Hussein visited Washington, Chicago, Annapolis, Norfolk, Williamsburg, and Knoxville, among other cities, and made anti-Communist speeches before receptive audiences.

Hussein's sincerity and passion were instrumental in convincing a superpower which doubted the viability of Jordan as a state to fund the kingdom.[9] A Foreign Office report summarised Washington's view: 'The prevailing opinion is still that the present regime in Jordan cannot be given a long lease of life, and they would therefore wish to avoid becoming any more involved with it.'[10] Nevertheless, the Jordan's skilful diplomacy, coupled with its proven ability to weather crises, convinced the Eisenhower administration to fund Jordan to the tune of $47.8 million in 1960.[11]

The US trip was important for Jordan's future security because it established the basis for personal relationships between Hussein and other Jordanian decisionmakers with their US counterparts. Throughout the coming decades, Jordanian decisionmakers learned to 'sell' and 'market' the Hashemite Kingdom as a strategic asset for the US. Not only was Jordan an ally in the Cold War, the Jordanians argued, but it was the most important state actor involved in the Palestine issue. Thus, Washington had clear geopolitical incentives for providing Jordan with economic and military aid.

The last coup attempt

The Washington trip coincided with – and indeed, provided the cover for – one faction to undercut its rivals through the discovery of yet another attempt to launch a coup d'état. The genesis of the clash can be found in the increased empowerment of the army following the 1957 and 1958 crises.[12] Hussein's dilemma, one which would plague him for several years, was how to balance the army's role as the ultimate guardian of the Hashemite state with its constant search for increased input in security policymaking. In short, Hussein needed to keep his military strong enough to protect the throne, but not strong enough to challenge the throne.

Two factions had crystallised during the 1958 crisis and were vying for predominance in the national security establishment. The Sharif Nasser faction included Chief of Staff Habis al-Majali, had links with Hazza` al-Majali, and was generally considered pro-British. The al-Shar`a faction included Deputy Chief of Staff Sadiq al-Shar`a, Salih al-Shar`a, and `Akif al-Fayiz of the Bani Sakhir. This clique had links with Prime Minister Samir al-Rifa`i and was considered pro-American.[13] At stake were rival security policies and competition for political and economic power. The Sharif Nasser faction advocated a hardline stance toward the UAR and Iraq and wanted the Hashemites to increase their regional role. The al-Shar`a faction advocated a less confrontational policy and believed that Jordan should reach an accommodation with the radical Arab states.

Each faction wanted to restrict the other's access to Hussein, the ultimate arbiter of power, and each sought greater input in policy formulation. Hazza` al-Majali, for instance, was in the habit of circumventing Prime Minister al-Rif`ai and presenting his ideas on security directly to King Hussein.[14] Sharif Nasser, similarly, was very influential with the king. As Hussein's uncle, the Sharif had been a prominent figure during the king's boyhood. Moreover, Sharif Nasser had been at Hussein's side throughout the 1957 and 1958 crises.

Al-Rifa`i, for his part, was trusted by the king as a long-time leading light of Jordan's political elite. However, al-Rifa`i resented the dominant role the military had been playing in security policymaking in the past two years. Accordingly, he wanted to augment the power of the defence ministry and reduce the army's leverage in the decisionmaking process. Al-Rifa`i began crafting a Defence Reorganisation Bill that would bring the armed forces under a degree of civilian control.[15]

One of the best methods of swaying Hussein was to present him with evidence of disloyalty to the Hashemite state. Sharif Nasser's faction had attempted to undercut the al-Shar`a faction in 1958, but had failed to muster convincing proof of the latter's perfidy. By March 1959, however, the Sharif Nasser group – which dominated the security and intelligence services – had mustered enough evidence to suggest that members of the al-Shar`a faction were not wholly committed to preserving the monarchy's principal position in policymaking.

Like most attempted coups in Jordanian history, the 1959 conspiracy is difficult to untangle. Today, Salih al-Shar`a disavows any involvement in a plot. 'There was no coup planned', he says.[16] However, Sadiq al-Shar`a admits he planned a coup d'état. He says the objective of the proposed mutiny was to unite Jordan with the UAR. When asked what his faction planned to do with Hussein when they seized power, al-Shar`a replied, 'we had no time to decide because we were caught.'[17]

Sadiq al-Shar`a's acknowledgment of complicity is interesting given the statements he has made through the years. In 1959, for example, he insisted he was trying to foil a coup attempt by the Sharif Nasser faction; his group planned to launch a countercoup by capturing the Amman radio station and securing the capital.[18] In 1971, though, al-Shar`a told Peter Snow he never conspired against Hussein, but wanted 'to make some changes in the Army in the interests of efficiency, and this must have led his opponents to denounce him, falsely, to the King.'[19]

Al-Shar`a's current version of events is probably closest to the truth. Like the 1957 and 1958 coup attempts, it is likely that his scheme was in its embryonic stages when a rival faction intervened. There was more evidence linking al-Shar`a to a plot than there had been in the Ali Abu Nuwar case, but, similarly, there existed no proof of a well-planned conspiracy. As the British army advisor, Brigadier Mike Strickland, argued, the affair represented an opportunity for competing factions to settle accounts.[20]

The Sharif Nasser faction adroitly executed its plan to dislodge its chief competitor from the national security establishment by insisting that Hussein take Sadiq al-Shar`a on the trip to Washington. Salih al-Shar`a had been appointed military attaché in Bonn in 1958, so he was out of the picture.[21] The only obstacle was the formidable Prime Minister al-Rifa`i, who had an alliance with Sadiq al-Shar`a based on shared interests and opposition to what they considered the reactionary, 'tribal' policies of the Sharif Nasser group.

On 14 March, the Sharif Nasser faction arrested Brigadier General Adib al-Qassim, commander of West Bank forces, and Dr Rifa`t `Udeh. Also detained were various junior officers stationed in Jerusalem. `Udeh was allegedly the liaison between the Jordanian plotters and the UAR.[22] Sadiq al-Shar`a was incriminated since he regularly met `Udeh, a medical doctor known for his radical views.[23]

The Sharif Nasser group next presented Prime Minister al-Rifa`i with lists of people to be arrested for 'security reasons', including Sadiq al-Shar`a. Predictably, al-Rifa`i balked at imprisoning people on the basis of flimsy evidence assembled by his political enemies. Al-Rifa`i initially defended his ally: 'if General Shara goes,' he argued, 'the Jordan Army will cease to exist and only a Beduin mob will be left.'[24]

Al-Rifa`i soon realised he was playing a losing hand and admitted that some action had to be taken against Sadiq al-Shar`a.[25] First, Sharif Nasser had the backing of the formidable Queen Zein, who wanted al-Rifa`i sacked.[26] So powerful was Zein that she was widely considered 'one of the strongest pillars of the Jordanian monarchy.'[27] Second, Sharif Nasser had a government-in-waiting with Hazza` al-Majali standing by to form a cabinet. Al-Majali, in fact, had 'started to throw his weight about' as soon as Hussein departed for Washington – he had told rival Hikmat al-Masri 'that he had better watch his step because he, Hazza` had been specially charged by the King with the duty of controlling all disloyal elements in the King's absence.'[28] Third, Sharif Nasser had the backing of critical sectors of the armed forces, including Colonel Abdullah Majelli (from Jerash), Brigadier `Akash al-Zabn, and Major-General Bahjat Tabbara. The last straw came when Habis al-Majali confronted al-Rifa`i and demanded his resignation.[29]

Al-Rifa`i made a final effort to sway Hussein when the king returned from the US on 2 May.[30] He told Hussein 'he wished to speak to him not as Prime Minister but father.' He argued against dismissing the second-in-command of the army and emphasised that al-Shar`a had detailed knowledge of Jordan's defence strategy and had participated in high-level negotiations with American and British decisionmakers.

Al-Rifa'i 'overplayed his hand', however, and resigned on 5 May.[31] As American Ambassador Thomas Wright noted, 'Rifai's decision to sacrifice Shara instead of defending him to the (political) death is just another example he is in [the] last analysis [a] ruthless political realist.'[32]

The al-Rifa'i government was the only administration in Jordanian history to be toppled, albeit peacefully, by a military faction. The crisis ended when Sadiq al-Shar'a was arrested on 17 May. Unlike the Free Officers, the al-Shar'a faction lacked a popular base, so there was little outcry when a military tribunal sentenced the al-Shar'a brothers to death.[33] (The sentences were later commuted to prison terms. Sadiq al-Shar'a was pardoned in 1971 and appointed director-general of the passport office. Salih al-Shar'a became interior minister in the military government of Brigadier Muhammad Daoud in September 1970.)

The Hazza' al-Majali administration

The undoing of the al-Rifa'i government symbolised the temporary eclipse of a part of the security establishment which advocated a non-confrontational approach toward Arab radicalism and the advent of a wing which championed an assertive policy of confrontation with the Arab nationalists. Whereas al-Rifa'i had generally been reactive to Arab radicalism, the Sharif Nasser group promoted a more proactive approach.

Hazza' al-Majali's new cabinet, formed on 7 May, included six East Bankers and four West Bankers and met with general approval among Jordanians. Despite his entrenched position in the national security establishment, al-Majali was remembered for his membership in Suleiman al-Nabulsi's National Socialist Party (few seemed to hold al-Majali accountable for his pro-Baghdad Pact views).[34] Further, his cabinet was considered less corrupt than al-Rifa'i's administration.[35] Whereas al-Rifa'i's greatest accomplishments had been, first, to maintain internal security and, second, to manage the transition from British to American patronage, al-Majali's objectives were to concentrate on political and economic reforms. He believed that the Hashemite state would be best served by building a strong domestic base. His political goals were to decrease the military's role in politics (this, despite his links with Sharif Nasser and Habis al-Majali) and reduce corruption. He promised to evince 'greater respect' for parliamentary procedure.[36]

A problem for the new premier was his alliance with powerful military officers. While the Sharif Nasser camp was largely responsible for al-Majali's return to office, the prime minister knew he had to keep the army in check.[37] Al-Majali realised his affiliation with Sharif Nasser and Habis al-Majali put him in a precarious position. Consequently, he told senior army officers that they should concentrate their activities in the military, rather than the political, sphere.[38] Al-Majali particularly opposed the military intelligence service's strongarm tactics. He hoped to curtail the authority of Khalid al-Yawar and Salam al-Mahawish, who were known for conducting brutal 'interrogation' and torture sessions.

Al-Majali, however, was limited in his ability to control the Sharif Nasser faction, which had close relations with Hussein's younger brother, Crown Prince Muhammad. Mentally unstable and impressionable, Prince Muhammad was cultivated by decisionmakers seeking royal support for their policies. Both Queen Zein and Samir al-Rifa`i warned Hussein that Muhammad was being encouraged to take a more active role in security policymaking.[39] Yielding to the advice of Samir al-Rifa`i, Hussein sent Muhammad on holiday abroad to remove him from 'the clutches' of the Sharif Nasser clique.[40]

The 'Third Force' concept

The influence of the Sharif Nasser faction on security policy manifested itself in the development of the 'Third Force' concept. Little has been written of Jordan's search for regional aggrandisement in the early 1960s. Most observers accept the notion that small states such as Jordan have no choice but to respond to the policies of larger states. On this reading, Jordan's policies have been merely reactive, not proactive. Jordan's actions under the Hazza` al-Majali and later the Wasfi al-Tell administrations prove otherwise.

The Third Force concept envisaged Jordan providing an alternative to UAR or Iraqi leadership of the Arab world. While not a formal doctrine or document, the Third Force concept influenced decisionmaking in the 1959–60 period. The Hashemites had always hoped to unify the Fertile Crescent under their leadership. Hussein, like King Abdullah I, dreamed of ruling a kingdom comprising Jordan, Syria, Iraq, and, in a perfect world, Palestine. The split between republican Iraq and the UAR polarised the Arab world, and Jordan hoped to establish a middle ground between Baghdad and Cairo.[41]

Rather than wait for external forces to break the status quo, the hardliners urged Hussein to take the initiative and, in effect, implement the Third Force idea by military means. The Sharif Nasser faction's understanding of Hussein's psyche and its aptitude for swaying him were crucial ingredients in the decisionmaking process. The group played on Hussein's yearning to avenge his Hashemite cousins who had been murdered during the Iraqi revolution and his desire to expand his authority on a regional level. The hardliners were also trusted by Hussein, having proved their loyalty during the 1957 and 1958 crises.

Several factors convinced Hussein to sanction a Jordanian military assault against Iraq. First, instability in Iraq – including an assassination attempt against Qassim (as an historical aside, one of the gunmen was future Iraqi leader Saddam Hussein) and an uprising in Mosul – led the hardliners to the conclusion that the Baghdad regime could easily be toppled. Jordanian intelligence reports indicated that Hussein had a modicum of support among Iraqi opposition groups and even more among Iraqi tribes. Second, the king wanted to avenge the deaths of the Iraqi Hashemites. 'The fact was that King Hussein and his uncle, Sharif Nasir, were fundamentally keen to pursue the family vendetta against the present Iraqi Government.'[42] Third, a rebellion in Iraq might have a knock-on effect in Syria and possibly lead to the dissolution of the UAR. American policymakers argued that the 'ultimate objective of Hussein and Majali is covertly to assist what they regard as [the] inevitable break-away of Syria from [the] UAR.'[43] British officials reported that the idea of 'some kind of Jordanian intervention in Iraq, or perhaps preferably in Syria, is of course a favourite one with King Hussein and his advisers.'[44]

The Jordanian assault would be spearheaded by an armoured brigade of Charioteers, a regiment of M47 tanks, and a regiment of mounted infantry in Saracen armoured personnel carriers. The second wave would comprise the three regiments of the 2nd Infantry Brigade (based at Khaw), a strong artillery group consisting of three regiments of 25-pound howitzers, and one medium regiment of 155mm howitzers. The final wave would contain an infantry brigade comprising three battalions. Major General Fawaz Maher would command the force, accompanied by Sharif Nasser. Planners reckoned that Jordan enjoyed the support of many of Iraq's tribesmen, who would rally against the Qassim regime.[45]

Jordan failed to win British support for its planned expedition. Britain believed that Hussein had no following in Iraq. Moreover, 'the Jordanian plan to send half their army across the desert without air cover was madness.'[46] Without effective air support, the Jordanian onslaught was doomed. The invasion force was equivalent to a division, but would be vulnerable to Iraqi aerial bombardment as it advanced eastward from H4 on the desert road to Baghdad. As Sadiq al-Shar`a put it: 'Anyone who knows anything about military strategy would never dream of such an operation.'[47] In the end, London effectively scuttled the operation by refusing to allow its advisors to the RJAF participate in the operation. On 13 October, Hussein called off the planned invasion.

Western versus Jordanian concepts of security

The invasion crisis highlighted the differences between the West's conception and the current Jordanian concept of the kingdom's security needs. Britain and America wanted Jordan to concentrate on the economic, rather than the military, dimensions of national security. Development of the economy, not the army, was the best long-term guarantor of Jordan's stability. The US and Britain recommended that Jordan implement military reforms and reduce defence spending. For example, between 1955 and 1960, foreign aid had increased by 147 per cent, and military spending had increased by 74 per cent.[48] US defence experts argued that Jordanian domestic security had improved to the point where the army could reduce its role in politics. They maintained that Jordan needed to concentrate on upgrading its current defence capabilities, rather than expanding its forces.[49] A British proposal recommended reducing the size of the army and standardising armoured units.[50]

Although Premier al-Majali believed the military was the backbone of Jordan's security system and maintained close relations with the army leadership, he understood the need to appease the kingdom's external backers. He comprehended military cutbacks were necessary to maintain Western goodwill and economic support. In addition, al-Majali believed that the kingdom's long-term security could be assured by creating more efficient civil and security services. Accordingly, al-Majali agreed to cut defence spending from JD 19 million to 15.5 million, while simultaneously lobbying the US for new weapons to replace Jordan's stocks.[51] Al-Majali's cuts were minor, though, and did not reduce the Sharif Nasser faction's power. As one colonel boasted, the army 'had plenty of money tucked away.'[52]

However, al-Majali's ability to bring Jordanian security policy in line with Washington's conception of Jordanian national security needs won the kingdom a $13.5 million US arms package.[53] The military's economic well-being was further bolstered by the US decision in May 1960 'to continue to subsidise Jordan for the time being' due to is 'pivotal' position in the Middle East.[54] At Anglo-American talks in London, Britain and the US agreed to extend their economic assistance to Jordan for another year, while encouraging the Jordanians 'to keep overall expenditure within its present level.'[55]

Reforms enter the security equation

By 1960, Prime Minister al-Majali had begun to root out the more blatant cases of corruption and mismanagement, partly to please the Western donor states and partly to streamline the national security establishment by undercutting his rivals. For example, al-Majali took action against Ganj Shukri – the finance director for the Development Board and brother-in-law of Samir al-Rifa`i – for having 'feathered his nest pretty thoroughly' with US aid.[56] Other political figures were sacked or transferred for financial improprieties.[57]

Al-Majali, however, could not eliminate corruption from government since he derived his power from alliances with powerful, but less-than-honest, policymakers. For example, al-Majali had included `Akif al-Fayiz in his government to ensure the support of the powerful Beni Sakhir tribal confederation.[58] As minister of agriculture, al-Fayiz reportedly made thousands of dinars by selling government wheat and animal fodder on the open market. He also diverted resources allocated to southern tribes during the drought of 1959 to his own tribes in the north.[59] Sharif Nasser, too, was heavily involved in smuggling activities and took commissions from arms deals. Another scandal involved Radi Abdullah, a close confidante of King Hussein, who was accused of embezzlement and placed under house arrest for several years.[60]

Al-Majali also managed to enact a degree of political reform. Stories of torture and detention without trial circulated the kingdom and eroded the government's legitimacy. In late 1958, for example, a young prisoner named Shama` Kayali was tortured to death by members of Sharif Nasser's 'intelligence group'. Kayali was suspected of working for the Syrians and had been beaten and burned to death after having his fingernails ripped out.[61] By July 1960 – 18 months after martial law was lifted – some 260 political prisoners (many of whom were unrepentant Communists) still languished in Jordanian jails. Most had been imprisoned in 1957 and had not been tried due to lack of evidence.[62] Such incidents prompted al-Majali to limit the security machine's powers of arrest by insisting that prisoners be tried by military courts.

Although Jordanian domestic security seemed to have improved slightly during al-Majali's government, relations with the radical Arab states remained poor. In March 1960, the security services uncovered a plot to assassinate al-Majali. A Colonel Qassim Nasser and others were seized by the security forces and accused of plotting against the government.[63] Cairo denounced Hussein as the 'Judas of the Arabs', a 'brilliant scholar of the London school of treason.' Al-Majali was condemned as

Hussein's 'chief eunuch', another 'descendent of high treason.'[64] *Sawt al-`arab* broadcast: 'You, Hussein, are nothing but a cog in the machinery of imperialism. We can almost discern the British fingerprints in your statements.'[65] Radio Cairo also devoted an entire programme, entitled 'Know your Enemies', to the Hashemite family.[66] The government retaliated with a harsh anti-UAR propaganda campaign.[67] The Arabic version of Hussein's memoirs sums up Jordanian attitudes at the time: 'The leaders of the Arab states which were attacking us [were] tools in the hands of Moscow.' Hussein suggests that a more appropriate moniker for Abdel Nasser would have been 'Abdel Moscow'.[68] Western officials, however, worried that Jordan's confrontational policies would goad the UAR into action. In a meeting with Hazza` al-Majali, Ambassador Johnston urged him to take security precautions to protect himself. The premier replied, 'we Majalis are used to killing and being killed.'[69] That meeting was to prove portentous.

The assassination of Hazza` al-Majali

At 11:30 AM on 29 August 1960, a bomb planted by Syrian intelligence agents killed Prime Minister Hazza` al-Majali and 12 others who were in his Amman office.[70] Twenty minutes later, a second explosion – designed to kill King Hussein – rocked the building. The army cordoned off the area and arrested and shot several people suspected of planting the bomb.[71] Amman was placed under curfew. Israeli intelligence asserted that 'these outrages were part of a coordinated plan to seize power' and reported that Syria had reinforced its forces on the border with Jordan.[72]

A new government was quickly formed under Bahjat al-Talhuni, a close ally of Samir al-Rifa`i.[73] Al-Talhuni's ascendancy signalled that the al-Rifa`i camp was moving back into Hussein's good graces and had been forgiven for its role in the 1959 intrigues. But al-Talhuni's appointment was also a matter of expedience; al-Talhuni was ensconced in the inner circle and could hastily assemble a cabinet. The national security establishment's ability to form a government so quickly 'played a large part' in its ability to weather the assassination crisis.[74] Once again, Jordan demonstrated that it could close ranks in the face of a common security threat.

The security apparatus quickly arrested the bombers. Salah al-Safadi, a bookshop owner, had been paid 1000 Syrian pounds to install two time-bombs in the prime minister's office. Zakaria Yusef al-Taher, an Amman merchant, had contributed money to the scheme.[75] Several others, including a member of the al-Dabbas clan from al-Salt, were implicated.

Four people were eventually hanged in a public execution. As one British official noted, the 'complicity of the condemned men in the bomb plot was never in doubt.'[76] The affair did not end, though, until August 1961, when a relative of Zakaria al-Taher was killed in revenge by a member of the al-Majali clan. Hussein personally mediated the dispute, and the two sides reconciled their differences.[77]

After al-Majali's assassination, Hussein 'really had to do something if he was not to lose all support from the Majalis and other loyalist and anti-Nasser elements in the Army.'[78] The Sharif Nasser faction, of which Chief of Staff Habis al-Majali was a leader, demanded that Syria be punished. Hussein, distraught over the loss of his premier, said he preferred 'death in battle to assassination' and ordered the army to mobilise on the Syrian border.[79]

A number of decisionmakers opposed the military operation. Prime Minister al-Talhuni and Samir al-Rifa`i believed that Jordan's national security would be endangered by confronting the UAR. However, they lacked clout with the army and were unable to counterbalance the senior officers who thirsted for revenge and a chance to flex their military muscles. The authoritative Queen Zein opposed the operation, but she was travelling in Europe and unable personally to influence Hussein. In the army, Circassians Fawaz Maher and Izzat Hassan urged restraint, but were ignored by the hawks in the Sharif Nasser faction, who had 'the king's ear' and wanted to even scores with the UAR.[80]

Operational planning was confined to the Sharif Nasser group. Sharif Nasser, Habis al-Majali, `Akash al-Zabn, `Atif al-Majali, Abdullah Majelli, and Minister of Defence `Akif al-Fayiz massed armour, tanks, artillery, and infantry in the al-Mafraq and al-Ramtha regions.[81] The plan was to launch a lightning strike against Syrian positions and drive directly to Damascus. Western defence experts believed Jordanian ground forces would acquit themselves well against the Syrians, but Jordan lacked the air power to provide cover for its forces.[82] The Sharif Nasser group, however, was confident it would be in Damascus in 24 hours. Moreover, they believed they could rally the support of the southern Syrian tribes.

The planners needed to protect their western flank before launching their offensive and sought an Israeli assurance of non-intervention.[83] As UN Secretary-General Dag Hammarskjöld commented, the 'Israelis would never accept Israel as complete until they had moved up to the River' and taken the West Bank.[84] Despite their hawkish security policy, no member of the Sharif Nasser group considered Jordan a match for Israel, and all were constantly aware of the potential Israeli military threat.

A Jordanian officer was dispatched to meet Israel's chief of military intelligence, General Chaim Herzog. The Jordanian told Herzog, 'we are about to invade Damascus' and asked that Israel not strike Jordan.[85] Prime Minister David Ben-Gurion had authorised Herzog to assure Jordan that Israel would not intervene. Herzog told the Jordanian: 'I think that an independent Jordan under the leadership of Hussein is in the interest of Israel.'[86] The Jordanian representative replied that his country recognised that it had shared interests with Israel. As Moshe Zak writes: 'This exchange of words over mutual recognition epitomized the partnership that was established between the two countries.'[87] Ben-Gurion reinforced his support in a message sent to Hussein through a Turkish intermediary 'to the effect that if there were fighting Israel would stand aside.'[88]

Western diplomats pressured Jordan to cancel the assault. Queen Zein, who had 'more influence on King Hussein than anyone else', was asked by Whitehall to telephone her son to dissuade him.[89] British Ambassador Charles Johnston confessed to being 'really shaken' by Hussein's uncompromising attitude and pleaded with the king to demobilise his forces.[90] The king told US Deputy Chief of Mission Eric Kocher that Jordan had to find al-Majali's assassin and 'tear him apart just as he tore Hazza Pasha apart. This is the only revenge we can accept.'[91]

It took firm pressure from the Eisenhower administration – coupled with entreaties from local United Nations Representative Pier Spinelli – to convince Hussein to abort the operation.[92] Hussein tried to coax Western officials into supporting the invasion by insisting that 'he had no greater Syrian ambitions.'[93] Washington rejected the Jordanian claim that Jordan's national security could be enhanced by attacking the UAR. As Malik Mufti argues, 'opposing the pan-Arab ambitions of the Hashemites' was a cornerstone of US Middle East policy.[94] Washington preferred to accept the regional status quo – even if it meant accommodating Nasserism – rather than encourage potentially destabilising Hashemite policies. Accordingly, the US warned Hussein and al-Talhuni to 'weigh most carefully' the 'consequences' of their actions.[95]

The affair illustrated the limits of Jordan's regional reach and signalled the collapse of the Third Force concept. A small country with few economic and military resources, Jordan could protect its borders and preserve its monarchial system. But when Jordan over-extended itself and attempted to project its military power, it risked losing the external economic and political support which underpinned its national security. An attractive proposition in theory, the Third Force concept worked less well in practice and was abandoned for a more cautious security policy.

Hussein's UN speech

Acknowledging the futility of influencing Arab politics through military means, Hussein decided to confront the UAR in the diplomatic arena and secured an invitation to address the UN General Assembly on 3 October 1960. In the speech, the young Hussein castigated Nasser and condemned the Soviets. He rejected the idea of neutralism and said there was one choice for the nations of the world: whether to accept freedom or whether to bow 'to the dictates of the Supreme Council of the Soviet Union.'[96] Soviet leader Nikita Khrushchev and the UAR delegation pointedly walked out of the room when Hussein began speaking.

Hussein's speech was clearly crafted for his American audience. On 7 October, King Hussein was warmly received at the White House. President Eisenhower praised Hussein's support of 'Free World principles' and denunciation of Communism.[97] Eisenhower was particularly impressed with Hussein's disavowal of neutralism. Washington showed its appreciation by announcing that it would give Jordan $56.5 million in budgetary and economic development aid for the 1961 fiscal year. Moreover, the US would provide the kingdom with 106 000 tonnes of wheat, flour, and barley.[98]

The UN visit coincided with a restoration of diplomatic relations with Iraq. For several months, Iraq had cultivated Jordan as an ally against the UAR. Iraqi leader Abdel Karim Qassim apologised to Hussein for the murder of his Hashemite cousins and expressed his desire to build fruitful ties with Amman. Appreciating the necessity of counterbalancing the UAR, Hussein agreed to restore links with Iraq and appointed Wasfi al-Tell as Jordan's first ambassador to republican Iraq.[99] Iraq set up a commercial office in Amman and began developing trade links with the Jordanian port of al-Aqaba.[100]

Easing tensions with the UAR

At this point, the time seemed right for an improvement in Jordanian–UAR relations. King Hussein felt that Jordan should move from a policy of confrontation to one of coexistence. Several factors prompted the policy shift. First, Jordan's room for manoeuvre had increased with the reestablishment of ties with Iraq. The kingdom was no longer completely isolated, so Jordan could afford to make overtures to the UAR without endangering Jordanian security. Second, Hussein became convinced of the merits of Samir al-Rifa`i and Bahjat al-Talhuni's policy of non-aggression. The anti-Nasser Wasfi al-Tell was in Baghdad, the Sharif

Nasser faction was busy with the army, and Hazza` al-Majali was dead, so there were few articulate anti-Nasserites in the inner circle. Third, Hussein hoped to regain the domestic popularity he had lost with his denunciations of Nasser. Finally, Hussein hoped to harmonise his policies with those of the newly inaugurated Kennedy administration. Unlike the Eisenhower administration, the Kennedy team tended to view Nasser as a progressive force and opposed confronting the Egyptian leader.

Hussein's accommodating stance toward Nasser was popular throughout Jordan.[101] Opposition leaders held public demonstrations to celebrate the new policy. The gatherings, however, were more pro-Nasser than pro-Hussein. In Nablus, 16000 pictures of Nasser were seized by authorities, and 60 people were arrested by the security forces. Army leaders warned Hussein that his move could backfire unless he took action. Not only were there rumblings in the military about the country's arch-enemy becoming a friend virtually overnight, but officers complained that opposition groups would be encouraged by the new policy. Accordingly, the al-Talhuni government warned newspaper editors to keep their editorials from praising the UAR too slavishly, and the security apparatus discouraged further popular demonstrations.

Playing the military card

Most Jordanian decisionmakers, regardless of their view on what role the military should play in formulating national security policy, agreed that the armed forces were the ultimate guardians of the Hashemite state. The West, however, believed that Jordan could best protect security by scaling down its military ambitions and channelling its energies into economic development.

Hussein, for one, was bitter that he had 'stood up on the side of the West in the United Nations against Communism' and was being ordered to reduce the size of his army.[102] He told the US and Britain that he might have to form a military government unless he got 'something which would enable him to show his Army that he was getting tangible support' from the West.[103] Commander-in-Chief Habis al-Majali, seen in Figure 5.1 with Hussein, was also coming under pressure from army commanders. After his return from London in April 1960, al-Majali had boasted in speeches that he had convinced Britain to provide additional aid to the military.[104] However, the army had seen no visible signs of increased military aid, and some officers blamed al-Majali.

Figure 5.1   King Hussein and Chief of Staff General Habis al-Majali (right) at the Army Day parade, 25 May 1961.

By early 1961, the military elements of the Sharif Nasser faction had split into two camps, each united primarily by tribal interests. Habis al-Majali and his supporters squared off against the Bani Sakhir group led by Minister of Defence ʾAkif al-Fayiz and ʾAkash al-Zabn. The al-Majalis had strong links with Sharif Nasser, while the Bani Sakhir had ties with Samir al-Rifaʾi, who was constantly searching for a solid base of support in the armed forces. The Bani Sakhir faction took advantage of Habis al-Majali's absence – he had departed in late January for a six-week tour of military establishments in Europe and Asia – to force a showdown with the al-Majali supporters.

Events came to a head on the night of 28 March, when al-Zabn's armoured brigade broke radio contact with headquarters. Tank units from the two factions confronted each other, and there was a threat of a fire-fight erupting. Hussein heard of the impending confrontation and rushed to the scene. He dismissed ʾAkash al-Zabn and fired Defence Minister al-Fayiz. Under the watchful eye of Sharif Nasser and ʾAtif al-Majali, the Bani Sakhir faction was purged from the army. Sharif Nasser split the armoured brigade in half and assumed overall control of both units.[105] Hussein sent a message to the armed forces in which he called for unity 'without distinction or discrimination between a Beduin or an urban citizen, or between a citizen of the North, South, East or West of Jordan.'[106]

While not a coup attempt in the conventional sense, the incident was used by Hussein to illustrate to Western policymakers the dangers he might face if he could not satisfy his army. The crisis, he argued, was a firm reminder that the military remained the backbone of the state, and any defence cuts or reductions in US and British military aid would adversely impact national security. The implication, of course, was that the West should increase, not decrease, its commitment to Jordan.

The chief domestic consequence of the Bani Sakhir crisis was to consolidate further the power of the Sharif Nasser faction. The removal of the Bani Sakhir from government and the army was a blow to Samir al-Rifaʾi, who had hoped his association with Defence Minister al-Fayiz would improve his relations with the army. By extension, the purges undercut al-Rifaʾi's associate, Prime Minister al-Talhuni, who also lacked sturdy links with the military. With his rivals removed from power, Sharif Nasser assumed greater control of the army and began lobbying strongly for a shift from British army trucks to American vehicles. Because Sharif Nasser was hand-in-glove with the Jordanian agent for Ford Motors, he planned to make a sizeable commission from the deal.[107]

Sharif Nasser was proving to be both an asset and a liability for Jordanian national security. The Sharif fervently believed in the ultimate end of Jordanian security policy and was instrumental in maintaining cohesion in the ruling coalition. Those decisionmakers Sharif Nasser considered inimical to the Hashemite monarchy and its territorial base were quickly dislodged from the inner circle and often removed from the national security establishment through peaceful or coercive means. In essence, Sharif Nasser acted as King Hussein's sergeant-at-arms, constantly searching for signs of disloyalty or independent political ambitions among policymakers.

But Sharif Nasser's powerful position and heavyhanded tactics created animosities among policymakers and sometimes threatened unity among the elite. The Sharif's distrust of many Palestinians and urban Transjordanians produced discord in the political elite and, to a lesser extent, the military.[108] British Ambassador Henniker-Major summed up the position of Sharif Nasser thus: He was 'a considerable source of weakness to the throne,' but it was 'dangerous for the King to take steps to clip his wings.'[109]

Despite his often-controversial role in the national security establishment, Sharif Nasser understood the vital need for Jordan to maintain external alliances with the conservative Arab states. He was thus a steadfast advocate of Jordan contributing troops to an Arab League force being assembled to protect Kuwait from a possible Iraqi border incursion in 1961. Other decisionmakers – such as Samir al-Rifa`i – felt that Jordanian security would be better served by waiting to see what Iraq intended to do in Kuwait. Al-Rifa`i was in no hurry to embroil Jordanian forces in a war. Court Chief Ahmad Tarawneh (from al-Karak) also opposed sending forces.[110]

Most Jordanian military commanders, on the other hand, favoured sending troops. Sharif Nasser was convinced that the Iraqi army was not a cohesive fighting force and believed his men would be in no danger. Circassian commander Fawaz Maher, who was sent to Cairo to sound out Arab attitudes towards Kuwait, believed Jordan needed to send troops to boost its influence in the Arab world. It would be foolish for Jordan to stand aside and watch another Arab state be swallowed up.[111]

Hussein tilted toward his military advisors and agreed to dispatch 1200 troops to the amirate. Hussein liked the idea of an Arab collective security force in which Jordan could play a part. Jordanian participation would raise the kingdom's image in the Arab world and hopefully contribute economically by convincing the Gulf states that Hussein was a reliable ally. Indeed, Hussein was willing to dispatch a larger Jordanian force to the Gulf and wanted to include two battalions from the Palestinian national guard in order to reassure Jordanians of Palestinian origin working in Kuwait that they had protection and to 'give the West Bank some stake in any hostilities in which the Jordanian forces might be involved.'[112] While the Kuwait issue did not erupt into inter-Arab military conflict, the incident reflected the growing Jordanian belief that closer ties with the Arab Gulf states were in the kingdom's interests.

The collapse of the UAR

The dissolution of the UAR after the Syrian army coup on 28 September 1961 checked the major regional threat to Jordan's security and was the last nail in the coffin for the Third Force idea of direct military intervention in the domestic affairs of other Arab states. The collapse of the UAR also paved the way for a perceptible shift in Jordanian national security policy.[113] With the major external threat to Jordanian security out of the way, Jordanian decisionmakers had to turn their attention inward and concentrate more on domestic issues.

King Hussein, in particular, felt the need to reform Jordanian security policy in order to bolster his reign. As one British official put it after the collapse of the UAR, 'King Hussein's survival may from now on depend more on his performance and less on his indispensability.'[114] Most Jordanians believed the 25-year-old monarch had been a hostage to powerful factions and had invariably blamed Sharif Nasser, Samir al-Rifa`i, Bahjat al-Talhuni, and other leaders for Jordan's problems. Now they were starting to condemn Hussein personally. Writing in 1961, one Western observer commented: 'The King and the people of Jordan have now reached the stage when the re-establishment of democracy in Jordan is the most important matter that confronts them.'[115]

A first step was to hold parliamentary elections. An elected assembly which had popular legitimacy, but did not defy the royal prerogative, could act as a safety valve for diffusing tensions. In its bid to secure more US aid, Hussein could claim that he was responsive to the needs of his citizens. During crises, Jordan had used the threat of disorder to garner American patronage. Now it would stress economic security and political development in its pitch to Washington.

The elections, however, were far from free. With the possible exception of the October 1954 polls, the October 1961 elections produced the most unrepresentative Lower House in Jordan's history. As British Ambassador John Henniker-Major reported: 'It would be a gross understatement to say that parliamentary democracy has not taken root in Jordan.'[116] The majority of seats were uncontested, and polling took place in only six constituencies. The government interfered with the election campaign by firmly 'suggesting' that certain candidates not stand. Recalcitrant candidates were excluded by not being granted election certificates. In some constituencies, the government ordered election officials to ensure that certain candidates should win and others lose.

Hussein realised that many of his closest advisors were unable or unwilling to expand their conceptions of national security to political participation. In fact, he had often complained that 'he could not find men who could take responsibility or exercise it properly.'[117] The Sharif Nasser faction was concentrated in the military and could provide no prime ministerial candidate. The al-Rifa`i camp was based in the political elite and had a wealth of governing experience, but was widely unpopular and 'not acceptable to the Army.'[118] Jordan needed a leader who was both committed to reforms and had the backing of the military.

Conclusion

The dissolution of the UAR and the rapprochement with Iraq removed the chief justifications for authoritarian rule in Jordan. Both Western donor states and ordinary Jordanians wanted a more accountable, less corrupt, government in Amman. The al-Majali government's efforts to expand the prevailing fairly narrow definition of security needs to include some limited political and economic reforms had given the population a taste for greater freedoms. However, opposition from the national security establishment's old guard and renewed intra-Arab tensions would make the task of implementing reforms a difficult one.

6
From Reforms to Rapprochement

This chapter illustrates how seeds of instability were planted by shifts in Jordan's national security policy between January 1962 and December 1963. Prime Minister Wasfi al-Tell tried to protect the Hashemite state's long-term stability by redefining security policy to include civil and military reforms. But al-Tell's unpopular Yemen policy played into the hands of opposition groups and several policymakers who advocated rapprochement with Egyptian President Gamal Abdel Nasser.

'The birth of modern Jordan'

Hussein's decision to appoint Wasfi al-Tell as prime minister was predicated on his perception that the young politician could transform security policy to match the changing regional and international political order. The Cold War had ebbed slightly with the advent of the administration of American President John F. Kennedy, who advocated coexistence rather than confrontation between nations. The new US administration pressed Hussein to appoint a reformer who would concentrate less on military, and more on economic, affairs.[1] The al-Majali government had started the process of redefining Jordanian national security policy to include reforms, but it had made limited progress.

Al-Tell was the ideal candidate for the new age. He wanted to create an efficient modern state in Jordan – a task postponed by the years of constant crisis. Integrated economic development and social welfare plans – widely considered in the 1960s to be benchmarks of successful developing states – had not been implemented in Jordan. The kingdom had no comprehensive income tax structure, no universities, few long-term water development plans, and a poorly developed infrastructure.[2]

Uriel Dann writes that Wasfi al-Tell's first government, formed on 28 January 1962, represented 'the birth of modern Jordan.'[3] Never before (or since, for that matter) had a prime minister been so ambitious in reforming the kingdom's political system. Never before had a politician struck so directly at vested interests in the national security establishment. Never before had a leader evinced such a willingness to speak his mind, even at the risk of angering Hussein.[4] Al-Tell's first government would become known – in one British official's words – as 'the best Government Jordan had ever had.'[5] Al-Tell (seen in Figure 6.1 with Hussein), a forthright leader with 'a magnetic personality', would come to be regarded by many as Jordan's premier statesman.[6]

Shortly after forming his cabinet, al-Tell began what the *Financial Times* called 'a peaceful revolution'.[7] The al-Tell government contained no former ministers and comprised young technocrats known for their efficiency. The government began purging the bureaucracy of crooked and inefficient civil servants. Without regard for family affiliation or political connections, al-Tell removed hundreds of bureaucrats, including members of his own clan. Approximately 700 people were

Figure 6.1   A soldier of the famed Arab Legion guards King Hussein and Prime Minister Wasfi al-Tell (right) as they ride through Amman, 1962.

dismissed, retired or transferred during the initial reforms.[8] To end selection based on nepotism and patronage, al-Tell established minimum educational requirements for civil service positions.[9]

Al-Tell also believed that modern communications could be mobilised to create allegiance to the Hashemite state. He thus used the Hashemite Broadcasting Service to inculcate Jordanian citizens with a sense of pride in their country. With the assistance of Salah Abu Zaid (from Irbid) and others, al-Tell mobilised tribal and religious themes to create songs and poems about Hashemite Jordan.[10] He also relied on symbols from Islamic and Arab history. On radio programmes such as *hadith al-balad* ('Talk of the Town') and 'Jordanian Hour', colloquial Arabic was spoken and newly created anthems based on traditional village and desert chants were broadcast. Many of the patriotic anthems and nationalist songs heard on Jordanian radio and television today date from the al-Tell era.

The White Paper on Palestine

Wasfi al-Tell's first foreign policy initiative concerned the Palestine problem, an issue with which he would become associated later in his career. Although he would acquire an anti-Palestinian reputation after 1970, al-Tell actually began his career fighting for the Palestinian cause. As British Ambassador Roderick Parkes (who replaced John Henniker-Major in late 1962) noted, 'Wasfi shares the distinction, rare amongst Arab leaders, of having contributed something more than eloquence to the Palestine cause.'[11]

After service in the British army, al-Tell had drawn up a viable plan for a coordinated Arab attack against the Zionist forces in Palestine in 1948. While the plan was never implemented, al-Tell felt he could contribute to the Palestinian cause and joined the ill-fated Arab Salvation Army. He proved a brave soldier, distinguishing himself in battle and suffering wounds during fighting in eastern Galilee.[12]

After the war, al-Tell censured the Arab states for their ineptitude and poor planning. Whereas the Zionist forces had planned and trained for battle, the Arab states had wasted time squabbling among themselves and had made no concerted effort to win the war. Al-Tell was among the first to recognise that Gamal Abdel Nasser's brand of anti-Zionism was based on rhetoric, not on military strength. Accordingly, al-Tell denounced the Egyptian leader as a false prophet and insisted that Jordan, and Jordan alone, should spearhead the struggle to liberate Palestine.

This background led the al-Tell government to release a White Paper on Palestine in July 1962. The paper, described by one British official as 'an eminently sensible document', staked out Jordan's pivotal position in any resolution of the Palestinian problem.[13] Al-Tell argued that Jordan's lengthy frontier with Israel, large refugee population, and history of ties to the West Bank gave the kingdom the right to direct the Palestinian liberation effort.

Predictably, the radical Arabs rejected the White Paper, which they considered another example of Jordan pursuing a proactive security policy. Few Arab states were willing to recognise Jordan's central role in resolving the Palestine question. Like King Abdullah I, Hussein was widely viewed as an ambitious monarch who was willing to compromise with the Israelis in order to expand his domain. Nasser was especially opposed to any initiative which failed to take into account his wishes and which circumvented the Egyptian-controlled Arab League.

Rival security policies

From the start, it was clear that Wasfi al-Tell's reformist security policy would inevitably clash with that of Jordanian hawks, particularly strongmen Sharif Nasser and Habis al-Majali. 'Security under the old order meant the exclusion from power of all whose loyalty was suspect' and 'the pre-eminent authority of the Army.'[14] Al-Tell avoided a direct confrontation with army leaders by spending his initial months in office concentrating on civil reforms. British Ambassador Parkes, however, wondered 'how far such a Prime Minister can pursue liberal policies in the face of the illiberal [royal] family and other personal influences to which the King is subjected.'[15]

Hussein, however, was convinced by his prime minister that a leaner, tougher army was better suited to protect security than the unwieldy force the military had become since Arabisation. The king gave his blessing to reforms which involved retiring and transferring ageing and corrupt officers, decentralising command and control functions, and formalising the army's promotion and officer selection procedures.[16] Two Front headquarters were established, one on the West Bank and one on the East Bank.

On the one hand, al-Tell's military reorganisation established a degree of civilian control over the security apparatus. In Ambassador Parkes' estimation, 'responsibility for security has been taken out of the amateur, blundering and dangerously inefficient hands of the Army.' Al-Tell's reforms created 'a technically effective security system' and 'eased up on the old senseless practice of wholesale, prejudiced and virtually indiscriminate detention.'[17]

On the other, al-Tell's reforms had a limited effect on the army's role in security policymaking. The military remained the paramount guardian of the Hashemite state, and defence spending continued to consume the largest portion of the national budget. Further, the intelligence services were still active. Military intelligence, *al-istikhbarat al-`askari*, kept an eye on the military and reported directly to Habis al-Majali.[18] The General Intelligence Directorate, known as *al-mukhabarat al-`amma*, was responsible for compiling intelligence dossiers on civilians and reported directly to King Hussein. (Muhammad Rasul al-Gaylani, Jordan's first *mukhabarat* chief, had made his name interrogating Communists and other dissidents, a job he assumed from a former Nazi named Kunz.)

The controversial Yemen policy

Wasfi al-Tell's military reforms coincided with the outbreak of a war in Yemen in September 1962 which further polarised the Arab world into pro-Nasser and anti-Nasser camps. Like the Baghdad Pact, the Yemen war forced the Arab states to choose between a 'revolutionary' or a 'reactionary' position. The conflict between the Yemeni republicans and royalists became 'one of the dominant features of Arab politics' until 1967.[19]

Under the guidance of al-Tell (and supported by King Hussein), Jordan adopted a fervently pro-royalist and anti-Nasserite stance over the Yemen war.[20] Jordan sent 62 military advisors to the region and roundly denounced the Egyptian intervention in the conflict in radio broadcasts and public speeches. Jordan also sent 12000 .303 rifles to the anti-republican forces. These actions convinced most observers that Jordan's role in the dispute was greater than it really was and served to inflame pro-Nasser sentiments throughout Jordan.

As co-architects of the Yemen policy, Hussein and al-Tell pursued their policy with zeal. When one reporter asked Hussein why Jordan adopted such a harshly anti-Nasser position, he snapped: 'Are you to blame me, after seven Egyptian attempts on my life before I was 26?'[21] Further, 'Hussein's ambitions were aroused, and the situation appealed to his love of adventure. He saw an opportunity to flex his muscles, and he had long been itching to use his small air force.'[22] Hussein, in sum, 'was now confidant enough of his political strength at home to indulge his wilder military fantasies abroad.'[23]

Although the policy was to prove profoundly unpopular in Jordan and would contribute to the downfall of al-Tell's government, the premier and the king were convinced that Jordan's security was best served by taking a resolute stand against the Egypt-backed republican regime in Yemen. In particular, al-Tell and Hussein wanted to diversify Jordan's sources of external aid and hoped the Arab Gulf states would supplement American assistance.

Jordan translated its Yemen policy into tangible capital with the signing of several security and economic cooperation agreements with Saudi Arabia in August–October 1962. Riyadh could provide Jordan with the economic wherewithal to modernise its army, something the West had been reluctant to finance. Saudi Arabia's goodwill was also necessary to ensure the continued flow of oil from Saudi Arabia through Jordan. Since 1960, Jordan had been getting crude oil at reduced rates from Tapline (the Trans-Arabian pipeline constructed in 1950). Further, Jordan received royalty payments for each barrel of oil that was shipped through its territory on its way to the Mediterranean Sea.[24]

To be sure, the Yemen policy had some advantages for Jordanian security, but it also diminished popular support for al-Tell's reforms. The policy of supporting the anachronistic, illiberal Yemeni royalists was unpopular among both East Bankers and West Bankers. To many, the policy seemed to contradict the reformist agenda of the al-Tell cabinet. Further, as Ambassador Parkes reported, 'the young and progressive elements which had welcomed the new liberalism were taken aback at this close association with a feudal Saudi monarchy.'[25]

Several incidents illustrated the schisms which were appearing among the Jordanian elite. In October 1962, Development Board Vice-Chairman Kamal al-Sha`ir resigned in protest over the Yemen policy. A Yale-educated Christian Ba`thist from al-Salt, al-Sha`ir was considered one of the brightest, and most efficient, technocrats in the al-Tell government.[26] Al-Sha`ir correctly divined that the decision to send arms to the Yemeni royalists was an economic burden on the country, one that weakened al-Tell's plan for Jordan to become economically self-sufficient. In addition, the commander of the Royal Jordanian Air Force and two pilots defected to Cairo in November to protest the Yemen policy.

Al-Tell, nevertheless, continued with his reform programme. One of al-Tell's declared aims on taking office was to hold free parliamentary elections. The 24 November elections were among the freest in Jordanian history.[27] Candidates were allowed to hold meetings in coffee shops and other public places and were able to distribute pamphlets. Some 166 candidates contested 57 seats, while three went uncontested. On polling day, the army was put on alert, but did not interfere directly in the electoral process. Although opposition leaders boycotted the elections over the Yemen policy and their fear of government interference, voter turnout was high. An estimated 60 to 70 per cent of the electorate voted, although the figure was substantially lower in opposition centres such as Nablus, where some 15 per cent of eligible voters cast ballots.[28]

The emergence of a fairly coherent opposition bloc in the newly elected Lower House contributed to the collapse of al-Tell's second government. Hussein decided he had to distance himself from the increasingly unpopular al-Tell. The necessity of changing governments was reinforced by the Ba`thist military coups in Baghdad on 8 February and Damascus on 8 March.[29] For the first time since 1958, there was a chance that Iraq and Syria might unite with Nasser. Jordan was surrounded by potentially hostile powers and further isolated in the Arab world. Hussein felt that Jordan could no longer afford to confront Egypt directly.[30]

Al-Tell was replaced by Samir al-Rifa`i on 27 March. Al-Rifa`i's return to power represented a restoration of the old guard to preeminence. Bahjat al-Talhuni returned as court chief, and Bani Sakhr chieftain `Akif al-Fayiz was back in office after a two-year absence. The key distinction between this and previous al-Rifa`i governments was that this one harboured more pro-Egypt sentiments than previous ones.

The Sharif Nasser faction, while not allied directly to the al-Rifa`i faction, breathed a sigh of relief at the demise of al-Tell's reformist government.[31] With al-Tell gone, Habis al-Majali regained his room for manoeuvre in the army. Nearly 50 officers 'of questionable loyalty' were dismissed in March, and Jordan's first parachute company was formed in April.[32] Army commanders convinced Hussein that the army's weaponry required updating. As Ambassador Parkes argued, the 'Jordanians are obviously intensely uneasy at their present virtual isolation in the Arab world and more determined than ever to get arms they want, and with minimum possible delay.'[33]

The April 1963 riots

The tripartite unity announcement on 17 April 1963 by Egypt, Syria, and Iraq led to the outbreak of violence in Jordan.[34] At the news that the three major Arab powers were to merge, pro-Nasser rallies were held throughout the West Bank and in Irbid. Disturbances erupted in Jerusalem, Jenin, and Hebron on 18 April, and the army was deployed. The demonstrations 'may have been encouraged by Samir Rifai's somewhat unguarded declaration in favour of the movement for Arab unity.'[35]

In parliament, meanwhile, al-Rifa`i sought a vote of confidence for his government. Despite his quest for a rapprochement with Nasser and his clear abandonment of al-Tell's reformist policy, al-Rifa`i came under fire from many deputies in the Lower House. He was attacked for his 'unclean past', nepotism, and heavy-handed policies.[36] When it became obvious that 31 deputies (out of a chamber of 60) opposed the government, al-Rifa`i conceded defeat and submitted his resignation to Hussein. Al-Rifa`i's public career was over, and his April government was the first to collapse under parliamentary pressure in Jordan's history. However, the veteran politician remained influential in security policy-making and 'stayed on at the King's urgent request as unofficial adviser in the palace.'[37]

After the ever-cautious Sa`id al-Mufti refused the job, Sharif Hussein, the king's great-uncle, agreed to form a caretaker government until elections could be held four months hence. (Sharif Hussein was regarded by some decisionmakers as Hussein's 'good uncle', while Sharif Nasser was considered his 'bad uncle'.[38]) The new government, however, was unable to stifle the pro-Nasser sentiments which gripped the country.

Between 20 and 24 April, the kingdom was rocked by riotous pro-unity demonstrations. As usual, schoolchildren formed the vanguard of the initial protests, organised by opposition activists. Agitators, equipped with Molotov cocktails, acid bottles, and machine guns, hid behind the crowds and fired on the army.[39] In Jerusalem, rioters attacked the governor's office and the broadcasting station, tore down Jordanian flags, and stoned the police. In Nablus, 4000 people demonstrated, and mosque loudspeakers broadcast anti-monarchy slogans and called for the establishment of a *jumhuria nabulsia* ('Nablus Republic'). Opposition leaders Hikmat al-Masri and Walid Shak`a tried unsuccessfully to calm the crowds; only after the army sealed off the city and cut electrical power did the protests begin to subside. In Irbid, a violent demonstration – incited by Ba`thist students – was quelled only by the deployment of armoured cars.[40]

The security services managed to restore order after several days of street fighting. Thirteen people were killed during the clashes, mostly by gunfire, and over 100 injured (the figure was probably much higher since most of those wounded avoided capture by seeking medical treatment at home rather than going to hospitals).[41] Curfews were imposed on West Bank towns and in Irbid, and 233 persons were arrested, including ten Lower House deputies. The army declared a state of emergency on Jordan's borders in the event of intervention by Syrian or Iraqi forces. Jordanians were not allowed to leave the country unless they were granted permission from military governors.[42]

On 26 April, US intelligence sources received information that a possible Egyptian-supported coup d'état would soon occur in Jordan.[43] The Kennedy administration decided to move the Sixth Fleet to the eastern

Mediterranean in a show of force for Hussein. Most worrying to US policymakers was the prospect of an Israeli seizure of the West Bank, which could lead to an Arab–Israeli war. The US warned the Ben-Gurion government to 'take no military action.' In addition, the US cautioned Damascus, Baghdad, and Cairo against supporting a coup in Jordan since this would provoke Israel.[44]

The US ambassador in Amman, William B. Macomber, reaffirmed America's support for Jordan and sounded out Hussein on whether he planned to request external assistance. Although the Western powers were willing to consider a possible intervention in Jordan, policymakers decided against associating themselves so openly with outside forces. Moreover, the Jordanians felt they could weather the crisis without UN backing. Hussein said he wanted to avoid creating the 'public impression in this or other ways that Jordan [was] prematurely seeking outside help.' He believed Jordan could 'ride out the present storms without major outside assistance.'[45]

The Israeli factor

The threat of an Israeli intervention in Jordan was heightened considerably as a result of the crisis. Indeed, the fear of Israeli occupation – coupled, to be sure, with the effectiveness of the army – contributed to the restoration of order on the West Bank. Israel radio broadcast a warning by Prime Minister David Ben-Gurion that 'Israel cannot remain indifferent if Jordan falls under Nasser's domination.'[46] Israel believed that 'Jordan is decisive, not just for the security of Israel but for the future of the area.'[47]

Before, during, and after the rioting, Israeli officials made no bones about their intention to occupy the West Bank in the event of Hussein's downfall. Israel told Britain that its 'often repeated threat to occupy the West Bank if the regime Jordan became subservient to the UAR' still applied.[48] Israel warned the US that it 'reserved complete freedom of action in case Hussein was overthrown.'[49] As Israeli diplomat Abba Eban put it to UN Secretary-General U Thant, Israel's action would be 'prompt and drastic.'[50]

Israel translated its warnings into action by firming up military plans to strike Jordan. Operation Granite, the plan to occupy the West Bank, was devised by general staff planners.[51] To facilitate its possible administration of Arab civilians in the event of occupying the West Bank, Israel finalised 'a blueprint for units of military administration.'[52] Israel also requested security guarantees from the US.[53] Washington, finding itself increasingly involved in Southeast Asia, was unwilling to grant the Jewish state explicit assurances of support, but agreed to warn Nasser that Israel was serious about seizing the West Bank.[54] Neither the US nor Britain, however, believed they could stop Israel should Ben-Gurion decide to capture the West Bank.[55]

Jordan's furtive diplomacy with Israel remains a sensitive issue in the kingdom, despite the signing of a peace treaty between the two countries in 1994. King Abdullah I had relations with Zionist leaders, but officially Jordan and Israel remained at war. The only acknowledged channel between the two sides was the UN Mixed Armistice Commission which met in Jerusalem on a regular basis to resolve security disputes.

Hussein held his first secret meeting with Israeli officials in London in September 1963.[56] Meeting with the deputy director for Middle Eastern affairs for Ben-Gurion, Ya`acov Herzog, Hussein asked (1) for Israeli assistance in securing additional US aid; (2) for Israeli backing for Jordan's request for American tanks; and (3) that Israel slow the pace of its plans to exploit the Jordan River. A written agreement regarding Jordan's promise not to deploy American Patton tanks on the West Bank was drawn up.[57]

Several factors influenced Hussein's decision to meet with the Israelis.[58] First, the king had inherited his grandfather's pragmatic approach to politics. While Hussein would have probably preferred to see Israel disappear, he was, in the last analysis, a realist who understood that the Jewish state was there to stay. Second, Hussein understandably feared Israel's military might, its demonstrated willingness to strike Jordan, and its ability to do so with impunity. On several occasions, Israel had launched preemptive strikes on West Bank towns, creating domestic instability. Finally, Hussein wanted Israel as a counterweight to the hostile regimes in Syria, Iraq, and Egypt. As shown previously, it was Israel – not the Arab states – which aided Jordan when the chips were down in 1958.

Rapprochement with Egypt

Even as Jordan was quietly building closer ties with Israel, the kingdom was repairing relations with Egypt. The decision to seek a truce with Egypt in late 1963 was neither unexpected nor unanimous. It was not unexpected given Jordan's regional position by late summer 1963. While the Egypt–Syria–Iraq merger had collapsed, Jordan was isolated from the Arab world. Moreover, both Jordan and Egypt feared the newly installed Ba`thist regimes in Baghdad and Damascus and hoped to forestall an

Iraqi–Syrian merger. As Patrick Seale put it in October 1963, a 'redrafting of Middle East alliances is thus taking place.'[59] The rapprochement policy was not unanimously accepted, especially by al-Tell and his supporters. However, Bahjat al-Talhuni, Samir al-Rifa`i and Jordan's UN representative, Abdel Mun`im al-Rifa`i, encouraged Hussein to patch up relations with Cairo.[60] Hussein, with 'no strong Prime Minister to guide or restrain him,' was 'in some danger of regarding himself as infallible' and he plunged ahead with his plan to improve relations with Nasser.[61]

Jordan's opportunity to reconcile with Egypt came on 23 December 1963, when Nasser publicly called for the convening of the first Arab summit. His justification for calling for a summit was to formulate a joint Arab plan to prevent Israel from diverting water from the Jordan River. In reality, his motivations were deeper. Nasser had seen the centre of gravity of Arab politics shift perceptibly to the Ba`thists in Syria and Iraq and needed a bold stroke to consolidate his regional position. Nasser's call for a summit laid the groundwork for events that would shake the Arab world for decades to come.

Conclusion

This chapter charted the rise and fall of a reformist national security policy predicated on economic growth and political development. Wasfi al-Tell's ambitious programme was designed to protect Jordan's long-term stability by building the foundations of a leaner, more self-reliant state. However, al-Tell's efforts to broaden the prevailing concept of Jordanian national security needs were scuttled, in part, by his unpopular Yemen policy and by Jordan's rapprochement with Egypt. Amman's alignment with Cairo would have weighty consequences for the security of the Hashemite state.

7
In Nasser's Grip

Jordan's policy of rapprochement with Egypt would increase instability by creating new challenges to national security. Linking Jordan's security to Egyptian interests effectively made the kingdom hostage to Nasser and produced new threats in the form of the Palestine Liberation Organisation (PLO) and the United Arab Command (UAC). Although Jordan managed to distance itself from the PLO, King Hussein failed to appreciate the long-term dangers inherent in subordinating Jordan's armed forces to the UAC.

The first Arab summit

The Arab summit held in Cairo between 13 and 17 January 1964 was a watershed in Arab politics. For Jordan, the summit had two important consequences for national security. The first was the creation of an independent Palestinian movement, the PLO. The second was the formation of the UAC to coordinate Arab military efforts. In retrospect, Jordan's acceptances of the summit's decisions were errors. Both the PLO and the UAC would endanger the stability of the Hashemite state by pushing Jordan toward an unnecessary war in 1967.

Although Hussein was initially uneasy about accepting the summit decisions, he felt that Jordan could not oppose Nasser. First, rapprochement with Cairo could shore up Hussein's waning popularity in Jordan and the Arab world. Hussein was always more concerned about legitimacy and public opinion than were others in the national security establishment. For them, popularity was a luxury, not a necessity. Hussein, on the other hand, genuinely wanted to be liked and admired by his subjects; he genuinely wanted to be accepted as an Arab leader by the Arab world.

Second, having been the first Arab leader to accept Nasser's invitation to Cairo in late 1963, Hussein would have isolated himself even further in the Arab world had he refused to go along with the summit's anti-Israel resolutions. As a Foreign Office briefing paper acknowledged in April 1964, 'Jordan cannot afford to appear less zealous in this cause.'[1] In short, accepting the creation of a Palestinian liberation movement and an Arab collective defence organisation was the price Hussein paid for Nasser's blessing.[2]

The challenge of the PLO

Although the establishment of an Arab collective defence scheme played a key role in Jordan's decision to fight Israel in 1967, more destabilising from a long-term perspective was the formation of the PLO. Whereas the UAC eroded Jordan's military capacity by making its army dependent on unreliable external powers, the PLO would challenge the very basis of the Hashemite state by creating an independent national movement which contested the monarchy's claim to represent the Palestinians. In security establishment member Adnan Abu `Udeh's words: 'The formation of the PLO interrupted the integration of the Palestinians into Jordan.'[3]

Acceptance of the organisation went against the grain of a long-standing Hashemite policy. Peter Mansfield summarises the policy thus: 'Jordan aimed both to combat Palestinian separatism and to maintain its right to speak for the Palestinians while proclaiming that one day an Arab Palestine would be restored.'[4] Since King Abdullah's time, the monarchy had discouraged the development of autonomous Transjordanian and Palestinian identities in Jordan. Abdullah used coercion and co-optation to torpedo the fledgling Transjordanian movement in the 1920s and tie local clans to the Hashemite state. He utilised similar tactics – coupled with a good deal of clandestine diplomacy with Zionist leaders – to scuttle the birth of a Palestinian entity in 1948 and incorporate the West Bank into his realm.

The monarchy's integrationist policies and the appeal of Nasserism and other ideologies inhibited the growth of Palestinian irredentism during the 1950s and early 1960s. As Kimmerling and Migdal write, Abdullah 'succeeded for a time in building significant support among many Palestinians.'[5] Nasserism, Ba`thism, and Islamism provided alternative political outlets for many Palestinians discontented with the status quo. In short, there was no Palestinian competitor for Palestinian allegiance.

The formation of the PLO created a new focus for Palestinian political aspirations and brought Jordan into conflict with the radical Arab states, which rejected the kingdom's right to govern the Palestinians.[6] Hussein – in Moshe Shemesh's words – 'made his first major error in the history of the struggle over the existence of the Palestinian Entity or the Jordanian Entity when he signed the summit decision.' Because Hussein was searching for 'short-term advantages', he failed to consider the long-term consequences of his actions.[7]

Egypt's Nasser, on the other hand, accrued political advantage from the formation of the PLO. He could use the organisation 'to co-opt and restrain the Palestinian resistance movement.'[8] By controlling the Palestinian liberation movement, Nasser could regain the political momentum he lost in the Arab world after the dissolution of the United Arab Republic. As Patrick Seale argues: 'Far from a call to arms, the PLO was a sort of corral in which the Palestinians could charge about harmlessly letting off steam. The whole idea was to placate nationalist sentiment while denying Israel a pretext for war.'[9]

The Palestine conference

Jordan hosted the first Palestine Entity conference in Jerusalem between 28 May and 2 June 1964. Attended by 388 delegates, 242 of whom resided in Jordan, the conference made several decisions. First, Ahmad al-Shuqayri – a Palestinian who had worked for the Arab League and for Saudi Arabia – was elected as the PLO's first chairman. Second, the PLO was to respect the territorial integrity of the Arab states – including the West Bank of Jordan – and not interfere in their domestic affairs. Third, the PLO would have its own flag and anthem and would establish offices at the United Nations and in various Eastern bloc and Arab countries.[10]

The most important ramification of the Jerusalem conference for Jordan's security was the ascendance of al-Shuqayri, who would soon challenge the legitimacy of the Hashemite state. Al-Shuqayri had eclipsed his chief rival for power, the ageing Hajj Amin al-Husseini, and packed the PLO's Executive Committee with his own supporters. (Notable members included Hikmat al-Masri from Nablus and Haidar Abdel Shafi from Gaza.) Al-Shuqayri assiduously cultivated an economic base to match his political position. Even before the conference, he had amassed £100 000 from Kuwait, £30 000 from Qatar, and £20 000 from Bahrain.[11]

Al-Shuqayri hoped to secure Arab diplomatic recognition of the PLO as the representative of the Palestinians. His long-term objective was the liberation of Palestine following the revolutionary model used by the

FLN in Algeria and the MPLA in Angola.[12] Al-Shuqayri, however, was neither warrior nor statesmen. He was a lawyer who had worked for various Arab governments and, as it turned out, was 'totally ineffectual.'[13]

While the Jerusalem conference was largely a success for al-Shuqayri, the PLO did not immediately enjoy the support of Jordan's heterogeneous Palestinian population. Nablus leaders such as Hikmat al-Masri and Walid al-Shak`a, both long-time Nasserites, supported the organisation. Nablus Mayor Hamdi Kan`an and Tulkarm's Hashim Jayusi sympathised with the Palestinian revolutionary idea, but would not cast their lot with the PLO. Palestinian leaders such as Abdel Ra`uf al-Faris and Rashid Agha al-Nimr, on the other hand, were Hashemite supporters and went as far as backing Hajj Amin al-Husseini in order to show their displeasure for al-Shuqayri.[14] As Mark Tessler writes, many Palestinian notables evinced 'little sympathy' for some of al-Shuqayri's radical ideas.[15]

Jordanian views on the PLO

While most security establishment figures opposed the very idea of an independent Palestine entity, many believed Palestinian irredentism could be kept in check. Hussein thought the PLO could be controlled, a task he was willing to perform if it kept Nasser and the radical Arabs on his side. In his estimation, Jordan possessed the security apparatus to keep the PLO under check. Samir al-Rifa`i and Bahjat al-Talhuni accepted the creation of the organisation as an unavoidable consequence of the reconciliation with Egypt. Prime Minister Sharif Hussein's view – echoed by the Foreign Office Eastern Department – was that Jordan could 'live with this form of organisation.'[16]

The most conspicuous, if not the first, Jordanian policymaker to recognise the dangers of creating an alternative political focus for Jordan's Palestinians was Wasfi al-Tell. While the PLO would not become a real hazard to Jordanian security until after the 1967 war, al-Tell felt the very acceptance of the PLO signified a negation of Jordan's right to represent the Palestinians. Al-Tell predicted that the PLO would never be strong enough to confront Israel and would ultimately make peace on the Jewish state's terms.[17] Former Ba`thist Kamal al-Sha`ir feels al-Tell's assessment of formation of the PLO was absolutely correct: It was 'a huge mistake … the greatest single mistake since the 1948 war.' Further, he argues, forming a Palestinian separatist movement made the 1967 war and the 1970 civil war inevitable.[18]

As al-Tell's White Paper of 1962 had indicated, his views on the Palestine problem had crystallised before the PLO was born. Al-Tell argued that the task of liberating Palestine was primarily Jordan's.[19] The Arab states, to be sure, had important roles to play in emancipating Palestine, but it was Jordan's duty to lead the way. Al-Tell insisted there was an innate incompatibility in two nationalisms – Hashemite and Palestinian – coexisting in Jordan.

Indeed, Al-Tell's policies toward the PLO from 1964 to 1966 (and during the civil war of 1970–71) were based on his conviction that the two identities were fundamentally irreconcilable. Despite the anti-Palestinian reputation he acquired after 1970, in truth al-Tell was an enemy of the PLO. This is a crucial distinction. Although he was a native Transjordanian, al-Tell cared little about a person's origins; what he cared about were one's actions. As director of the Hashemite Broadcasting Service, for example, al-Tell had hired West Bankers and gone out of his way to employ Palestinian luminaries (such as poet Fadwa Tuqan). If a person backed Jordan's position vis-à-vis Palestine, he was a compatriot. If he supported the PLO, he was an adversary. As one Jordanian put it, al-Tell 'was the best Palestinian I've ever known.'[20]

The pro-Egypt camp returns

After Sharif Hussein resigned as prime minister over the king's pro-Egypt stance, Bahjat al-Talhuni 'came to power with a Cabinet largely purged of opponents of an Egyptian-aligned policy and packed with [his] unsavoury or undistinguished proteges.'[21] Formed on 6 July 1964, the al-Talhuni administration planned to extend the pro-Nasser security policy to the domestic political sphere. British Ambassador Roderick Parkes, who argued that Hussein was no 'inspired judge of character', felt the new government boded ill for the king and for Jordan.[22]

Prime Minister al-Talhuni began pursuing the most pro-Nasser policy Jordan had followed since Suleiman al-Nabulsi's time. Whereas al-Nabulsi had crafted a political programme which ignored the throne, al-Talhuni was working in close concert with Hussein. The king and his government made several tangible gestures to the Arab radicals. First, Jordan reversed its pro-royalist policy by recognising the Yemeni republican regime several weeks after al-Talhuni took office. Second, the UAC commander, Egyptian General Abdel-Hakim `Amer, was given an enthusiastic reception during a visit to Jordan in mid-July. `Amer met with Jordanian officials and explained how his plans to coordinate Arab defence efforts would protect Jordan. Third, Hussein granted pardons to Nasserites and leftists held in Jordan's jails. In April, 50 Ba`thists and Communists had been released. Ali Abu Nuwar was pardoned in

September to demonstrate Jordan's seriousness in improving relations with Cairo.[23]

The second Arab summit, held in Alexandria between 5 and 12 September 1964, gave Hussein the opportunity to enhance his relations with the radical Arab states. Hussein reported that the summit 'continued the work of the first.'[24] The Arab leaders ratified the founding of the PLO and unanimously accepted Ahmad al-Shuqayri's chairmanship. The PLO would begin training military forces in Gaza and in Jordan. Further, the PLO would soon be able to impose an income tax on Palestinians employed by the Jordanian government. The summit also urged that the integration of the Arab armies under Egypt proceed apace. Jordan's army would be subordinated to General Abdel-Hakim `Amer's command.

After the Alexandria summit, Hussein and al-Talhuni decided to diversify Jordan's foreign relations. Alarmed by Ba`thist Iraq, Hussein quietly began improving ties with Ba`thist Syria and with Lebanon. At the non-aligned conference held in Cairo in early October, Hussein expressed Jordan's commitment to the non-aligned movement. The same week, Jordan announced the establishment of relations with Bulgaria (in 1964, relations were also established with Czechoslovakia and Poland).

Hussein's 'progressive' diplomacy was hailed by many Jordanians. The king was greeted by wild, enthusiastic crowds on visits to Irbid, Jenin, Tulkarm, Nablus, Ramallah, Jerusalem, Bethlehem, and Hebron. In Nablus, for example, Hussein's welcome in late October was 'quite extraordinary.' 'The Nabulsis mobbed the King and his accompanying Ministers and lifted first the King's car and then the King himself off the ground in a triumphal procession.'[25] Hussein felt that his decision to redefine security to include Egypt's wishes had been vindicated.

Dissension in the national security establishment

After nearly a year of the pro-Egypt security policy, cleavages began to appear among the ruling elite. Anti-Nasserite decisionmakers understood why Hussein felt compelled to go to Cairo and establish ties with Nasser. What they opposed was the zeal with which the king was revamping Jordan's security stance. British Ambassador Parkes agreed: 'My main criticism is that, once launched on this course, he has pursued it with characteristic over-enthusiasm though plenty of plausible excuses could have been found for not going full speed ahead.'[26] Kamal Salibi, in his otherwise uncritical history of Jordan, admits that Hussein 'was sacrificing sound political judgement for stability' in his overtures toward Nasser.[27]

Many army leaders also wanted to undercut al-Talhuni and return to the anti-Egypt policy. Neither the PLO nor the UAC boded well for security.[28] Of particular concern to some military commanders was the recent reduction in their role in formulating national security policy. In short, the 'old Trans-Jordanian Establishment [had] suffered a severe reverse. Their hold on the army [had] been significantly weakened' by recent events.[29] In July 1964, 93 officers, mostly East Bankers, had been retired to streamline the officers corps in line with UAC directives. Commander-in-Chief Habis al-Majali and his assistant, Major-General `Akash al-Zabn, blamed Egypt for the dismissals and threatened to resign.[30]

The significance of Hussein's estrangement from the old guard in the national security establishment cannot be underestimated. In short, Hussein was alienating 'the very forces on which he has traditionally and historically relied.'[31] The anti-Nasserites believed that 'the King may have been taken in by Nasser who, it is feared, may be knocking away the Throne's main prop of East Bank support under the guise of disinterested friendship.'[32]

On 13 February 1965, Wasfi al-Tell replaced al-Talhuni as prime minister, a sign that the King Hussein was ready to put the brakes on Jordan's alignment with Egypt. Al-Tell sought to repair the damage of Jordan's dalliance with Nasserism by strengthening the kingdom internally. In particular, he hoped to 'deepen national consciousness' through improved relations with the press and through encouraging a sense of participation in domestic politics.[33] Al-Tell made immediate gestures to his detractors by urging Hussein to approve a far-reaching amnesty law in April to celebrate the appointment of his brother, Prince Hassan, as heir to the throne.[34] Hussein ordered the public burning of 20 000 intelligence files accumulated by the *mukhabarat*.[35] Nearly 2000 political prisoners were released from jail, and only 61 hardcore activists remained in custody. Those allowed to return from exile included Abdullah al-Tell (accused of complicity in King Abdullah's assassination), Ali al-Hiyari, Shafiq Irsheidat, Abdullah al-Rimawi, Na`im Abdel Hadi, and Abdel Rahman Shuqayr.

The emergence of al-Fatah

The appearance of the al-Fatah group in early 1965 would radicalise the PLO and exacerbate tensions between Jordan and the Palestinians for years to come. Formed by Palestinian exiles Yasser Arafat, Salah Khalaf, and Khalil al-Wazir, among others, in 1957–58, al-Fatah (a reverse acronym for *al-hakarat al-tahrir al-filastini*, or the Palestinian Liberation Movement) advocated conducting a guerrilla war of attrition against Israel.[36] There existed no formal link between al-Fatah and the PLO in early 1965, but al-Fatah militancy would force Ahmad al-Shuqayri into adopting a more combative stance as the year progressed.

The first indications of strain in the Jordanian–Palestinian relationship came in late February 1965, when al-Shuqayri held talks with the al-Tell government. Al-Shuqayri demanded that Jordan arm and fortify West Bank villages and asked that Palestinian 'popular resistance' units be trained in Jordan.[37] Further, he insisted that all Palestinians employed by the Jordanian government contribute 5 per cent of their salaries to the PLO and demanded that a PLO office be opened in Amman. Such requests, if granted, would create a rival political authority in Jordan with its own resource base and coercive powers.[38]

The government hence rejected al-Shuqayri's requests, while reiterating its support for the Palestinian cause. Al-Tell publicly invited Palestinians to join the Jordanian army if they truly wanted to liberate Palestine. The PLO's 'Voice of Palestine', broadcast from Cairo, responded by accusing Jordan of trying to undermine the PLO.[39] In a speech, Hussein tried to allay Palestinian fears by insisting that there existed no distinction between Jordanians and Palestinians. Not to be outdone, al-Shuqayri rejoined that 'our Jordanian brothers are in fact Palestinians' and that he hoped that Jordanians such as Wasfi al-Tell and Bahjat al-Talhuni would some day sit on the Palestine National Council.[40] (Later al-Shuqayri was not so charitable. In his memoirs, he dismissed al-Tell as 'a clerk of mine in the Arab office in Jerusalem in 1947.'[41])

Backed by military leaders, Hussein and al-Tell decided to weaken al-Shuqayri by disbanding the largely Palestinian National Guard. While Susser correctly deduces that the timing of the move was conditioned by Jordan's desire 'to forestall any penetration or control of the National Guard by the PLO or its sympathizers,' the plan to dissolve the unit had actually been formulated years before the PLO appeared on the scene.[42] In 1959, a British study had suggested integrating the National Guard into the army in the interests of efficiency. In 1963, an Anglo-American inquiry had recommended dissolving the unit and reorganising the military.[43] However, as British Ambassador Roderick Parkes commented at the time, disbanding the National Guard 'would be a great propaganda tool for Nasser.'[44]

Tensions at the Casablanca summit

Whereas the initial Arab summits had been typified by an outward display of solidarity between Jordan and the PLO, the summit held in Casablanca, Morocco in September 1965 brought their differences into the open. Hussein forcefully rejected al-Shuqayri's demand that the PLO be allowed to conscript Jordan's Palestinians into serving in a Palestinian army. Hussein disingenuously claimed 'that 60 per cent of the Jordanian army consists of Palestinians' and restated al-Tell's invitation to Palestinians to join forces with Jordan.[45] To Jordan's delight, the Arab states failed to endorse the PLO's demands and merely requested that Jordan continue negotiating with the Palestinians.

On 4 October, Hussein reiterated the tough line he had taken in Casablanca. Before a joint session of parliament, he asserted Jordan's key role in the Palestinian struggle and censured the PLO for its anti-Jordanian stance.[46] The address was the most detailed public statement to date of Jordan's grievances with the PLO. Having convinced the king that the PLO presented a security threat, the al-Tell government stepped up its efforts to cut al-Shuqayri and his followers down to size. Al-Tell instructed the security services to crack down on smugglers and local operatives who provided logistical support to al-Fatah guerrilla operations. Moreover, military intelligence increased its efforts to penetrate al-Fatah cells and expand its surveillance activities of hardcore PLO activists.[47]

By early 1966, Jordanian–PLO relations had deteriorated to the point where the Arab League decided to step in and mediate between the two camps. The Cairo agreement postponed, but did not end, the contest between Jordan and the PLO. In fact, some decisionmakers felt that it was only a matter of time before tensions with the PLO resurfaced. The Palestine issue was even discussed in the Lower House. In one session, deputies nearly came to blows when one Transjordanian accused the Palestinians 'of having run away at the time when the East Bankers were defending Jordan against the Jews in 1948.'[48]

The Cairo agreement alleviated tensions for several months before the pact dissolved in the summer of 1966. At the Palestine National Council meeting in Gaza in May, the PLO blasted Jordan for claiming to represent the Palestinians. On 14 June, Hussein publicly censured the PLO and publicly translated his rhetoric into reality by ordering the closing of the PLO's offices in Jordan, arresting PLO activists, and severing relations with the organisation in July. The new policy, in Uriel Dann's words, represented the 'PLO's virtual elimination from Jordan.'[49] The organisation would not resurface and become active in the kingdom until after the 1967 war.

The UAC and the military restructuring

While most decisionmakers eventually supported the decision to purge the PLO from Jordan, there existed no similar consensus concerning the UAC. Two factions, each with its own security policy, debated the merits of subordinating Jordan's army to Egypt's. The first faction, led by Commander-in-Chief Habis al-Majali, resisted any reduction of the army's role in security policymaking and firmly opposed the UAC. Backed by Prince Muhammad and composed of men who had defended the state since the 1920s and who had fought in Palestine in 1948, the al-Majali faction believed the Jordanian army, and no other, could safeguard the kingdom.[50] They distrusted Cairo and ridiculed Egypt's less-than-impressive combat record. Why, they asked, should the only Arab army which had acquitted itself well against the Israelis in 1948 join forces with an army which had been roundly defeated on several occasions by the Israelis? Moreover, what business did Jordan have forming an alliance with a country whose own military was tied down in a bloody civil war in Yemen? (Egypt had some 60 000 troops fighting there.)

Opposed to this contingent was a younger, pro-Egyptian group of officers led by Brigadier ʿAmer Khammash, whose family hailed from Nablus. Backed by many officers of Palestinian origin, Khammash was a bright, ambitious officer with 'progressive' views. He supported Hussein's pro-Egypt security policy partly out of ideological sympathy and partly because he felt Jordan had no other choice. The Khammash group understood the magnitude of the Israeli threat to the West Bank and argued that Jordan was incapable of defending itself, especially with its tiny air force. Jordan, therefore, needed the collective security umbrella provided by the UAC.[51]

Khammash had led the army's directorate of planning and organisation since 1962. His conception of operations was based on the notion of an 'offensive-defence' alignment of forces.[52] The West Bank would be designated a forward defence zone, while the East Bank would be a cushion or buffer. Khammash advocated discontinuing all direct commissions from the ranks (although he himself had been commissioned directly) and sending all cadets to a royal military college.

As ultimate arbiter in the national security establishment, Hussein inclined toward the Khammash faction. First, the king believed that Jordan's weakness meant it needed an Arab security shield. In particular, the kingdom lacked the air power to defend itself against Israel. Second, Hussein had given his pledge in Cairo that Jordan would adhere to the UAC's directives. In Arab eyes, openly challenging al-Shuqayri's PLO was forgivable, but forsaking Nasser's military plans was not. Third, Khammash had excellent contacts with the US defence industry and had proven adept in securing arms for Jordan. Fourth, Khammash had no tribal base and was thus immune to the sectarian politics which affected al-Majali and his followers.

The long-anticipated reorganisation (based roughly on the UAC plans drawn up in Alexandria in 1964) began on 5 May 1965, when the command group of the army was reshuffled. The two assistant commander-in-chief positions were abolished – Major-General `Akash al-Zabn was appointed an ambassador, and Major-General Izzat Qandur was retired. Sharif Nasser was designated deputy commander-in-chief, and `Amer Khammash became chief of staff.[53] Many other officers were transferred or retired. Wrote the British defence attaché in Amman: 'Although the details of this reconstruction are mainly the work of General Khamash, the timing is almost certainly King Hussein's own.' In sum, 'the Khammash faction has gained ground decisively' at the expense of the al-Majali faction.[54]

A major problem with the reorganisation is that it would replace Jordan's defensive strategy with an Egyptian plan. Jordanian military planners had long envisaged fending off an Israeli assault on the West Bank by employing a mobile defensive concept, whereby the kingdom would concentrate its forces in key tactical locations. The UAC plan, however, called for Jordanian forces to be deployed along the entire length of the armistice line. As the 1967 war proved, this strategy was an imprudent one.

In short, Hussein seemed to have weakened the paramount guarantor of the Hashemite state, the military, by redefining national security policy on Egypt's terms. As one British official remarked in 1965, the question remained 'whether this future Army, officered by younger and even more professionally qualified men, will provide the same sort of prop for the Hashemite regime that the Army has done in the past.'[55]

Conclusion

The increased role King Hussein played in policymaking and his quest for increased domestic and regional stature between 1964 and 1966 led him to accept – and even implement – several Arab Summit decisions that could endanger Jordan's long-term national security. Jordan's acceptance of the formation of the PLO and its subordination of its military strategy to the UAC put the kingdom in a precarious position and set the stage for disaster in 1967.

8
Jordan's March to War

This chapter argues that King Hussein's decision to link Jordan's national security policy to Egyptian interests was largely responsible for the loss of the West Bank in June 1967. Hussein's signing of a defence pact with Egypt's President Gamal Abdel Nasser, while understandable given the highly charged atmosphere of the time, was based on emotional rather than rational factors. The king's decision was taken with wide popular support, but without the backing of his experienced military professionals in the national security establishment.

The al-Sam`u raid

The devastating Israel raid on the West Bank village of al-Sam`u (located approximately ten miles south of Hebron) on 13 November 1966 had a major impact on Jordanian security policymaking and played a large part in driving the kingdom toward Egypt. In retaliation for an al-Fatah raid which had originated in Syria, Israel sent an armoured brigade to destroy al-Sam`u – believed to be sympathetic to the guerrillas – in its largest military action since the Suez war. Over 125 buildings, including houses, the local school, medical clinic, and mosque, were systematically destroyed by Israeli forces. When Jordanian army units rushed to the scene, they were ambushed and beaten back in a firefight. In all, 15 Jordanian soldiers and 30 civilians were killed.[1]

Mass demonstrations erupted across the West Bank as Palestinians took to the streets to protest the government's failure to protect them from Israel. On 19 November, riots rocked the towns of Nablus, Hebron, Jerusalem, Ramallah, Jenin, and Tulkarm. The army was deployed, and a number of protesters were killed. In Jerusalem, over 1000 demonstrators were dispersed by policemen wielding whips and batons.[2] Two weeks passed before the military restored order.

The PLO and the radical Arab states fanned the flames with incendiary broadcasts condemning the 'weakness' of Jordan's army and the 'corruption' of Jordan's leaders. PLO Chairman Ahmad al-Shuqayri called for the creation of 'a Palestinian republic'. Had Jordan permitted the formation of a Palestinian army, al-Shuqayri claimed, then the West Bankers could have defended themselves. Further, Jordan's acceptance of small quantities of American weapons over larger quantities of Soviet arms 'might well have weakened the Arab Legion.'[3]

Hussein took the al-Sam`u raid more personally than others in the national security establishment. Hussein felt betrayed by the Israeli leadership. He thought that his private meetings with Israel had afforded him a measure of security on his Western flank. Perhaps more upsetting was the Arab reaction. Hussein had gone to Cairo in 1964 in good faith and had fulfilled his commitment to the Arab summit decisions. Although he had been forced to admit that his acceptance of the PLO had been a mistake, Hussein still clung to the notion that Jordan's security depended on the collective defence provided by the UAC. When put to the test at al-Sam`u, however, the UAC failed to back its promises of military support. Rather than rallying to Jordan's aid by providing air or logistical support, the Egyptians had instead condemned Jordan for its military weakness.

Alarmed by events, Jordanian decisionmakers took several measures to protect national security. First, on 26 November Jordan introduced conscription for the first time in its history. The army had long prided itself on being a professional military force. But to blunt Palestinian and Arab criticisms, the king introduced a 90-day limited service law for able-bodied males between 18 and 40 years of age.[4]

Second, Jordan launched a propaganda offensive against the UAC and the Arab states for failing to come to Jordan's defence. Led by al-Tell, Jordan denounced Cairo and Damascus for betraying the promises enshrined in the UAC principles for collective defence. Jordan also castigated the PLO.[5] The Arab radicals responded in fury. Radio Cairo dismissed al-Tell as an agent of the British. The PLO urged Jordan's ministers to resign and leave al-Tell 'alone to meet his fate.'[6] Damascus staged 'popular' demonstrations calling for the overthrow of the Hashemite monarchy. Once again, Hussein had become the pariah of the Arab world.

Third, Jordan sought assurances of support from its chief external patron, the United States. President Lyndon Johnson's administration, although more pro-Israel than its predecessor, felt the Israeli attack at al-Sam`u had been unjustified and censured the Eshkol government for such an 'unwise Israeli action.'[7] The US voted along with the UN Security Council's overwhelming condemnation of the raid (New Zealand abstained).[8] President Johnson reassured Hussein privately of America's commitment to Jordanian security.[9] Washington backed its words by airlifting $4.7 million worth of military supplies into Jordan in December 1966.[10]

Al-Sam`u's effect on security policy

As far as al-Tell and the anti-Nasserites were concerned, the al-Sam`u crisis had proven beyond a shadow of a doubt that the UAC was a paper tiger. They wanted Hussein to renounce the agreement and concentrate on building up Jordan's defences from within. However, rather than drawing the conclusion al-Tell had drawn, some decisionmakers became convinced that Jordan needed the UAC more than ever. Paradoxically, the al-Sam`u incident persuaded many that Jordan should draw closer to, not further away from, Cairo.

Al-Tell's outspoken denunciation of the UAC and the PLO made him an unpopular leader among many in Jordan, especially on the West Bank. In parliament, over 40 deputies vowed to oppose the al-Tell government.[11] Al-Tell was also drawing criticism from 'a new opposition group among Palestinians, largely directed and led from outside Jordan, supported and financed by radical Arab states.' As Vatikiotis correctly predicted in early 1967, this new force would soon challenge 'the old, but now assimilated, Palestinian opposition in Jordan.'[12] Al-Tell eventually resigned in March and was appointed royal court chief. Hussein wanted al-Tell by his side, but out of the public eye, where the latter's anti-Egypt policies were unpopular with many Jordanians and Palestinians.

The gathering storm

By May 1967, Jordanian decisionmakers were sure that an Arab war with Israel was inevitable. The debate which had polarised the national security establishment since 1964 was renewed with intensity. The anti-Nasserite faction, led by Court Chief Wasfi al-Tell, pressured Hussein to renounce the collective Arab defence plans and concentrate on preparing Jordan's army to fight its own war. The Arab states had done nothing to support Jordan after the al-Sam`u attack, and the Egyptian and Syrian armies had always fared poorly in battle against the Israelis.

As one Israeli leader said of Egypt's army: 'Their officers are too fat, and their soldiers are too thin.'[13] It made far more sense for Jordan to rely on its own defence plans – prepared after the 1948 war – than to subordinate Jordan's army to the Egyptians.

Although al-Tell and his supporters would be vindicated after the fact when Jordan lost the West Bank and Jerusalem, their opinion was not a popular one with the king or among Jordan's population. Kamal al-Sha`ir recalls: 'Wasfi was one of maybe 12 people in Jordan who opposed going to war.'[14] Adnan Abu `Udeh says that al-Tell 'was fully aware of the extent of the local constraint on the King but argued that this would not be as disastrous as losing the West Bank.'[15] Abu `Udeh personally agreed with al-Tell's view, but was a captain in the *mukhabarat* in 1967 and unable to influence senior decisionmakers.[16]

The position embraced by King Hussein and Prime Minister Sa`ad Jum`a (who became Prime Minister in April) and supported by others in the political elite was that Jordan had no choice but to repair ties with Cairo. Jordan's thrashing at Israel's hands in November 1966, and Syria's poor performance in a skirmish with the Israeli air force in April 1967, convinced many decisionmakers that Jordan's security could only be protected with Egyptian assistance. Even former anti-Nasserites now favoured linking Jordan's security policy to Egypt. As Mutawi notes, 'a significant number of influential people in Jordan found themselves deluded into believing Egyptian boasts of their superior military capacity.'[17]

The conventional wisdom

The notion that Jordan had no choice but to fight alongside the Arab states in 1967 remains a powerful one today. Virtually every account of Jordanian or Middle Eastern politics insists that the kingdom had no option but to enter the war and that Hussein's decision was the correct one. This chapter argues that Jordan had several policy options, but that it made the wrong ones. Further, this chapter contends that it is a strange logic indeed which concludes that the loss of the West Bank and Jerusalem could be regarded as anything other than a failure in security policymaking.

Specifically, Jordan had four opportunities to pursue policies which might have protected national security in 1967. The first was the decision to sign a defence pact with Egypt. The second was the decision to place Jordanian forces under the direct command of Egypt. The third was the decision to abandon Jordan's mobile defence concept in favour of a linear defence scheme. The fourth was the decision to initiate hostilities with Israel on the first day of the war. Hussein's reliance on decisionmakers with little or no military experience and exclusion of others who understood warfare would cost him dearly.

The alliance with Nasser

While Hussein later presented his decision to fight as an unavoidable consequence of regional and domestic political trends, he was not entirely blameless and, in fact, had contributed to escalating the conflict by allying with Nasser. As one journalist put it in July 1967, 'Hussein did not really want to get into the war, but he must take some responsibility for starting it.'[18] Even the arch-opponent of the war, Wasfi al-Tell, had played a role in escalating the conflict by baiting Nasser for his cowardice and weakness in the months before hostilities erupted.

Jordanian media attacks forced Nasser to engage in brinkmanship in the last weeks of May and only heightened Jordan's sense of isolation. On 15 May, Nasser ordered his troops in the Sinai on alert after receiving a misleading Soviet report of an Israeli troop buildup on the Syrian border.[19] On 16 May, Nasser asked UN Secretary-General U Thant to remove the UN forces stationed in Sinai. On 19 May, Cairo took the provocative act of closing the Straits of Tiran to Israeli shipping.

With the stage set for war, Hussein felt he had no option but to arrange a defence agreement with Nasser. First, many decisionmakers now believed that Jordan needed the protection of the radical Arab states. Second, Hussein and many of his advisors were convinced that Israel would seize the West Bank regardless of what policy Jordan chose. The al-Sam`u raid had demonstrated beyond a shadow of a doubt that Israel was militarily strong and willing to use force against Jordan. Third, Hussein believed he could not protect internal security unless Jordan reestablished relations with the radical Arab states. Both West Bankers and East Bankers were cheering Nasser's confrontational policies toward Israel. Finally, Hussein felt he needed a rapprochement with Nasser to protect Jordan from the militant regime in Damascus. On 21 May, a bomb planted by Syrian intelligence agents exploded at Jordan's border post at al-Ramtha, killing 21 people.

Thus, Hussein sent Major-General Khammash to Cairo on 21 May to coordinate Jordan's defences with the UAC. When he arrived, Khammash discovered that the UAC had virtually ceased to function. Jordan's estrangement from Egypt became evident as Khammash was shunted from one Egyptian army commander to another. Nobody was willing to brief him on the Arab war effort. Alarmed, Hussein decided that he himself had to make a powerful symbolic gesture to Nasser by going personally to Cairo.

On 30 May, Hussein flew to Cairo with Prime Minister Jum`a, Foreign Minister Ahmad Tuqan, and Khammash to conclude a defence agreement with Nasser. In Egypt, Hussein signed without fanfare an agreement similar to the Egypt–Syria pact signed in 1966 (see Figure 8.1). The Egypt–Jordan treaty committed the two states to the defence of the other and stipulated that Jordan's armed forces would be placed under Egyptian control. During the negotiations, Nasser persuaded Hussein to mend fences with PLO Chairman Ahmad al-Shuqayri, who accompanied the Jordanian delegation back to Amman.

When Radio Cairo announced that Jordan had signed a military pact with Egypt, Jordanians rejoiced as they never had before. Thousands of Jordanians dashed to the airport to meet Hussein's airplane, while thousands more held mass demonstrations of support for the king throughout the kingdom. Amman Radio broadcast: 'Blessed be Hussein as redeemer and redeemed.'[20] Not since the expulsion of Glubb had the Hussein adopted a policy so in tune with popular sentiments.

Figure 8.1   King Hussein and Egypt's Gamal Abdel Nasser sign the mutual defence treaty in Cairo, 30 May 1967.

Placing the army under Egyptian command

The next decision Hussein made which contributed to defeat was to honour the terms of the Egypt–Jordan pact by placing Jordanian forces under Egyptian command. As Hussein saw it, Jordan had no choice but to accept Egyptian military commanders. Egypt was the driving force behind the Arab collective defence effort and was already linked to Syria by treaty. Besides, Jordan was dependent on Egyptian air power for any defence of the West Bank. Egyptian General Abdel Mun`im Riyad, accompanied by Major-General Hosni Mekki, Brigadier Mustafa al-Hinawi, and several other staff officers, arrived in Amman on 1 June to take command of Jordan's armed forces.

Al-Tell and many senior army officers believed Hussein was making another mistake.[21] Jordan, in effect, was surrendering its control of the pivotal institution in Jordan to a foreign commander. It was one thing to sign a defence pact with Egypt to placate pro-Nasser popular opinion. It was quite another actually to abide by the agreement and subordinate the military to the leadership of a country which had lost every war it had fought against Israel. As one Western diplomat, John Phillips, had put it back in 1964, 'the risk to the regime in subordinating almost the entire Jordanian Armed Forces to the UAC and integrating the air force within the UAC air defence system needs no stressing.'[22]

Now that the decision had been made to place Jordan's armed forces under Egyptian control, al-Tell and his army allies concentrated their efforts on convincing King Hussein and General Riyad of the necessity of adhering to Jordanian defence plans for the West Bank. Al-Tell, Western Front Commander Major-General Muhammad Ahmad Salim, and Colonel `Atif al-Majali argued that Jordanian commanders were better placed than Egyptian officers to defend the West Bank. Jordan understood the topography of the West Bank and had defended the territory effectively since 1948.

Two factors dictated the type of defence Jordan had adopted after the 1948 Palestine war. First, Jordanian planners had identified at least 33 well-concealed points from which Israel could launch an offensive against the West Bank and formulated their defences accordingly.[23] Second, Jordanian planners realised that Jordan lacked the manpower to cover the whole of the 630-kilometre armistice line on the West Bank and the 400-kilometre border on the East Bank.

To offset these disadvantages, Jordan's commanders formulated a 'defence in depth' or mobile defence plan, whereby the kingdom concentrated its forces in key strategic locations and along likely avenues of

Israeli attack. Although militarily realistic, the mobile defence concept was politically contentious because it involved temporarily sacrificing certain parts of the West Bank to defend other parts. In 1955, Glubb and Hussein had clashed over the merits of the scheme. Glubb insisted that Jordan lacked the forces to defend the entire border, but Hussein said: 'I will not surrender one hand's-breadth of my country.'[24] Nevertheless, Jordan's defences continued to be predicated on the mobile defence concept.

A centrepiece of the mobile defence plan was Operation Tariq (`amaliyat tariq). This manoeuvre was the most important of several limited plans army planners devised to protect the West Bank. The plan called for concentrating Jordanian forces in and around Jerusalem, where Israel could not use its air power for fear of destroying the Old City, and seizing the Jewish sector of the city. Jordan knew it could not hold Jerusalem indefinitely, but was confident it could hold the city until the UN imposed a ceasefire. The kingdom would thus have a valuable pawn to use in negotiations with Israel.

Comprising military professionals with combat experience against Israel in 1948, the al-Tell faction had an accurate assessment of Israel's military power and knew that Jordan was far weaker than the Jewish state. While they remained wholly dedicated to upholding the territorial integrity of Jordan, this group believed the only way to salvage something from a war with Israel was by prioritising Jordan's defensive objectives. If Israel so desired, it could snatch the West Bank within hours.

Western experts shared the al-Tell faction's view of Israel's military power. As a US National Intelligence Estimate noted in 1963, 'Israel will probably retain its overall military superiority vis-à-vis the Arab states for the next several years.'[25] Britain's military attaché in Amman argued in 1963 that Jordan would lose the West Bank 'in a very short time' unless the UN stepped in.[26] In 1965, another British official noted that a 'takeover of the West Bank would present few military problems to the Israelis.' Even if the other Arab states intervened, Israel could complete the operation 'within 24 to 48 hours'.[27] US Defence Secretary Robert McNamara believed that Israel could take the West Bank 'in 24 hours'.[28] In May 1967, the director of the CIA reported to President Johnson that 'Israel would win a war against one or all of the Arab countries, whichever struck the first blow, in about a week.'[29]

Abandoning the mobile defence concept

The chief problem with Operation Tariq – and, indeed, with the entire mobile defence concept – was that it was militarily feasible, but politically unthinkable from Hussein's viewpoint since it involved temporarily sacrificing parts of the West Bank to retain Jerusalem and surrounding areas. In Hussein's estimation, launching Operation Tariq or similar plans was tantamount to forsaking the Hashemite claim to the West Bank. Why, Hussein reasoned, should he reject the Arab collective defence scheme and embrace a plan which asked him to sacrifice parts of the West Bank to the Israelis? To him, the Arab plan would allow Jordan to demonstrate that it was not surrendering an inch of Arab territory to Israel.

Hussein decided to stick with the decision to follow the Arab collective defence plan which called for Jordan to hold the entire West Bank. Hussein was backed by many members of the political elite and some members of the military. Prime Minister Jum`a believed that Hussein had made the right decision. Bahjat al-Talhuni and the pro-Egypt camp also backed the decision. `Amer Khammash supported the decision as the only alternative Jordan had to defend its territorial integrity.

The Egyptian defence plan formulated in Cairo necessitated Jordan defending the entire West Bank as opposed to key strategic locations as envisaged by Jordanian planners. The al-Tell faction insisted that the 'thinning of the Jordanian army along the border with Israel had placed it in a weak position and minimised its ability to stave off an Israeli attack in one area.'[30] Snow concurs: 'Hussein's objective was to fight a defensive action, but his infantry were strung out along the frontier in a manner which gave him little defence in depth.'[31]

That the Egyptian command disagreed with the al-Tell group is not surprising given General Riyad's interpretation of the political situation. For some time, Riyad had insisted that Israel 'would not occupy the West Bank even if Hussein were deposed.'[32] When Wasfi al-Tell had condemned the UAC for failing to provide air cover for the Jordanians at al-Sam`u, Riyad had retorted that this task had been Jordan's responsibility.[33] He even went as far as saying that King Hussein should sack al-Tell as prime minister.[34]

The final mistake

While Jordan's decisions thus far provided textbook examples of how not to prepare for war, the loss of the West Bank was not yet a foregone conclusion. Al-Tell and his army supporters argued that Jordan should not engage the Israelis until it was certain that the Arab armies had the battlefield momentum. Then Jordan could concentrate its forces in areas of Israeli weakness.

The long-anticipated war erupted on 5 June, when Israel's air force obliterated the Egyptian air force on the ground. Despite their devastating losses, the Egyptian military leadership in Cairo and President Nasser himself urged Jordan to enter the war. Egypt disingenuously claimed it had destroyed 75 per cent of Israel's air power capability.[35] It was only a matter of time, Cairo boasted, before Israel surrendered to the Arabs.

Jordan's senior military commanders and al-Tell suspected the Egyptians were lying and pleaded with Hussein to wait before permitting General Riyad to engage Israel. The sceptics seriously doubted that Egypt had annihilated Israel's powerful air force and insisted that Jordan wait for independent confirmation of Egypt's claims. The Western Front commander, Major-General Salim, wanted to delay 48 hours before committing Jordan to the war.[36] Sharif Nasser advised Hussein to wait at least 12 hours in order to confirm the Egyptian reports.[37] Brigadier `Atif al-Majali, in the command post with General Riyad, also insisted that Jordan corroborate the Egyptian account.

Jordan's final mistake was made when Hussein disregarded the advice of his commanders and allowed General Riyad to order an artillery barrage of Israeli positions near Jerusalem. Riyad next launched Jordan's tiny air force into action against Israel. The king mistakenly believed Nasser's triumphant claims that Egypt had the tactical advantage over Israel. Hussein felt he had no other choice but to join the war effort at this stage.

Israel reportedly dispatched several messages to Hussein urging Jordan to stay out of the war. According to Golda Meir, Israel sent Hussein 'constant messages promising that if he kept out of the war nothing would happen to him.' Hussein's disregard of these communications, in Meir's estimation, was an 'error of judgement.'[38] Yitzhak Rabin says that Israel sent warnings through three channels: (1) the Israeli representative to the joint Military Assistance Command; (2) UN General Odd Bull; and (3) the US embassy in Tel Aviv.[39] US Secretary of State Dean Rusk also warned Hussein not to open another front on 5 June, but 'Hussein replied that he was sorry but his honor left him no choice.'[40]

Was Israel's warning to Hussein sincere? On the one hand, at al-Sam`u Israel had violated its private assurances to Hussein that it would not attack Jordan.[41] Consequently, there were sufficient grounds for Jordan to doubt Israel's intentions. Moreover, Israel had never made any bones about its willingness to seize the West Bank for security reasons. Israeli leaders had made numerous public and private statements to that effect since the 1950s. On the other hand, had Hussein actually accepted Israel's warning at face value and not entered the war, he at least would have had a strong case to put before the international community and the UN. Jordan, he could claim, had been invaded by Israel and had not provoked the battle.

Hussein's response to the Israelis was a brave one, but it sealed Jordan's fate: 'They started the battle, and now they are receiving our reply by air.'[42] As Hussein saw it, he had little reason to trust Israel. The Israelis had broken their commitments to Jordan at al-Sam`u, so why should he believe them now? As CIA Director Richard Helms put it – 'Hussein's trip to Cairo marked Jordan, in Israeli eyes, for elimination.'[43]

A catalogue of errors

Hussein's miscalculations became starkly evident during the 72 hours Jordan fought Israel. The course of Jordan's military campaign was determined when 'General Riad, following orders from Field Marshall Amer in Cairo, completely abandoned the carefully laid plans of the Jordanians and instead issued a series of commands which spelt disaster for the Jordanians.'[44] As Major-General James Lunt, who served with the Arab Legion in the 1950s, writes: 'The real scapegoat, if one needs to be found, must surely be Field Marshal Abdel Hakim Amer. From beginning to end he made mistake after mistake.'[45]

The Egyptian command's decision to adhere to the linear defence scheme determined the outcome of the war for Jordan. During the opening stages of the fighting, General Riyad rejected persistent Jordanian advice to conduct limited operations along the defensive line and instead initiated hostilities along the entire front. In effect, Cairo forced Jordan to adopt an offensive posture which needlessly exposed Jordanian forces to the full brunt of Israel's ground and air power.

Reacting to commands issued by the central command in Cairo, General Riyad's conduct of the war was lamentable. Snow summarises some of Riyad's tactics thus: 'His juggling of the armoured brigades in the Jordan valley, in full daylight, and without air cover, almost surpasses belief.'[46] It was bad enough that Riyad implemented the wrong decisions several times, but worse that he countermanded several orders he had given previously, forcing West Bank commanders into confusion.

Throughout the war, Major-General Salim and Brigadier `Atif al-Majali, among others, demanded that General Riyad attempt to salvage something by implementing Operation Tariq. Then, at least, Jordan would have a bargaining chip to use in postwar negotiations with Israel. Further, the symbolic value of having saved Arab Jerusalem and captured the Jewish sector of the city would boost Jordan's regional standing immeasurably. When Riyad flatly refused to implement the plan and announced that he was sticking with the Egyptian strategy, al-Majali yelled at the Egyptian general, threw his headdress to the ground, and stormed out of the command post.[47]

Another controversial decision was Riyad's decision to withdraw from the West Bank while the bulk of Jordan's forces remained intact. Although overwhelmed by Israel's air power, Jordanian infantry units acquitted themselves fairly well in battle. In Nablus and Jenin, the 'Jordanians man for man, and tank for tank, gave as good as they got, and often better.'[48] In Jerusalem, too, Jordanian ground forces put up fierce resistance. Consequently, most Jordanian commanders felt they could have made a stand in certain locations. Commander-in-Chief Habis al-Majali – who successfully held out against Israeli forces in Latrun in 1948 – argued that Jordan could have fought longer than it did.[49] Eastern Front Commander Mashour al-Haditha thought the order to withdraw from the West Bank had come entirely too quickly – 'I was not defeated. I did not even take part in the fight.'[50] While Jordan could not have kept the entire West Bank, it is highly probable it could have saved key strategic points.

Other mistakes were made. Hussein's conversations with Nasser took place over open telephone lines. There had been no time to install specialised communications between Cairo and Amman, so the Israelis easily intercepted the conversations between Jordan and Egypt (the transcripts of which were released after the war, to Jordan's embarrassment). Jordan did not have a single liaison officer in Cairo to coordinate with the Egyptians and was entirely dependent for information on General Riyad in Amman. Riyad, for his part, reported directly to the Arab command in Cairo and was not accountable to a single Jordanian decisionmaker. Hussein refused to override Riyad's orders, even when advised to do so by Jordanian commanders who opposed the way the war was being conducted.

After the storm

Jordanian historian Suleiman Musa writes that there 'is no doubt that the defeat the Arabs suffered in 1967 was much worse than the results of the 1948, 1956, and 1973 wars.'[51] Jordan's three-day clash with Israel resulted in the destruction of the kingdom's air force and 80 per cent of its armoured capability.[52] Only four of the army's 11 brigades remained operational. The military's command structure was reorganised to streamline the senior leadership. Major-General Salim was retired, while Major-General Khammash – who many officers condemned for his cooperation with the Egyptians before the war – was promoted and made chief of the general staff.[53] Egyptian General `Amer reportedly committed suicide, and General Riyad was killed in March 1969 by an Israeli shell while directing Egyptian artillery fire near the Suez Canal. Even more disastrous, Jordan lost the highly populated and agriculturally fertile West Bank to Israel. The West Bank contributed nearly 40 per cent of Jordan's Gross National Product and comprised 25 per cent of the kingdom's arable land and almost half its industrial capacity.[54] Moreover, Jordan lost control of the West Bank's valuable water resources and the income generated by the territory's vibrant tourism sector. In addition, the East Bank became burdened with the influx of another 300 000 refugees, who strained scarce resources and created an additional burden for relief agencies.

As the paramount figure in the national security establishment, King Hussein must bear ultimate responsibility for Jordan's defeat in 1967. As he remarked (with some understatement) immediately after the war: 'It is apparent that we have not yet learned well enough how to use the weapons of modern warfare.'[55] Through the years, Hussein has maintained that his decision to go to war was the correct one. As he said in an interview in 1983, 'I had no choice. Passions were too high.'[56] Others concur. Kamal al-Sha`ir argues: 'At the time, I was convinced that Wasfi al-Tell was right and that we should have stayed out of the war. Now I'm not so sure we had any choice.'[57] Major-General Ma`an Abu Nuwar says that Jordan could not have altered the war's outcome due to Israel's superior military power: 'Israel could have occupied the West Bank anytime since 1949 if it wanted.' Even plans such as Operation Tariq could not have saved Jerusalem. Abu Nuwar argues that Israel could have surrounded the city and cut power and water. Jordan had insufficient ammunition supplies in Jerusalem and would have been unable to fight. 'We could have caused casualties,' Abu Nuwar recalls, 'but we had only our bodies and our training. Israel had everything.'[58]

Some observers understand why Jordan felt compelled to fight in 1967, but wonder why Jordan fought the way it did. Indeed, given Hussein's belief that Israel was determined to seize the West Bank regardless of Jordanian policy, his desperate flight to Cairo is certainly comprehensible. However, he still had plenty of time to backtrack and to adopt a more sensible battle posture. Indeed, recently declassified Western diplomatic records indicate that Hussein adhered to the notion of Arab collective defence, even though he lost faith in the UAC after the al-Sam`u attack.[59]

As Snow argues, Hussein's decision to go to war was at least understandable, but 'judged in cold military terms, his acceptance of Riad's *conduct* of the war was deplorable.'[60] Indeed, any 'rational analysis would have told him that the odds were overwhelmingly against Jordan and the other Arabs, however close their alliance, and that the risk of civil war was preferable to the loss of much of his country.'[61] Vatikiotis wondered in 1967:

> If King Husayn had everything to lose, including a large part of his army which has been the main prop of his regime and dynasty, the question is why did he proceed to engage the Israelis in battle from the very first day of hostilities?[62]

Fawaz Gerges asks: 'The puzzling question is, why did King Hussein decide to join Nasser's war coalition? After all, Nasser and Hussein had been bitterly attacking each other during the preceding eighteen months.'[63]

One theory advanced by some observers, including some Jordanians, is that Hussein was lured into a trap by the pro-Israel Johnson administration. At the very least, so the theory goes, Hussein was given misleading assurances by Washington that Israel would not seize the West Bank. According to Andrew and Leslie Cockburn, the CIA chief of station in Amman gave Hussein 'an urgent message' on 4 June:

> Israel would attack Egypt the following morning. It would be a short war. Israel would win. Jordan should stay out of the fight, but if Hussein felt he had to demonstrate Arab solidarity, he should confine himself to a pro forma demonstration. Jordan would be left alone by the Israelis.[64]

Hussein supposedly telephoned Nasser to warn him, but Nasser refused to believe the story. After Jordan's losses during the first two days of fighting, Hussein confronted the CIA station chief:

> 'Didn't you tell me that Israel was not going to attack Jordan?' Hussein reportedly asked. The CIA man agreed this was so. 'Have they not taken over half my country?' Again, the American agreed. 'Well,' said the shattered monarch, 'what the fuck do I do now?'[65]

Amman's belief in American complicity manifested itself in Jordanian accusations that US and British pilots were conducting bombing raids against Arab targets during the war. Even military realists such as al-Tell were convinced that the Israeli air force had foreign assistance.

Al-Tell argued that the sheer number of enemy aircraft launching simultaneous attacks on numerous Arab targets could only mean that Israel was being supported by the major powers.[66]

While it is true that the Johnson administration pursued policies favourable to Israel and even gave Israeli leaders 'a yellow light' in 1967,[67] there is no available evidence confirming that Jordan was 'trapped' by the US or even by Israel. The kingdom's own blunders, not an Israeli–American ruse, cost Jordan the West Bank and Jerusalem. As Mutawi concludes, by 'attempting to place Arab interests above all others King Hussein allowed Egyptian interests to prevail over Jordan's.'[68]

Further, even if Jordan had been beguiled into fighting by other powers, it could have pursued a policy of damage limitation by fighting its own war. While it is undeniable that Jordan could not have defeated its powerful neighbour, it certainly could have acquitted itself better in battle than it did. Hussein himself privately admitted that Glubb's mobile defence concept might have saved the West Bank.[69] In fact, he personally told Glubb that the British general's assessment of Israel's army had been accurate.[70]

Several British officers who served in the Arab Legion and who knew Jordan's military capabilities better than most criticised the way the kingdom fought. Writing in September 1967, Brigadier Peter Young argued of the Jordanians:

> If they were going to fight – which was obviously a mistake – they could do much better by launching a vigorous offensive, than by sitting in their defensive positions, harassing the Jewish part of Jerusalem, Tel Aviv and Ramat David with shell fire and, once their air force had been shot out of the sky, being bombed with napalm.[71]

Even after the Egyptian air force had been destroyed, 'the Jordanians had one advantage': they could launch a 'vigorous thrust' into Jewish Jerusalem, where the Israelis 'would be reluctant to use their air power' for fear of inflicting civilian casualties on Israeli citizens.[72] In essence, Young is describing Operation Tariq which, as Major-General James Lunt argues, 'was based purely on military considerations.' Although the plan meant 'abandoning certain areas in order to ensure the security of … Jerusalem,' it 'made sense'.[73]

Jordanian commanders also concurred that the kingdom could have at least salvaged key pieces of territory, although they recognise that Jordan was no match for Israel. Today many of these commanders point to the fact that the same Jordanian army which fought in 1967 successfully defended the East Bank town of al-Karama against a large-scale Israeli assault in March 1968. During that battle, the Jordanian First Infantry Division and the 60th Armoured Brigade held off an Israeli force of 15 000 troops backed by supporting arms, inflicting relatively heavy casualties on the Israelis.[74] The al-Karama battle proves, the Jordanians argue, that the kingdom had the military capability to acquit themselves well in June 1967.

Finally, on the 30th anniversary of the Six Day War, King Hussein publicly admitted that Jordan should not have fought. In a televised speech before the nation, the king criticised the Arab armies for failing to mobilise properly for war and for poor coordination during the actual fighting. 'It was probably our duty,' King Hussein concluded, 'to try to prevent this country from being part of that battle.'[75]

Conclusion

The king's handling of the 1967 war jeopardised national security more than any other crisis since the Abu Nuwar and al-Nabulsi factions dominated the national security establishment. The territorial integrity of the Hashemite Kingdom was altered by the loss of the West Bank, and a new inflow of refugees would add to Jordan's security difficulties. Like the 1956–57 crisis, the 1967 crisis can be traced, in large part, to the dominant role Hussein exercised in decisionmaking. Hussein responded to Jordan's pro-Nasser public opinion and relied on decisionmakers who would not oppose him. The series of blunders made by Hussein and the pro-Egypt camp cost Jordan half its territory and the bulk of its resources.

Conclusion

This study has sought to broaden the focus of the existing scholarship on Jordanian stability by concentrating less on the personality of King Hussein and more on the underlying establishment that has guided Jordan since its creation in 1921. Jordan's inherent security weaknesses necessitated the creation of a ruling coalition that needed to accommodate domestic urban and tribal interests if the Hashemite state were to survive.

This book argues that Jordan overcame the challenges of the Cold War, radical pan-Arabism, Israeli hostility, and internal opposition due largely to the cohesion of its national security establishment. A ruling coalition comprising the institutions of the monarchy, the political elite, and the military, the national security establishment was the paramount policymaking body in Jordan from 1955 to 1967. While decisionmakers often disagreed over the means of protecting national security, they agreed on the ultimate end of this policy: the preservation of the Hashemite monarchy and the territorial integrity of Jordan.

What set Jordan's ruling establishment apart from many Arab elites was its long record of governing experience and its deep-rooted commitment to the state. The same set of political and military leaders who ruled Jordan after state formation in 1921 were still in power at independence in 1946. The Palestine war in 1948 further demonstrated the security establishment's cohesiveness. Jordan deployed its entire army to Palestine, where it performed better than any other Arab force, and managed to incorporate the West Bank and Jerusalem into Jordan in the face of widespread Arab hostility.

When King Hussein ascended the throne in 1953, Jordan's ruling establishment was entering its fourth decade in power. However, although Jordan's national security establishment had an 'institutional' longevity that few Arab ruling elites could match, most observers were convinced that Hussein could not survive the external, regional, and domestic challenges he faced. Numerous Arab and Western commentators predicted the demise of the Hashemite state and its replacement with a republican state.

This book has demonstrated that such fears were not realised given the cohesiveness of Jordan's ruling establishment. This cohesion becomes evident when one realises that Jordan was virtually the only state in the Levant to make the transition from independence with its ruling elite intact. The same officials who collaborated with the British remained powerbrokers in autonomous Jordan. Jordan's establishment was also one of the few that survived the fallout from the Palestine war. By contrast, Syria experienced the first of many military coups in 1949; the Egyptian monarchy was toppled in 1952; and Iraq became a republican state in 1958. In each case, the pre-revolutionary structures of government were purged. Land reforms, 'popular' committees, and new legislative assemblies ensured that a new cast of characters ruled. Even Lebanon, widely regarded as a bastion of stability in the region, faced a civil war in 1958. In Jordan, no such upheaval obtained.

The absence of a successful coup d'état in Jordan underscored the ruling coalition's cohesion. As argued, those officers not wholly committed to the Hashemite state represented a minority in the armed forces. While a revolutionary impetus existed among small segments of the officer corps, the army, by and large, did not regard itself as a force for political change in Jordan. Those officers accused of intriguing against the monarchy never enjoyed a wide following, and the only time they constituted a security threat was during the immediate post-Arabisation period when they displaced officers of proven loyalty. Hence, the various coup attempts between 1957 and 1959 are better viewed as manoeuvres by rival officers hoping to regain their prerogative in national security policymaking than as well-laid conspiracies against the throne.

The national security establishment's cohesion was also evident during times of domestic turmoil. Rather than abdicating in the face of rioting that erupted in 1955–56, 1957, 1963, and 1966, the security establishment closed ranks and acted decisively to restore order. While some decisionmakers advocated the use of less heavy-handed tactics toward demonstrators, few questioned the morality of using force to break up rallies. Indeed, every decisionmaker understood the importance of preventing opposition leaders from gathering a critical mass of support from 'the street'.

Another indicator of the national security establishment's cohesive-ness was its ability to weather the assassination of Prime Minister Hazza` al-Majali at the hands of the Syrians in August 1960. Rather than disin-tegrating as its enemies hoped, the ruling coalition quickly formed another government and reinstated public order. Further, Jordan sent a message to the United Arab Republic that Jordan was willing to use mil-itary means to protect its national security by deploying a large invasion force on the Syrian border.

Perhaps the most vivid example of the national security establish-ment's cohesion came after Jordan lost the West Bank in June 1967. While the decision to go to war had been a divisive one, decisionmakers put aside their animosities and quickly shored up their authority on the East Bank. Some observers predicted that the loss of the West Bank sig-nalled the beginning of the end of the Hashemite state. Yet the national security establishment retained its grip on power and easily consolidated its rule, despite the serious errors it made before and during the war with Israel. The national security establishment's successful regrouping was illustrated by its ability to overcome a major armed challenge from the Palestinian resistance movement during the civil war of 1970–71.

In addition to helping the Hashemite state weather crises, the national security establishment's cohesion contributed to Jordan's abil-ity to influence its relationship with regional and international powers. Despite the widely held view that small states have little leverage over larger states, this study has shown that the opposite was often true of Jordan. Rather than merely reacting to external events, Jordan pursued policies designed to influence regional and international politics. The Third Force and Yemen War policies were examples of the kingdom pro-jecting its power on a regional level. Jordan's handling of the Baghdad Pact, Ali Abu Nuwar, and 1958 crises were instances of playing the Cold War card to attract and maintain US support.

Only twice during the 1955 to 1967 period did the lack of cohesion in the national security establishment create or exacerbate instability in Jordan. The first instance occurred in 1956–57 when the radical Suleiman al-Nabulsi faction entered the inner circle of the security establishment, and the Ali Abu Nuwar group took control of the armed forces. The second was in 1966–67, when the pro-Egypt faction helped steer Jordan toward an alliance with the radical Arab states. In the first instance, Jordan nearly lost its identity as a Hashemite state and, in the second, the kingdom entered a war that cost it the West Bank.

The ruling coalition's lack of cohesion during the 1957 and 1967 crises can be traced, in large part, to the dominant leadership role

King Hussein exercised on both occasions. The king's position in the decisionmaking process was normally that of ultimate arbiter between competing factions. That is, he took final decisions based on policy advice from his closest civil and military advisors. The 1957 and 1967 crises were anomalous because they were times when the king took unilateral policy decisions. Instead of playing his usual mediating role and choosing policies formulated by his long-time advisors, Hussein set the pace and dragged the rest of the national security establishment with him.

Hussein's decisions in the months before both crises were taken with a narrow base of support in the national security establishment. The king ignored policymakers who had proven their reliability in previous crises and turned to those who were less inclined to oppose him. In 1956, Hussein's decision to sack General John Glubb and Arabise the armed forces was backed primarily by the faction of the untrustworthy Ali Abu Nuwar. Most civil and military leaders, however, had reservations about the king's decision. In 1967, Hussein sought support for his decisions from a group of pro-Egypt advisors, rather than from his senior military officers. Comprising professionals who had successfully defended Jerusalem and Latrun during the 1948 war, this group could not see the logic of turning the Jordanian army over to Egyptian officers who had never won a battle.

King Hussein's failure to allow the national security establishment to function in 1956 and 1967 is compounded by the fact that he made poor decisions on both occasions. In each instance, Hussein mistakenly believed that the Hashemite state could reach an accommodation with radical pan-Arabism. Whereas in 1956 Hussein calculated that tilting toward Egyptian President Gamal Abdel Nasser and the Arab radicals was the best way of protecting his throne, in 1967 he calculated that it was the only way. On both occasions, his affiliation with Nasser sorely disappointed him.

The king's decisions may not have been so destabilising had he pursued a policy of damage limitation. For example, expelling Glubb and Arabising the national security establishment were not injurious to national security per se. What was dangerous was the way in which Hussein went about Arabising Jordan. Rather than promoting senior officers with decades of service to the Hashemite state, he promoted young officers of doubtful loyalty. Rather than reading the riot act to the al-Nabulsi government at an early stage, the king permitted events to spiral out of control before he acted in April 1957.

Likewise, for all its faults, Hussein's decision to fight Israel in 1967 was comprehensible given regional and domestic circumstances at the time.

However, there was no reason for Jordan to fight the way it did. Alone of the Arab states that fought in the June war, Jordan enjoyed covert relations with Israel and good ties with the US. Alone of the Arab states, Jordan had a proven record of success in battle against the Israelis. While Jordan lacked air power, its infantry was probably the best in the Arab world. Of the Arab regimes that fought, Jordan's leadership had the longest record of success in power. Unlike Egypt, Syria, and Iraq, Jordan had never faced a popular revolution, a military coup, or large-scale domestic disorder. In fact, despite much contemporary hysterical reporting that Jordan had no choice but to fight or face a civil war, the ruling coalition had overcome numerous crises over the years, and there was no reason it could not do so in 1967.

Hussein's propensity to take the lead in forming security policy stemmed from the increasing significance of the monarchy in policymaking from 1955 to 1967 and from an impetuous streak in his nature. The throne was overshadowed in the early days of Hussein's reign, but it acquired strength as the young monarch gained confidence and maturity. By the early 1960s, Hussein was apt to insert himself more forcefully in the policymaking process. While strong leaders such as Wasfi al-Tell and Queen Zein were usually able to dissuade Hussein from taking rash decisions, the king's increased assurance led him to take a more active role in formulating policy by the mid-1960s.

The king's increased powers came from his ability to remove rivals from the national security establishment. The first step in Hussein's consolidation of his authority came with his expulsion of Glubb. In one fell swoop, the king removed the most powerful figure in Jordanian political life. The next step Hussein took was to purge the national security establishment of anti-royalists in 1957, a move he followed by declaring martial law, banning political parties, and securing a commitment of American support for his reign. The final stages of Hussein's consolidation came after the army purges of 1958 and 1959. By the early 1960s, Hussein was starting to play such a visible role in the decisionmaking process that he was in danger of weakening the chief foundation of his rule, the national security establishment.

Another factor explaining Hussein's increased role in decisionmaking was his impulsive and often stubborn nature. The king's impetuosity did not result from a mere personality quirk or from his family's history of mental instability, but from his energetic personality. Active by nature, Hussein grew frustrated waiting for others to formulate policies that affected the security of the Hashemite state. Consequently, he was inclined to take decisions without consulting his advisors. Although

Hussein often wavered over policy options and could be easily swayed by other decisionmakers, once he took a decision he was difficult to budge.

Hussein's active leadership role during the 1957 and 1967 crises reveals a key weakness of Jordan's national security establishment, its lack of checks and balances. Unlike systems of rule that contain mechanisms to prevent one policymaker from becoming disproportionately powerful, the Jordanian system depended ultimately on the king. Hence, there were no systemic restraints to prevent the ultimate arbiter of political power, Hussein, from making bad decisions. On occasion, the United States and Britain could deter Hussein from taking potentially disastrous decisions – for example, when the West dissuaded him from attacking Iraq and Syria between 1958 and 1960 – but without firm external pressure, the king was relatively free to do as he chose.

Conversely, the aftermath of the 1957 and 1967 crises reveals the national security establishment's greatest strength, its ability to remain focused on the chief objectives of national security policy. When Hussein wanted to shore up his reign in April 1957, he turned back to the old guard whose advice he had rejected in 1956. Similarly, when Hussein wanted to restore the Hashemite state's authority in September 1970, he turned to the very men whose cautions he had ignored in 1967. Decisionmakers understood that their futures were inextricably linked to the Hashemite state and thus united to confront the common threat (e.g. Arab radicalism in 1957 and Palestinian separatism after 1967).

Just as Jordan's national security establishment's shared commitment to the Hashemite state protected Jordanian stability between 1955 and 1967, that same coalition will contribute to Jordan's national security under King Abdullah II. The smooth transition from King Hussein to his son in 1999 demonstrates the continued existence of a cohesive Jordanian ruling establishment. This cohesion remained even after former Crown Prince Hassan (King Hussein's brother) was passed over at the 'last minute' in favour of the relatively inexperienced Abdullah.

Abdullah's challenge will be to develop an understanding of when and how he should rely on Jordan's national security establishment, while seeking to broaden his base of popular support. While the national security establishment has proven to be an effective guardian of the Hashemite state, the power of information technology, modern communications, and universalist ideologies such as democratisation and economic liberalisation will increase demands for a more inclusive system of rule in the Hashemite Kingdom.

Appendix: Biographical Sketches

The following biographical sketches are compiled from declassified Western and Jordanian diplomatic records, interviews with surviving decisionmakers, and secondary Arabic and English sources.

Tawfiq Abul Huda

Born in Acre, Palestine in 1895, Tawfiq Abul Huda was co-opted by King Abdullah in the early 1920s after service in the Ottoman army and in Prince Faisal's ill-fated Damascus government. Abul Huda served in various Jordanian administrations in differing capacities and, as prime minister, opposed some of the young King Hussein's policies. Abul Huda's suicide in 1956 sparked unfounded rumours that he had been assassinated by the British for adopting anti-Western policies.

Ali Abu Nuwar

Ali Abu Nuwar, born in al-Salt to a Circassian mother, occupies a notorious place in Jordanian history. Abu Nuwar was commissioned as an artillery officer in 1944 and commanded an infantry company in 1946. He served as a lieutenant in the 1948 Palestine war and was a member of the Jordanian delegation to the Rhodes armistice negotiations. A graduate of Britain's staff college at Camberly, Abu Nuwar was posted to Europe by General John Glubb, where he formed close ties with King Hussein (then at school in England). Abu Nuwar became involved with the Jordanian Free Officers and helped Hussein sack Glubb. After his meteoric rise to chief of staff after Arabisation, Abu Nuwar was linked to a coup attempt in 1957 and purged from the national security establishment.

Salah Abu Zaid

Salah Abu Zaid was born in Irbid and related through marriage to the al-Tell family. He was plucked from obscurity by chance and became influential in decisionmaking by virtue of his close friendship with King Hussein. A colourful figure, Abu Zaid was reputed to have arranged relationships between Hussein and various women. He was known in Jordan as *gadahat al-malik*, or 'the king's lighter', because whenever Hussein wanted a cigarette, Abu Zaid was supposedly there to light it for him. A fervent anti-Nasserite, he found common cause with Wasfi al-Tell. The two masterminded Jordan's vitriolic radio campaigns against Cairo, but fell out in the early 1960s.

`Akif al-Fayiz

`Akif al-Fayiz was the son of the paramount sheikh of the powerful Beni Sakhir tribal confederation in northern Jordan. Born around 1920 and married to an ex-wife of King Saud, Al-Fayiz shifted his political alliances throughout his tenure in the national security establishment. He rose to prominence in 1957 with his flamboyant deployment of beduin irregulars in Amman in support of Hussein. Considered corrupt by many, he used his sinecure in the security establishment to divert funds to his own tribal supporters. He and the Bani Sakhir clashed politically with southern tribal elements, and al-Fayiz's faction was purged from the ruling coalition in 1961 only to return several years later.

General Sir John Bagot 'Glubb Pasha'

Born in 1897, Glubb served in the British army during the First World War and was posted to France and Iraq. Glubb was transferred to the Arab Legion in 1930 and became commander-in-chief in 1938. Glubb was retained under contract by the Hashemite state, but most Jordanians considered him the British pro-consul in Amman. Although Glubb's troops had successfully captured the West Bank in 1948, he was blamed by opposition groups for the Arab defeat in the war. King Hussein's sacking of Glubb in 1956 removed his chief rival for power in Jordan and paved the way for the Arabisation of the national security establishment.

Ibrahim Hashim

Born in Nablus, Palestine in 1884, Ibrahim Hashim served in the Ottoman civil service before joining King Abdullah's government in the early 1920s. As a West Bank notable, Hashim had no real base in Transjordan and was empowered through his affiliation with the Hashemite state. A holder of the MBE – an award which did little to endear him to anti-British opposition groups – Hashim was the quintessential 'king's man' who became a perennial caretaker prime minister in charge of various interim governments. Hashim remained a reliable security establishment player until his murder by the Baghdad mobs during the Iraqi revolution in 1958.

Hussein bin Talal

Born in Amman in 1935, King Hussein was educated at Victoria College (Alexandria, Egypt), Harrow, and Sandhurst military academy before succeeding his father as king in 1953. Surrounded by much older, more experienced political and military leaders, the young Hussein worked hard to consolidate his position as the ultimate arbiter in the national security establishment. His sacking of General Glubb in 1956 and undercutting of the anti-royalists in 1957 and 1958 went a long way toward establishing his leadership credentials. The 1960s witnessed a series of political successes on Hussein's part. However, Jordan's poor performance in the 1967 war and expulsion of the Palestinian commandoes in 1970 dented Hussein's regional credibility. Nevertheless, Hussein managed to overcome the threats to his throne and eventually became one of the most respected leaders in the modern Middle East.

`Amer Khammash

`Amer Khammash hailed from al-Salt, although he had familial links in Palestine. After being commissioned as an officer in the Arab Legion in 1944, he qualified as Jordan's first Arab pilot in 1949. After serving as an aerial observation officer and battery commander, Khammash was aide-de-camp to various prime ministers between 1953 and 1956. Khammash gradually became regarded as the military's chief theoretician and planner. Influenced by American military doctrine, Khammash spearheaded the reorganisation of Jordan's armed forces in the mid-1960s and was instrumental in supporting King Hussein's decision to go to war against Israel in 1967.

Habis al-Majali

Born in 1913, Habis al-Majali was the first Jordanian officer in the Arab Legion and rose to become one of the most influential military leaders in Jordanian national security policymaking. Al-Majali came to prominence in 1948 due to his performance in the war against Israel. He was known as the 'hero of Latrun' for his successful defence of Latrun against the Israeli forces. In the 1950s and the 1960s, al-Majali allied with the powerful Sharif Nasser and became a fervent opponent of any reductions in the army's role in security policymaking. Although al-Majali lost some influence after 1965, he regained his position with a successful appointment as commander-in-chief and military governor during 'Black September' 1970.

Hazza` al-Majali

Born in al-Karak in 1916, Hazza` al-Majali played a prominent role in Jordanian political life until his death. Al-Majali was educated at Damascus University and practised law until he entered government in 1947. Al-Majali, like his ally, Wasfi al-Tell, believed that Jordan needed reliable external backers and that Britain could fulfil such a role. Al-Majali's first, short-lived government was formed in 1955 with the express purpose of bringing Jordan into the Baghdad Pact. His second administration, formed in 1959, initiated Jordan's first civil and economic reforms. A supporter of a proactive security policy, al-Majali was assassinated in August 1960 by Syrian intelligence agents.

Sa`id al-Mufti

Sa`id al-Mufti was a Circassian whose family had fled Czarist Russia. Like most minority elements in the ruling coalition, al-Mufti did little to rock the boat and was considered a steady, but unimaginative, prime minister. Like Ibrahim Hashim, al-Mufti often played the role of caretaker premier. Al-Mufti played a part in the succession crisis following King Talal's abdication and proved his loyalty in 1957 by backing the royalist purge of the national security establishment.

Suleiman al-Nabulsi

Born in al-Salt in 1910, Suleiman al-Nabulsi became one of the most controversial figures to enter the ranks of the Jordanian ruling coalition. After being educated at the American University of Beirut, al-Nabulsi served in various ministerial positions before becoming prime minister and head of the National Socialist Party in 1956. Due to his alliance with radical anti-royalists and pursuit of policies that challenged the monarchy's primacy in policymaking – most notably, his conclusion of an alliance agreement with Egypt and Syria and his termination of the Anglo-Jordanian Treaty – al-Nabulsi was purged from power by a royalist faction. Al-Nabulsi spent his remaining years in political isolation, often under house arrest during times of crisis.

Sharif Nasser bin Jamil

Sharif Nasser, Hussein's maternal uncle, exercised a major influence on Jordanian security policy throughout the 1950s and 1960s. A man of prodigious strength and impressive stature, Sharif Nasser was both feared and respected by his rivals. The Sharif believed in maintaining a strong policymaking role for the army and was responsible for many of the purges that occurred in the armed forces. Allied to Habis al-Majali and other officers of tribal origin, Sharif Nasser often advocated a proactive national security policy which involved Jordan seizing the political initiative in regional politics. Sharif Nasser's strength diminished in 1966 – after his reputation for corruption and smuggling activities forced the king to confront his uncle – but he maintained an active role in security policy formulation until 1974–75.

Samir al-Rifa`i

Born in Safad, Palestine in 1896, Samir al-Rifa`i became a major national security establishment powerbroker, serving in numerous posts until his death in 1967. Al-Rifa`i was known for his political pragmatism and willingness to steer Jordan toward closer ties with Egypt. His closest political allies were Bahjat al-Talhuni and his brother, Abdel Mun`im al-Rifa`i. Al-Rifa`i and his camp often clashed with Hazza` al-Majali and the Sharif Nasser faction. Although al-Rifa`i was unpopular with opposition groups due to his advocacy of heavy-handed security policies, he remained a powerful influence in policymaking. His son, Zaid, rose to a similar position in Jordanian political life in the years following the 1967 war.

Sadiq al-Shar`a

Sadiq al-Shar`a was born in 1917 in Irbid and gained prominence during his career in the military. He was bright, articulate, and supported by his brother Salih and a phalanx of other army officers. Until his downfall in 1959, his patron in the political sphere was Samir al-Rifa`i. Although he had helped oust Glubb in 1956 and Abu Nuwar in 1957, his increased role in army decisionmaking led to conflict with the powerful group led by Sharif Nasser and Habis al-Majali. After being implicated in an attempted coup in 1959, al-Shar`a was released from prison in 1963 and appointed military advisor in Kuwait.

Kamal al-Sha`ir

Kamal al-Sha`ir was a Christian from al-Salt who, although a technocrat, became prominent in the national security establishment in the 1960s and 1970s. Educated at Yale and Cambridge universities, al-Sha`ir had ties with opposition circles and was a Ba`thist. The British considered him the most able leader in Jordanian government. He enjoyed close relations with Wasfi al-Tell, but his defection from government in protest to Jordan's Yemen policy in 1962 was a blow to al-Tell. Al-Sha`ir successfully translated his government skills into commercial success and went on to head Jordan's largest engineering firm.

Bahjat al-Talhuni

Born in 1913, al-Talhuni hailed from an established Ma`an family. Trained as a lawyer at Damascus University, al-Talhuni rose to prominence in policymaking in the 1950s and served in numerous positions throughout the 1960s and early 1970s. Allied with Samir al-Rifa`i and opposed to Wasfi al-Tell and Hazza` al-Majali, al-Talhuni was more pro-Nasser than most national security establishment figures. Moreover, al-Talhuni was considered pro-PLO during the Jordanian–Palestinian tensions of 1968–71. Nevertheless, al-Talhuni was loyal to the Hashemite state and was at the king's side throughout Jordan's most turbulent years.

Wasfi al-Tell

Wasfi al-Tell was born in 1920 to the noted Transjordanian poet and political activist, Mustafa Wahabi al-Tell, and a Kurdish mother. Reared in Irbid, al-Tell was educated at the American University of Beirut, where he was active in the Arab nationalist movement. From 1942 to 1945, he served as a captain in the British army. From 1945 to 1947, he served in the Arab Office in Jerusalem. During the 1948 Palestine War, al-Tell served in the *jaysh al-inqadh* (Army of Salvation) and suffered wounds in battle. He joined the Jordanian civil service in 1949 and served in various posts until being appointed prime minister in January 1962. He headed several governments before being assassinated by Palestinian guerrillas in Cairo in November 1971. Throughout his career, al-Tell was a fervent anti-Nasserite and a proponent of creating a modern, self-sufficient Jordanian state.

Queen Zein

The formidable Queen Zein was perhaps the most influential informal decision-maker in the national security establishment. Since the reign of her husband, King Talal, Zein had exerted strong leverage on Hussein. Fluent in French, she proved adept at marketing the Jordanian cause to foreign diplomats. She also had strong opinions regarding who was and who was not suitable for promotion in the national security establishment. She had close links with her brother, Sharif Nasser, and Hazza` and Habis al-Majali. Zein often opposed Samir al-Rifa`i, Bahjat al-Talhuni, and Wasfi al-Tell for having too much influence on the king. A good-natured woman, Zein dubbed al-Rifa`i 'ad-ad-ad' due to his slight speech impediment, referred to the British – whose embassy adjoined the Palace compound – as 'the neighbours', and called Sadiq al-Shar`a 'la petite'.

Notes

1 Jordan's National Security Establishment

1. A survey of the 'theoretical' literature on Middle Eastern and other developing states is beyond the scope of this book. For a more detailed discussion of
   some of the political science and international relations scholarship on security in developing states and in Jordan, see Lawrence Tal, 'Politics, the
   Military, and National Security in Jordan, 1955–1967', doctoral thesis,
   University of Oxford, 1997.
2. See Mary C. Wilson, *King Abdullah, Britain and the Making of Jordan.*
   (Cambridge: Cambridge University Press, 1987), p. 225.
3. On this idea, see Rex Brynen, 'Economic Crisis and Post-Rentier
   Democratization in the Arab World: the Case of Jordan', *Canadian Journal of
   Political Science*, 25:1 (March 1992), 74.
4. Rex Brynen, 'Economic Crisis and Post-Rentier Democratization in the Arab
   World', 78. For most of the period covered by this study, 1 Jordanian Dinar
   (JD) = 1 Pound Sterling (£) = 2.8 American Dollars ($).
5. Alan S. Milward, *War, Economy and Society, 1939–1945* (London: Penguin,
   1977), p. 347.
6. Mary C. Wilson, 'King Abdullah and Palestine', *British Society of Middle
   Eastern Studies Bulletin*, 14 (1987), 37.
7. Naseer H. Aruri, *Jordan: a Study in Political Development (1921–1965)* (The
   Hague: Martin Nijhoff, 1972), 63. Details on the Eisenhower Doctrine can be
   found in Paul E. Zinner (ed.), *Documents on American Foreign Relations, 1958*
   (New York: Council on Foreign Relations Press, 1959) and United States
   Department of State, Historical Office, *American Foreign Policy, Current
   Documents, 1958* (Washington: US Government Printing Office, 1962).
8. Harry N. Howard, 'Jordan in Turmoil', *Current History* (January 1972), 16.
9. Brynen, 'Economic Crisis and Post-Rentier Democratization in the Arab
   World', 78.
10. See E. Kanovsky, *The Economy of Jordan: the Implications of Peace in the Middle
    East* (Tel Aviv: University Publishing Projects, 1976); Bichara Khader and
    Adnan Badran, *The Economic Development of Jordan* (London: Croom Helm,
    1987).
11. As Jordanian historians Munib al-Madi and Suleiman Musa put it: 'The
    Palestinian disaster affected Jordan more than any other country.' See their
    Tarikh al-urdunn fi al-qarn al-`ashreen [The History of Jordan in the Twentieth
    Century] (Amman: n.p., 1959; 2nd edn, Amman: Maktaba al-Muhtasab,
    1988), p. 627.
12. For more on the integration of West Bank land into the Jordanian system,
    see Michael R. Fischbach, 'The Implications of Jordanian Land Policy for the
    West Bank', *Middle East Journal*, 48 (Summer 1994), 493.
13. Samir Mutawi, 'Jordan in the 1967 War', doctoral thesis, University of
    Reading, 1985, p. 104.

14. The figures in this paragraph are from Aruri, *Jordan: a Study in Political Development*, p. 64.
15. See Lawrence Tal, 'On the Banks of the Stormy Jordan: the Coming Middle East Water Crisis', *Contemporary Review*, 260 (April 1992), 169–74.
16. See the chapter on Jordan by Lawrence Tal in Yezid Sayigh and Avi Shlaim (eds), *The Cold War in the Middle East* (Oxford: Oxford University Press, 1997), pp. 102–24.
17. See Galia Golan, *Soviet Policies in the Middle East: From World War II to Gorbachev* (Cambridge: Cambridge University Press, 1990).
18. Moscow to FO, 4 September 1958, FO 371.133797, Public Record Office (PRO), London.
19. James Lunt, *Hussein of Jordan: a Political Biography* (London: Macmillan, 1989), 65–6. Other examples of Hussein's philosophy can be found in *Al-majmu`a al-kamila li-khutub jalalat al-malik al-Hussein bin-Talal al-mu`adhim, 1952–1985* [Complete Collection of the speeches of His Majesty King Hussein bin Talal the Great, 1952–1985] (Amman: Ministry of Information, Directorate of Press and Publications, n.d.).
20. See Benny Morris, *Israel's Border Wars, 1949–1956: Arab Infiltration, Israeli Retaliation, and the Countdown to the Suez War* (New York: Oxford University Press, 1993), pp. 227–62.
21. Michael Oren, 'A Winter of Discontent: Britain's Crisis in Jordan, December 1955–March 1956', *International Journal of Middle East Studies*, 22 (1990), 174.
22. Anthony Parsons, *They Say the Lion: Britain's Legacy to the Arabs* (London: Jonathan Cape, 1986), p. 42.
23. Mutawi, 'Jordan in the 1967 War', 88.
24. See 'Awni Jadu`a al-`Abidi, *Hizb al-tahrir al-islami* [Islamic Liberation Party] (Amman: Dar al-Liwa` Press, 1993). Also, translation of the ILP's 'Political Tenets of the Islamic Liberation Party in Jordan', in Jacob M. Landau (ed.), *Man, State, and Society in the Contemporary Middle East* (London: Pall Mall Press, 1972), pp. 183–8. Also, Interview with Muhammad Sa`ad, 14 April 1995, Irbid.
25. A survey of the Arabic and English literature on the Brotherhood can be found in Lawrence Tal, 'Dealing with Radical Islam: the Case of Jordan', *Survival*, 37:3 (Autumn 1995), 139–56.
26. Interview with Abdel Ra'uf Abu al-Rasa`, 19 April 1995, Amman.
27. See Joel S. Migdal, 'Dispersal and Annexation: Jordanian Rule', and Shaul Mishal, 'Conflictual Pressures and Cooperative Interests: Observations on West Bank–Amman Political Relations, 1949–1967', in Joel S. Migdal (ed.), *Palestinian Society and Politics* (Princeton: Princeton University Press, 1979), pp. 34–43 and 169–84, respectively; and Baruch Kimmerling and Joel S. Migdal, *The Palestinians: the Making of a People* (New York: The Free Press, 1993), p. 102.
28. Avi Plascov, *The Palestinian Refugees in Jordan, 1948–1957* (London: Frank Cass, 1981).
29. Adam M. Garfinkle, 'Jordan and Arab Polarization', *Current History* (January 1982), 24.
30. Dana Adams Schmidt, *Armageddon in the Middle East* (New York: The John Day Company, 1974), p. 59.
31. For more on the 'Jordan first' or 'East Bank first' school of thought, see Valerie Yorke, *Domestic Politics and Regional Security, Jordan, Syria, and Israel: the End of an Era?* (Aldershot: Gower for IISS, 1988); Yossi Nevo, 'Is there a

Jordanian Entity?', *Jerusalem Quarterly*, 16 (Summer 1980), 98–110; Lawrence Tal, 'Is Jordan Doomed?', *Foreign Affairs*, 72:5 (November/December 1993), 45–58; and Jamal al-Sha`ir, *Siyassi yatadhakkir* [A Politician Remembers] (London: Riyad al-Rayyes Publishers, 1987).

32. On this theme, see Lisa Anderson, 'Absolutism and the Resilience of Monarchy in the Middle East', *Political Science Quarterly*, 106 (1991), 14.

33. See S.H. Amin, *Middle East Legal Systems* (Glasgow: Royston Limited, 1985), pp. 244–68. Also, Kamel S. Abu Jaber, 'The Jordanian Parliament', in Jacob M. Landau (ed.), *Man, State, and Society in the Contemporary Middle East* (London: Pall Mall Press, 1972), p. 116.

34. Interview with Salah Abu Zaid, 15 April 1995, Amman.

35. Ali E. Hillal Dessouki and Karen Aboul Kheir, 'The Politics of Vulnerability and Survival: the Foreign Policy of Jordan', in Bahgat Korany and Ali E. Hillal Dessouki (eds), *The Foreign Policies of Arab States: the Challenge of Change* (Boulder: Westview Press, 1991), p. 227.

36. Quoted in ' "Boy King" Grows Up', *US News and World Report*, 10 May 1957.

37. Jill Crystal, 'Authoritarianism and its Adversaries in the Arab World', *World Politics*, 46 (January 1994), 274.

38. Bassel F. Salloukh, 'State Strength, Permeability, and Foreign Policy Behavior: Jordan in Theoretical Perspective', *Arab Studies Quarterly*, 18:2 (Spring 1996), 55.

39. Quoted in Samuel P. Huntington, *Political Order in Changing Societies* (New Haven: Yale University Press, 1968), p. 179.

40. Samir Mutawi, *Jordan in the 1967 War* (Cambridge: Cambridge University Press, 1987), p. 46.

41. Figure cited in economic tables in *Middle Eastern Affairs* (May 1961), 148.

42. Oral communications and radio were especially important given Jordan's low literacy rate. The Human Relations Area Files estimated that approximately 20 per cent of Jordan was literate in 1958. See George L. Harris, *Jordan: Its People, Its Society, Its Culture* (New York: Grove Press, 1958), p. 193.

43. Quoted in the article, 'The Last Unreasonable Arab', *Time*, 14 July 1967.

44. Parkes to Home, 8 February 1963, FO 371.170265/EJ 1015/23, Public Record Office (PRO), London.

45. Naseer H. Aruri, *Jordan: a Study in Political Development (1921–1965)* (The Hague: Martinus Nijhoff, 1972), p. 69. One of the best sources for following the careers of Jordan's political elite are the charts in Marius Haas, *Husseins Königreich* [Hussein's Kingdom] (Munich: Tuduv Buch, 1975), pp. 571–605. I wish to thank Sabine Gerson for her translation assistance.

46. Interview with Kamal al-Sha`ir, 25 April 1995, Amman.

47. For a discussion of 'units of informal organization', see Robert Springborg, 'Patterns of Association in the Egyptian Political Elite', in George Lenczowski (ed.), *Political Elites in the Middle East* (Washington, DC: American Enterprise Institute, 1975), pp. 83–107.

48. Korany, 'The Take-Off of Third World Studies?', 487.

49. Selwyn Lloyd quoted in Alan Rush, obituary of 'Queen Zein of Jordan', *The Independent*, 28 April 1994, 14.

50. Dana Adams Schmidt, *Armageddon in the Middle East*, p. 59.

51. Vatikiotis argues that the army 'virtually created the state of Jordan.' See P.J. Vatikiotis, *Politics and the Military in Jordan: a Study of the Arab Legion, 1921–1957* (London: Frank Cass, 1967), p. 137.

52. J.C. Hurewitz, *Middle East Politics: the Military Dimension* (Boulder: Westview Press, 1982), table 18.
53. Michael P. Mazur, *Economic Growth and Development in Jordan* (London: Croom Helm, 1979), p. 92.
54. Parkes to Home, 3 July 1963, FO 371.170311/EJ 1195/5, PRO.
55. Merriam to DOS, 18 November 1957, DOS 785.00/11-1857, NA.
56. Anthony H. Cordesman, *After the Storm: the Changing Military Balance in the Middle East* (Boulder: Westview Press, 1993), p. 296.
57. Gavin Kennedy, *The Military in the Third World* (London: Gerald Duckworth, 1974), p. 181.
58. Haim Gerber, *The Social Origins of the Modern Middle East* (London: Mansell Publishing, Limited, 1987), p. 159.
59. Eliezer Be'eri, *Army Officers in Arab Politics and Society* (London: Praeger, 1970), p. 229–30.
60. Be'eri, *Army Officers in Arab Politics and Society*, p. 345.

2 Between Imperialism and Arabism

1. Michael B. Oren, 'A Winter of Discontent: Britain's Crisis in Jordan, December 1955–March 1956', *International Journal of Middle Eastern Studies*, 22 (1990), 171.
2. For details on the decision to move the British Middle East headquarters to Cyprus, see Minute by R. Allen, 6 September 1952, FO 371.96977/JE 1194/85/G; Minutes of cabinet meeting, 3 December 1958, CAB 128/25 CC(52), both Public Record Office (PRO), London. I wish to thank Michael Thornhill for bringing these documents to my attention.
3. Mallory to DOS, 22 October 1955, DOS 785.00/10-2255, National Archives (NA), Washington, DC. Nasser's speech announcing the arms deal can be found in C.H. Dodd and Mary Sales (eds), *Israel and the Arab World* (London: Routledge and Kegan Paul, 1970), pp. 106–11.
4. See Memorandum of Conversation, White House, 30 January 1956, in *Foreign Relations of the United States, 1955–1957, Near East: Jordan and Yemen, Volume XIII* (Washington: US Government Printing Office, 1988), 20. (Hereafter cited as FRUS, 1955–1957, Volume XIII.)
5. Mallory to DOS, 22 October 1955, DOS 785.00/10-2255, NA.
6. P.J. Vatikiotis, *Politics and the Military in Jordan: a Study of the Arab Legion, 1921–1957* (London: Frank Cass, 1967), p. 76.
7. Vatikiotis, *Politics and the Military in Jordan*, p. 75.
8. Glubb's views on Jordanian national security can be found in his *A Soldier with the Arabs* (London: Hodder and Stoughton, 1957) and 'Violence on the Jordan–Israel Border', *Foreign Affairs*, 32 (July 1954), 552–62.
9. Interview with James Lunt, 17 March 1993, Oxford.
10. Johnston to Beith, 5 May 1960, FO 371.151080/VJ 1121/18, PRO.
11. As Glubb put it in his memoirs: If 'Jordan had joined the Baghdad Pact, her safety from any attack by Israel would have been absolutely assured.' See *A Soldier with the Arabs*, p. 394.
12. Asher Susser, *On Both Banks of the Jordan: a Political Biography of Wasfi al-Tall* (London: Frank Cass, 1994), p. 25. For Hazza' al-Majali's political views, see his *Mudhakkarati* [My Memoirs] (Beirut: Dar al-'ilm lil-Malayeen Press, 1960).

13. Hussein bin Talal, *Uneasy Lies the Head* (London: Heinemann, 1962), p. 89.
14. Robert B. Satloff, *From Abdullah to Hussein: Jordan in Transition* (New York: Oxford University Press, 1994), p. 116. Also, Glubb, *A Soldier with the Arabs*, p. 393.
15. Uriel Dann, 'The Foreign Office, The Baghdad Pact and Jordan', *Asian and African Studies*, 21 (1987), 258.
16. Memorandum from the Director of the Office of Near Eastern Affairs to the Assistant Secretary of State for Near Eastern, South Asian, and African Affairs, 9 December 1955 in FRUS, 1955–1957, Vol. XIII, p. 8.
17. Richard Parker, who was posted to the American embassy in Amman at the time, recalls that many Jordanians were 'indifferent' to the Pact. It was the 'politically active minority' that mobilised students and leftists against the Pact. Personal correspondence with Ambassador Richard B. Parker, 24 February 1997.
18. Satloff, *From Abdullah to Hussein*, p. 123. Al-Sadat himself claims: 'I was able to persuade [Hussein] not to join the pact.' See Anwar El-Sadat, *In Search of Identity: an Autobiography* (London: Fontana, 1978), p. 167.
19. Oren, 'A Winter of Discontent', 176. For more on Templer's efforts to cajole the Jordanian government, see Keith Kyle, *Suez* (London: Weidenfeld and Nicolson, 1991), p. 90.
20. Said K. Aburish, *The St. George Hotel Bar* (London: Bloomsbury, 1989), p. 141.
21. Mallory to DOS, 18 December 1955 in FRUS, 1955–1957, Vol. XIII, p. 10.
22. See Parker to DOS, 31 December 1955, DOS 785.00/12-3155, NA. Glubb described his troops' actions thus: 'whenever they were obliged to fire, they showed perfect steadiness and discipline. The officer in charge would give a quiet command, two or three single shots rang out, one or two men fell, and the incident was over. Nearly all the wounded were injured in the legs – proof of the calm discipline with which the soldiers aimed.' Glubb, *A Soldier with the Arabs*, p. 399.
23. Parker to DOS, 31 December 1955, DOS 785.00/12-3155, NA. Suleiman Musa argues that al-Majali favoured the Pact as a means of strengthening Jordan (particularly against Israel), but opposed using violence to force Jordanian accession. See Suleiman Musa, *Al-'alam min al-urdunn: safhat min tarikh al-'arab al-hadith* [Prominent Personalities from Jordan: Pages from Modern Arab History] (Amman: Dar al-Sha'ab, 1986), pp. 30–1.
24. Duke to Lloyd, 16 January 1956, FO 371.121464/VJ 1015/92, PRO.
25. Mallory to DOS, 26 January 1956 in FRUS, 1955–1957, Vol. XIII, p. 22.
26. Elizabeth Monroe, *Britain's Moment in the Middle East, 1914–1956* (London: Chatto and Windus, 1963), p. 189.
27. Duke to Lloyd, 16 January 1956, FO 371.121464/VJ 1015/92, PRO. Also, Richard B. Parker, 'The United States and King Hussein', in David W. Lesch (ed.), *The Middle East and the United States: a Historical and Political Reassessment* (Boulder: Westview, 1996), p. 106.
28. For details of the violence, see Mallory to DOS, 10 January 1956 in FRUS, 1955–1957, Vol. XIII, p. 16.
29. Duke to Lloyd, 16 January 1956, FO 371.121464/VJ 1015/92, PRO. Parker believes that Glubb was initially hesitant about deploying his forces, but did so when ordered to by the king. See Parker, 'The United States and King Hussein', 107.

30. Glubb, *A Soldier with the Arabs*, p. 407.
31. Satloff, *From Abdullah to Hussein*, p. 132.
32. Al-Rifaʿi told the Lower House that 'it is not our policy to enter or become linked with any new alliances.' Quoted in Musa, *Al-ʿalam min al-urdunn*, p. 31. Saʿad Aboudia relies heavily on published English accounts in his assessment of the decision not to join the Pact. See ʿ*Amaliyat ittikhadh al-qarar fi siyassat al-urdunn al-kharijiyya* [The Foreign Policy Decisionmaking Process in Jordan] (Amman: n.p., 1983), pp. 191–211.
33. Satloff, *From Abdullah to Hussein*, p. 134.
34. Satloff, *From Abdullah to Hussein*, p. 138.
35. James Lunt, *Hussein of Jordan: a Political Biography* (London: Macmillan, 1989), p. 26.
36. See, for instance, Parker to DOS, 10 May 1956, DOS 785.5/5-1056, NA.
37. Glubb's claim that there were only six Free Officers (out of an officer corps of 1500) is dubious. See his *The Changing Scenes of Life: an Autobiography* (London: Quartet Books, 1983), p. 180.
38. Parker to DOS, 10 May 1956, DOS 785.5/5-1056, NA.
39. E.L.M. Burns, *Between Arab and Israeli* (London: George G. Harrap, 1962), p. 50.
40. Benjamin Shwadran, *Jordan: a State of Tension* (New York: Council for Middle Eastern Affairs Press, 1959), p. 317.
41. Naim Sofer, 'The Political Status of Jerusalem in the Hashemite Kingdom of Jordan, 1948–1967', *Middle Eastern Studies*, 12 (January 1976), p. 82.
42. Munib al-Madi and Suleiman Musa, *Tarikh al-urdunn fi al-qarn al-ʿashreen* [The History of Jordan in the Twentieth Century] (Amman: n.p., 1959; 2nd edn, Amman: Maktaba al-Muhtasab, 1988), pp. 628–30. For an analysis of Glubb's concept of operations, see Syed Ali el-Edroos, *The Hashemite Arab Army, 1908–1979: an Appreciation and Analysis of Military Operations* (Amman: The Publishing Committee, 1980), pp. 313–16.
43. Peter Snow, *Hussein: a Biography* (London: Barrie and Jenkins, 1972), p. 79.
44. Snow, *Hussein*, p. 83
45. Uriel Dann, *King Hussein and the Challenge of Arab Radicalism, 1955–1967* (New York: Oxford University Press, 1989), p. 32.
46. Mallory to DOS, 16 March 1956, DOS 785.00/3-1656, NA. Glubb also believes that Hussein made the decision. See *A Soldier with the Arabs*, p. 427.
47. See Shahir Yusef Abu Shahut, *Al-jaysh wa al-siyassa fi al-urdunn: dhikriyat ʿan harakat al-dubat al-urdunniyeen al-ahrar* [Army and Politics in Jordan: Memories of the Jordanian Free Officers Movement] (N.P.: al-Qabas Publishing, 1985).
48. Interview with Mahmud al-Maʿayta, 15 April 1993, Amman.
49. Hussein, *Uneasy Lies the Head*, p. 142.
50. James Morris, *The Hashemite Kings* (London: Faber and Faber, 1959), p. 186. Trevor Royle identifies Abu Nuwar as 'one of the main instigators of Glubb's removal' in his *Glubb Pasha* (London: Abacus, 1993), p. 467.
51. See Mallory to DOS, 16 March 1956, DOS 785.00/3-1667, NA.
52. Satloff, *From Abdullah to Hussein*, p. 146. According to Sharif Nasser, al-Rifaʿi was more than mildly upset by Glubb's sacking; in fact, he 'was *in tears* much of the time and deeply worried that, without Glubb, Jordan would be in jeopardy.' (Emphasis in original.) See Snow, *Hussein*, p. 85.
53. M.E. Yapp, 'Jordan's Englishman', *The Times Literary Supplement*, 6 November 1992, p. 12.

54. Hussein, *Uneasy Lies the Head*, p. 114.
55. Interview with Mahmud al-Ma`ayta, 15 April 1993, Amman. Today al-Ma`ayta claims that Operation Dunlop was named after the brand of his cigarette lighter. Also, Snow, *Hussein*, p. 84. It is doubtful that the Free Officers actually went as far as cutting the telephone lines to Glubb's house given that the British general apparently received phone calls during the night.
56. Mallory to DOS, 2 March 1956 in FRUS, 1955–1957, Vol. XIII, p. 27.
57. Snow, *Hussein*, p. 62.
58. Lunt, *Hussein of Jordan*, p. 26.
59. Satloff, *From Abdullah to Hussein*, p. 136.
60. See Anthony Nutting, *No End of a Lesson: the Story of Suez* (London: Constable, 1967), p. 18. Anthony Eden's version of events can be found in his *Full Circle* (London: Cassell, 1960).
61. Mohamed H. Heikal, *Cutting the Lion's Tail: Suez Through Egyptian Eyes* (London: Andre Deutsch, 1986), p. 97.
62. Aldrich to DOS, 5 March 1956 in FRUS, 1955–1957, Vol. XIII, p. 28.
63. Cited in Oren, 'A Winter of Discontent', 181.
64. Memorandum of Conversation between Acting Secretary of State and Jordanian Ambassador, 6 March 1956 in FRUS, 1955–1957, Vol. XIII, 30; also, Snow, *Hussein*, p. 90.
65. Burns, *Between Arab and Israeli*, p. 50. One retired official believes that '95 percent of the population supported the king's decision.' Interview with Ma`an Abu Nuwar, 13 May 1996, Amman.
66. Mallory to DOS, 16 March 1956 in FRUS, 1955–1957, Vol. XIII, p. 33.
67. Parker to DOS, 30 July 1956, DOS 785.11/7-3056, NA.
68. Parker to DOS, 10 May 1956, DOS 785.5/5-1056, NA.
69. Information from this paragraph comes from Parker to DOS, 10 May 1956, DOS 785.5/5-1056, NA. Today Parker remembers Mahmud al-Rusan as 'an inveterate, and very indiscreet, plotter.' Personal correspondence with Ambassador Richard B. Parker, 24 February 1997. Douglas Little mistakenly identifies Abu Nuwar as the first Jordanian chief of staff after Arabisation (it was actually Radi `Ennab). See 'A Puppet in Search of a Puppeteer?: The United States, King Hussein, and Jordan, 1953–1970', *The International History Review*, 17 (August 1995), 521.
70. Mallory to DOS, 2 March 1956 in FRUS, 1955–1957, Vol. XIII, p. 27.
71. Mallory to DOS, 6 May 1956, DOS 785.00/5-656, NA.
72. Israeli intelligence sources cited in Tel Aviv to DOS, 22 May 1956, DOS 785.00/5-2156, NA.
73. Parker to DOS, 10 May 1956, DOS 785.5/5-1056, NA.
74. Parker to DOS, 9 April 1956, DOS 785.00/4-956, NA. For more on Sharif Nasser's smuggling, see Urwick to Goodison, 28 September 1966, FO 371.18619/EJ 1941/9; and Roberts to FO, 3 November 1966, FO 371.186607/EJ 1671/9, both PRO.
75. As P.J. Vatikiotis puts it, al-Majali 'was not a technically very competent, up-to-date officer', but someone who rose in the officer corps due to his position as chief of King Abdullah's formal bodyguard. Personal correspondence with Professor P.J. Vatikiotis, 24 May 1997.
76. Mallory to DOS, 26 May 1956, DOS 785.551/5-2556, NA.
77. Vatikiotis, *Politics and the Military in Jordan*, pp. 128–9. Also, interview with Hikmat Mihayr, 13 April 1993, Amman.

78. Al-Madi and Musa, *Tarikh al-urdunn fi al-qarn al-`ashreen*, p. 635.
79. See Richard A. Gabriel and Alan Scott MacDougall, 'Jordan', in Richard A. Gabriel (ed.), *Fighting Armies: Antagonists in the Middle East, a Combat Assessment* (Westport: Greenwood, 1983), p. 28.
80. Israeli sources cited in Mallory to DOS, 21 May 1956, DOS 785.13/5-2156, NA.
81. Johnston to Lloyd, 19 March 1957, FO 371.127876/VJ 1011/1, PRO.
82. Johnston to Lloyd, 19 March 1957, FO 371.127876/VJ 1011/1, PRO.
83. Memorandum from the Director of the Office of Near Eastern Affairs to the Assistant Secretary of State for Near Eastern, South Asian, and African Affairs, 28 March 1956 in FRUS, 1955–1957, Vol. XIII, p. 34.
84. Dulles to Amman, 12 May 1956 in FRUS, 1955–1957, Vol. XIII, p. 41.
85. Memorandum of a Conversation between the Secretary of State and the Ambassador to Jordan (Mallory), 10 September 1956 in FRUS, 1955–1957, Vol. XIII, p. 49.
86. Jerusalem to DOS, 30 November 1956, DOS 785.00/11-3056, NA.
87. Israel would strike Jordan if (1) the kingdom aided Egypt, if (2) 'terrorists' attacked Israel from Jordan, and if (3) the Iraqi army entered the kingdom. See Moshe Dayan, *The Diary of the Sinai Campaign 1956* (London: Sphere, 1967), p. 33.
88. For details, see Zeid Raad, 'A Nightmare Avoided: Jordan and Suez 1956', *Israel Affairs*, 1 (Winter 1994), 289; also, Kyle, *Suez*, p. 92.
89. Raad, 'A Nightmare Avoided', 290.
90. For a discussion of Jordanian security calculations during the Suez crisis, see, al-Madi and Musa, *Tarikh al-urdunn fi al-qarn al-`ashreen*, pp. 642–5.
91. Satloff, *From Abdullah to Hussein*, p. 151.
92. Dayan, *Diary of the Sinai Campaign 1956*, p. 28.
93. Details in this paragraph are from Raad, 'A Nightmare Avoided', 291.
94. For a survey of Israeli reprisal raids during this period, see Benny Morris, *Israel's Border Wars, 1949–1956* (Oxford: Clarendon Press, 1993).
95. Parker to DOS, 26 July 1956, DOS 785.5/7-2, NA. Today Richard Parker believes that such raids 'could not have been mounted without at least the passive acquiescence of the Jordan military along the border.' Personal correspondence with Ambassador Richard B. Parker, 24 February 1997.
96. Mallory to DOS, 29 September 1956 in FRUS, 1955–1957, Vol. XIII, p. 55.
97. Memorandum of Conversation, 15 October 1956, DOS 785.5/101556, NA.
98. Raad, 'A Nightmare Avoided', 295. Also, on British warnings to Israel, see Nutting, *No End of a Lesson*, p. 110; and Burns, *Between Arab and Israeli*, p. 175.
99. Tel Aviv to DOS, 27 September 1956 in FRUS, 1955–1957, Vol. XIII, p. 55, n. 2.
100. Gallman to DOS, 29 September 1956 in FRUS, 1955–1957, Vol. XIII, pp. 53–4.
101. Al-Madi and Musa, *Tarikh al-urdunn fi al-qarn al-`ashreen*, p. 647. Moshe Zak's claim that Israel's threat to intervene militarily in Jordan if Iraqi troops entered the kingdom 'rescued Hussein from confronting hostile Iraqi troops' is fallacious. It was not Hashemite Iraq, but Israel which endangered Jordan's national security in 1956. See Moshe Zak, 'Israel and Jordan: Strategically Bound', *Israel Affairs*, 3:1 (Autumn 1996), 44.
102. Raad, 'A Nightmare Avoided', 298; also, Kyle, *Suez*, pp. 399–400. This strategy was similar to the Arab League plan devised by Captain Wasfi al-Tell before the 1948 Palestine war. See Avi Shlaim, *The Politics of Partition: King Abdullah, the Zionists and Palestine, 1921–1951* (Oxford: Oxford University Press, 1990), pp. 154–6.

103. Lunt, *Hussein of Jordan*, p. 33. Al-Madi and Musa write that Hussein called an emergency meeting of the Lower House to discuss Jordanian intervention. The al-Nabulsi government, however, refused to intervene. In addition, Hussein personally contacted Gamal Abdel Nasser and offered him military aid, but the Egyptian leader declined the king's offer. See *Tarikh al-urdunn fi al-qarn al-`ashreen*, p. 647.
104. Snow, *Hussein*, p. 100. It seems that al-Nabulsi never regretted his decision to oppose Hussein over the Suez war. See his comments to Suleiman Musa, *Al-`alam min al-urdunn*, p. 72.
105. Raad, 'A Nightmare Avoided', 298.

3 Radicals versus Royalists

1. Peter Snow, *Hussein: a Biography* (London: Barrie and Jenkins), p. 98. Also, Mason to Lloyd, 26 October 1956, FO 371.121470/10121/75/76, Public Record Office (PRO), London.
2. Mason to Lloyd, 26 October 1956, FO 371.121470/10121/75/76, PRO.
3. See Snow, *Hussein*, p. 98; Jamal al-Sha`ir discusses how 'external' candidates were able to win in other districts. For instance, Communist leader Ya`qub Zayadin, from al-Karak, won in Jerusalem, where the left was fairly strong. See Jamal al-Sha`ir, *Siyassi yatadhakkir* [A Politician Remembers] (London: Riyad al-Rayyes, 1987), p. 70.
4. Robert B. Satloff, *From Abdullah to Hussein: Jordan in Transition* (New York: Oxford University Press, 1994), p. 152. Elie Podeh discusses the impact the Suez crisis had in the Arab world in 'The Struggle over Arab Hegemony after the Suez Crisis', *Middle Eastern Studies*, 29:1 (January 1993), 91–110.
5. See Mason to Hadow, 23 January 1957, FO 371.127878/VJ 1015/5, PRO.
6. Memorandum of Conversation between the Secretary of State and the Ambassador to Jordan, 10 September 1956 in *Foreign Relations of the United States, 1955–1957, Near East: Jordan–Yemen, Volume XIII* (Washington: US Government Printing Office, 1988), p. 50. (FRUS, 1955–1957, Vol. XIII.)
7. Memorandum of Conversation at Ambassador's Residence, Paris, 10 December 1956 in FRUS, 1955–1957, Vol. XIII, p. 73.
8. Satloff, *From Abdullah to Hussein*, p. 154. For detailed lists of the al-Nabulsi and other governments discussed in this study, see *Al-watha'iq al-urdunniyya: al-wazarat al-urdunniyya, 1921–1984* [Jordanian Documents: Jordanian Ministries, 1921–1984] (Amman: Ministry of Information, Directorate of Press and Publications, 1984); and Hani Salim Khayr, *Al-sajl al-tarikhi al-musawwar, 1920–1990* [The Illustrated Historical Record, 1920–1990] (Amman: Al-Ayman Printing Press, 1990).
9. Snow, *Hussein*, p. 100. In his short biography of al-Nabulsi, Suleiman Musa discusses the difficulties of writing on such a controversial figure. See *Al-`alam min al-urdunn: safhat min tarikh al-`arab al-hadith* [Prominent Personalities from Jordan] (Amman: Dar al-Sha`ab, 1986), pp. 57–94. Also, Jamal al-Sha`ir, *Siyassi yatadhakkir*, p. 181–218.
10. Satloff, *From Abdullah to Hussein*, p. 154.
11. Johnston to FO, 20 May 1957, FO 371.127878/VJ 1015/13, PRO.
12. Sanger to DOS, 19 March 1956, DOS 785.00/3-1956, National Archives (NA), Washington, DC.

13. Interview with Kamal al-Sha`ir, 21 April 1995, Amman.
14. Satloff, *From Abdullah to Hussein*, pp. 152–3.
15. Mason to Hadow, 16 January 1957, FO 371.127878/VJ 1015/4; also, see al-Rimawi's statements to Charles Johnston, Johnston to FO, 31 January 1957, FO 371.127889/VJ 1023/5, both PRO.
16. Mason to Lloyd, 26 October 1956, FO 371.121470/10121/75/76, PRO.
17. Uriel Dann, 'Regime and Opposition in Jordan since 1949', in Menachem Milson (ed.), *Society and Political Structure in the Arab World* (New York: The Humanities Press, 1973), p. 163.
18. Amman to DOS, 13 February 1957, DOS 885.10/2-1357, NA.
19. Memorandum of Conversation, Ambassador's Residence, Paris, 10 December 1956, in FRUS, 1955–1957, Vol. XIII, p. 73.
20. Amman to DOS, 25 July 1956, DOS 885.00-TA/7-2556, NA.
21. Amman to DOS, 25 July 1956, DOS 885.00-TA/7-2558, NA. The text of the ASA can be found in Munib al-Madi and Suleiman Musa, *Tarikh al-urdunn fi al-qarn al-`ashreen* [The History of Jordan in the Twentieth Century] (Amman: n.p., 1959; 2nd edn, Amman: Maktaba al-Muhtasab, 1988), pp. 649–50.
22. Amman to Regional Information Office (Beirut), 30 January 1957, FO 371.127979/VJ 1671/1, PRO; al-Madi and Musa, *Tarikh al-urdunn fi al-qarn al-`ashreen*, p. 664.
23. British diplomat Heath Mason reported: 'One of the more disturbing developments in the political scene in Jordan recently has been the increased activity of the extreme Muslim groups.' See Mason to Hadow, 23 January 1957, FO 371.127878/VJ 1015/5, PRO.
24. This paragraph is based on information from Walstrom to DOS, 27 February 1957, DOS 785.21/2-2757, NA.
25. Johnston to FO, 1 February 1957, FO 371.127878/VJ 1015/6, PRO.
26. Mason to Hadow, 20 February 1957, FO 371.127878/VJ 1015/8, PRO.
27. Mason to Hadow, 20 February 1957, FO 371.127878/VJ 1015/8, PRO.
28. Lebanese President Camille Chamoun believed Hussein adopted an anti-Communist stance because he had been 'shown scant courtesy' by the Egyptians when he went to Cairo to sign the ASA. See Middleton to Rose, 9 February 1957, FO 371.127989/VJ 1941/12, PRO.
29. Hussein bin Talal, *Uneasy Lies the Head* (London: Heinemann, 1962), p. 133. Al-Madi and Musa summarise the letter and its effects in *Tarikh al-urdunn fi al-qarn al-`ashreen*, p. 665.
30. Dulles to Amman, 6 February 1957, in FRUS, 1955–1957, Vol. XIII, p. 83.
31. Mallory to DOS, 4 February 1957, in FRUS, 1955–1957, Vol. XIII, p. 83, n. 2. National Front leader Abdel Rahman Shuqayr says that the national security establishment exaggerated the 'Communist threat' to bolster its own power. He also denies that his party was funded by external sources: 'We had no foreign backing.' Interview with Abdel Rahman Shuqayr, 20 April 1993, Amman.
32. Mallory to DOS, 13 February 1957, in FRUS, 1955–1957, Vol. XIII, p. 86.
33. Johnston to FO, 4 February 1957, FO 371.127979/VJ 1941/5, PRO.
34. Johnston to FO, 8 February 1957, FO 371.127979/VJ 1671/2, PRO.
35. Amman to FO, 5 March 1957, FO 371.127979/VJ 1671/3, PRO.
36. Amman to FO, 29 March 1957, FO 371.127979/VJ 1071/4, PRO.
37. Snow, *Hussein*, p. 102.
38. Johnston to FO, 8 February 1957, FO 371.127989/VJ 1941/9, PRO. Al-Madi and Musa argue that the Communists had an 'unwritten understanding with

the National Socialist Party and the Ba`th Party' and that they and other parties were funded by external sources. See *Tarikh al-urdunn fi al-qarn al-`ashreen*, p. 662.

39. Mason to Hadow, 20 February 1957, FO 371.127878/VJ 1015/8, PRO.
40. Johnston to FO, 20 February 1957, FO 371.127990/VJ 1941/14; also, Johnston to FO, 1 February 1957, FO 371.127878/VJ 1015/6, PRO. Interview with Kamal al-Sha`ir, 21 April 1995, Amman.
41. Al-Madi and Musa suggest that Hussein was the impetus behind the termination agreement, whereas it was actually the al-Nabulsi government. See *Tarikh al-urdunn fi al-qarn al-`ashreen*, p. 649. Since 1945, Britain had provided Jordan approximately £82 million in subsidies and budgetary assistance. See Benjamin Shwadran, *Jordan: a State of Tension* (New York: Council for Middle Eastern Affairs Press, 1959), p. 343.
42. Amman to DOS, 13 February 1957, DOS 885.10/2-1357, NA. A full text of the agreement can be found in al-Madi and Musa, *Tarikh al-urdunn fi al-qarn al-`ashreen*, pp. 656–8.
43. See Jerusalem to DOS, 30 November 1956, DOS 785.00/11-3056, NA; also, Johnston to Lloyd, 27 March 1957, FO 371.127878/VJ 1015/15, PRO. Also, interview with Abdel Rahman Shuqayr, 20 April 1993, Amman.
44. Mallory to DOS, 29 March 1957, in FRUS, 1955–1957, Vol. XIII, p. 89.
45. Johnston to FO, 11 April 1957, FO 371.127878/VJ 1015/21, PRO.
46. Mason to FO, 19 July 1957, FO 371.127887/VJ 10110/1, PRO; Mason to FO, 29 July 1957, FO 371.127887/VJ 10110/2, PRO; Johnston to Lloyd, 9 October 1957, FO 371.127887/VJ 10110/7, PRO; and Merriam to DOS, 18 November 1957, DOS 785.00/11-1857, NA.
47. Al-Madi and Musa write that – according to `Akif al-Fayiz – Ali Abu Nuwar telephoned Sa`id al-Mufti and summoned him to a meeting in the al-`Abdali neighbourhood of Amman. Present were Abu Nuwar, Ali al-Hiyari, and Muhammad al-Ma`ayta. They told al-Mufti that the situation in the army was 'dangerous' and that a new government must be formed by Abdel Halim al-Nimr by 9:00 PM on 13 April. See *Tarikh al-urdunn fi al-qarn al-`ashreen*, pp. 669–71.
48. Merriam to DOS, 18 November 1957, DOS 785.00/11-1857, NA.
49. *Qarar al-mahkama al-`urfiyya al-`askariyya al-khassa* [Decision of the Special Military Court Martial], unpublished document, private collection of Mike Doran. Also, Johnston to Lloyd, 9 October 1957, FO 371.127887/VJ 101160/7, PRO.
50. Erskine B. Childers discusses a version of this plot in Appendix B of his *The Road to Suez: a Study of Western–Arab Relations* (London: MacGibbon and Kee, 1962). Childers' account was confirmed by many policymakers interviewed for this study.
51. Interview with Muhammad Ishaq Hakuz, 20 April 1995, Amman.
52. Johnston to FO, 11 April 1957, FO 371.127878/VJ 1015/21, PRO; interview with Mahmud al-Mu`ayta, 15 April 1993, Amman. Mu`ayta identifies Sa`ad Jum`a, Khalusi al-Khayri, and Samir al-Rifa`i as being the 'most prominent people' who symbolised the pro-US trend.
53. Mallory to DOS, 27 April 1957, in FRUS, 1955–1957, Vol. XIII, p. 100. Before al-Hiyari's defection, he apparently had a confrontation with Hussein in which he questioned the king's judgement. Hussein reportedly pounded the

table and shouted, 'I'm King! I do what I want! This is my country. I will join the Baghdad Pact if I want…This is my country.' Reported in 'Jordan: the Education of a King', *Time*, 6 May 1957.

54. 'Jordan: the Road to Zerka', *Time*, 29 April 1957.
55. Shwadran, *Jordan: a State of Tension*, p. 357.
56. Snow, *Hussein*, p. 116.
57. Abu Nuwar's version of events can be found in Chapter Ten of his memoirs. See Ali Abu Nuwar, *Hayn talashat al-`arab: mudhakarat fi al-siyassa al-`arabiyya (1948–1964)* [When the Arabs Decline: Memoirs of Arab Politics (1948–1964)] (London: Dar al-Saqi, 1990), pp. 301–46.
58. Ma`an Abu Nuwar says he was implicated by his relation to Ali Abu Nuwar, and that Operation Thabit was a routine exercise which had been planned some time before April 1957. He says that Ali Abu Nuwar told him shortly before he died that 'I did not plot against King Hussein in my mind, my heart or by my hand.' Interview with Ma`an Abu Nuwar, 14 May 1996, Amman.
59. Robert B. Satloff, 'The Jekyll-and-Hyde Origins of the US–Jordanian Strategic Relationship', in David W. Lesch, *The Middle East and the United States: a Historical and Political Reassessment* (Boulder: Westview, 1996), p. 117.
60. Both quotes from Satloff, *From Abdullah to Hussein*, p. 167.
61. Johnston to Lloyd, 9 October 1957, FO 371.127887/VJ 10110/7, PRO.
62. Satloff, *From Abdullah to Hussein*, p. 168.
63. Miles Copeland, *The Game of Nations: the Amorality of Power Politics* (London: Weidenfeld and Nicolson, 1969), p. 189.
64. Interview with Moraiwid al-Tell, 4 July 1996, Oxford.
65. Benjamin Shwadran, *Jordan: a State of Tension*, p. 339.
66. Johnston to FO, 12 February 1957, FO 371.127989/VJ 1941/10, PRO.
67. Johnston to FO, 8 February 1957, FO 371.127989/VJ 1941/9, PRO.
68. See, for instance, Foreign Office Minute, 15 March 1957, FO 371.127878/VJ 1015/12, PRO.
69. Johnston to FO, 5 March 1957, FO 371.127878/VJ 1015/10, PRO.
70. Caccia to FO, 12 April 1957, FO 371.127878/VJ 1015/21, PRO.
71. Merriam to DOS, 18 November 1957, DOS 785.00/11-1857, NA.
72. Al-Madi and Musa, *Tarikh al-urdunn fi al-qarn al-`ashreen*, p. 667.
73. Johnston to Lloyd, 9 October 1957, FO 371.127887/VJ 10110/7, PRO.
74. Johnston to Lloyd, 9 October 1957, FO 371.127887/VJ 10110/7, PRO.
75. In the weeks before the showdown, royalists used American Point IV trucks to transport tribal irregulars into central Amman to bolster Hussein's support. Interview with Moraiwid al-Tell, 4 July 1996, Oxford.
76. 'Jordan: The Road to Zerka', *Time*, 29 April 1957.
77. 'Jordan: The Road to Zerka', *Time*, 29 April 1957. For CIA involvement, see Douglas Little, 'A Puppet in Search of a Puppeteer?: the United States, King Hussein, and Jordan, 1953–1970', *The International History Review*, 17:3 (August 1995), 524.
78. Eliezer Be`eri, *Army Officers in Arab Politics and Society* (London: Praeger/Pall Mall, 1970), p. 232.
79. Johnston to FO, 20 April 1957, FO 371.127879/VJ 1015/53, PRO.
80. Interview with Ma`an Abu Nuwar, 14 May 1996, Amman and personal correspondence with P.J. Vatikiotis, 24 May 1997.

81. Johnston to FO, 24 April 1957, FO 371.127879/VJ 1015/67, PRO; interview with Hikmat Mihayr, 13 April 1993, Amman; also, al-Madi and Musa, *Tarikh al urdunn fi al-qarn al-`ashreen*, p. 677.
82. For details of the conference, see Johnston to FO, 24 April 1957, FO 371.127879/VJ 1015/63, PRO; and Johnston to FO, 25 April 1957, FO 371.127878/VJ 1015/66, PRO. There was mass popular support for the conference. A former finance manager at the Foreign Ministry recalls: 'We all rushed into the streets and began shouting for Arab unity. It was complete chaos.' Interview with Yusef Abdel Qadir al-Tell, 10 April 1993, Irbid.
83. Transcript of Telephone Conversation between Eisenhower and Dulles, 24 April 1957, in FRUS, 1955–1957, Vol. XIII, p. 103.
84. Memorandum of Conversation, Department of State, 24 April 1957, in FRUS, 1955–1957, Vol. XIII, p. 106. Richard Parker recalls that Hussein's message was 'passed through the second-ranking CIA man in Amman.' See Richard B. Parker, 'The United States and King Hussein', in David W. Lesch (ed.), *The Middle East and the United States: a Historical and Political Reassessment* (Boulder: Westview, 1996), p. 112.
85. Memorandum of Telephone Conversation between Eisenhower and Dulles, 25 April 1957, in FRUS, 1955–1957, Vol. XIII, p. 109.
86. Foreign Office Minute, 25 April 1957, FO 371.127879/VJ 1015/80, PRO.
87. See ' "Boy King" Grows Up', *US News and World Report*, 10 May 1957.
88. See, for instance, Herter to Amman, 15 April 1957, FRUS, 1955–1957, Vol. XIII, p. 96.
89. Memorandum of Conversation, Department of State, 24 April 1957, in FRUS, 1955–1957, Vol. XIII, p. 105.
90. Text of Press Conference, 24 April 1957, in FRUS, 1955–1957, Vol. XIII, pp. 108–9. Also, 'Another Middle East Hot Spot: the Story of Jordan', *US News and World Report*, 26 April 1957, 34.
91. Shwadran, *Jordan: a State of Tension*, p. 358. Ten million dollars in 1957 was equivalent to $56 million in current dollars.
92. Bob Woodward, 'CIA Paid Millions to Jordan's King Hussein', *The Washington Post*, 18 February 1977. Eveland says that Kim Roosevelt chose the cryptonym, NOBEEF, to designate the American plan to 'beef up' Hussein, whose CIA pseudonym was NORMAN. See *Ropes of Sand*, p. 191. For more on Jordanian contacts with the CIA, see Jonathan Bloch and Patrick Fitzgerald, *British Intelligence and Covert Action: Africa, Middle East and Europe Since 1945* (Junction: London, 1983), p. 126; and Miles Copeland, *The Game Player* (London: Aurum, 1989), p. 208.
93. Zein was supposedly paid $12 million for influencing Jordanian policy in a pro-Western direction. See Leonard Mosely, *Dulles: a Biography of Allen and John Foster Dulles and their Family Networks* (New York: The Dial Press, 1978), p. 350.
94. FO to Baghdad, 14 April 1957, FO 371.127878/VJ 1015/26, PRO; also, Richard M. Saunders, 'Military Force in the Foreign Policy of the Eisenhower Presidency', *Political Science Quarterly*, 100:1 (Spring 1985), 97–116.
95. Memorandum of Conversation, Department of State, 24 April 1957, in FRUS, 1955–1957, Vol. XIII, p. 105.
96. Dulles to Beirut, 25 April 1957, in FRUS, 1955–1957, Vol. XIII, p. 114.
97. FO to Amman, 14 April 1957, FO 371.127910/VJ 1081/4, PRO.
98. Dulles to Riyadh, 25 April 1957, in FRUS, 1955–1957, Vol. XIII, p. 111.

99. Johnston to FO, 20 April 1957, FO 371.127879/VJ 1015/53, PRO.

100. Fawaz A. Gerges, *The Superpowers and the Middle East: Regional and International Politics, 1955–1967* (Boulder: Westview, 1994), p. 82.

101. Details can be found in the BBC Monitoring Report for 27 April 1957. Also, al-Madi and Musa, *Tarikh al-urdunn fi al-qarn al-`ashreen*, p. 679.

102. Personal correspondence with Robert Satloff, 23 June 1997.

103. Johnston to FO, 25 April 1957, FO 371.127879/VJ 1015/71, PRO.

104. Quoted in FO 371.127879/VJ 1015/92, PRO.

105. See John K. Cooley, *Green March, Black September: the Story of the Palestinian Arabs* (London: Frank Cass, 1973), p. 136.

106. See Walstrom to DOS, 31 July 1957, DOS 985.63/7.3157, NA; interview with Abdel Rahman Shuqayr, 20 April 1993, Amman.

107. See Johnston to FO, 6 May 1957, FO 371.127880/VJ 1015/106, PRO.

108. Merriam to DOS, 18 November 1957, DOS 785.00/11-1857, NA.

109. See Mason to Hadow, 17 July 1957, FO 371.127980/VJ 1681/1; and Johnston to FO, 15 April 1957, FO 371.127956/VJ 1431/3, both PRO.

110. Reported in *Mideast Mirror*, #2 (2 June 1957).

111. Memorandum from Rountree to Dulles, 7 June 1957, DOS 785.5-MSP 6-757; and Joint State-Defense Message from Dulles to Amman, 5 August 1957, DOS 785.56/8-557, both NA.

4 The July Crisis

1. Details of the crisis can be found in Lawrence Tal, 'Britain and the Jordan Crisis of 1958', *Middle Eastern Studies* (January 1995); Uriel Dann, *King Hussein and the Challenge of Arab Radicalism: Jordan, 1955–1967* (Oxford: Oxford University Press, 1989); Hussein bin Talal, *Mahnati ka-malik* [My Job as King] (Amman: The National Press, 1986); and Sa`ad Aboudia, `Amaliyat ittikhadh al-qarar fi-siyassat al-urdunn al-kharijiyya* [The Foreign Policy Decisionmaking Process in Jordan] (Amman: n.p., 1983), pp. 213–30.

2. See Amman to DOS, 12 August 1957, *Foreign Relations of the United States, 1955–1957, Near East: Jordan–Yemen, Volume XIII* (Washington: US Government Printing Office, 1988), p. 104. (FRUS, 1955–1957, Vol. XIII.)

3. This paragraph is based on various dispatches from FO 371.127881 and FO 371.127882, both Public Record Office (PRO), London.

4. A brief account of the party's history and activities can be found in Musa Zeid al-Kilani, *Al-harakat al-islamiyya fi al-urdunn* [The Islamic Movements in Jordan] (Amman: Dar al-Bashir, 1990), pp. 85–106.

5. See Kerr's excellent *The Arab Cold War: Gamal `Abd al-Nasir and his Rivals, 1958–1970* (London: Oxford University Press, 1971).

6. See Patrick Seale, *The Struggle for Syria: a study of Post-War Arab Politics, 1945–1958* (London: I.B. Tauris, 1986), p. 321.

7. For Jordan's relations with Egypt and Syria, see Munib al-Madi and Suleiman Musa, *Tarikh al-urdunn fi al-qarn al-`ashreen* [The History of Jordan in the Twentieth Century] (Amman: n.p., 1959; 2nd edn, Amman: Maktaba al-Muhtasab, 1988), p. 683.

8. For the economic benefits of such a union, see Mason to Hadow, 26 February 1958, FO 371.134026/VJ 10393/69, PRO.

9. Hussein was unquestionably the main impetus for the union. See Wright to Lloyd, 25 February 1958, FO 371.134025/VJ 10393/64, PRO.
10. On Nuri al-Sa`id's influence, see Michael B. Oren, 'Nuri al-Sa`id and the Question of Arab–Israel Peace, 1953–1957', *Asian and African Studies*, 24 (October 1990), 267–82.
11. James Lunt, *Hussein of Jordan: a Political Biography* (London: Macmillan, 1989), p. 47. Nuri al-Sa`id considered Samir al-Rifa`i a rival. Both were suspicious of the other. Al-Sa`id, however, got on well with rising political star Wasfi al-Tell. Interview with Moraiwid al-Tell, 9 April 1993, Amman.
12. For the complete text of the announcement, see *Middle Eastern Affairs* (August–September 1958), 267. Jamal al-Sha`ir discusses the background to the UAR in *Siyassi yatadhakkir* [A Politician Remembers] (London: Riad al-Rayyes, 1987), pp. 135–7.
13. Wright to FO, 11 February 1958, F0 371.134197/VQ 1015/11, PRO.
14. See Iskander M`arouf *Al-urdunn al-jadid wa al-ittihad al-`arabi* [New Jordan and the Arab Union] (Baghdad: The New Iraq Press, 1958). For a discussion of the negotiations and an assessment of the AU, see al-Madi and Musa, *Tarikh al-urdunn fi al-qarn al-`ashreen*, pp. 688–9.
15. Hussein bin Talal, *Uneasy Lies the Head* (London: Heinemann, 1962), p. 153. In his Arabic memoirs, Hussein claims: 'While Iraq and Jordan were equal partners in the Arab Union, Egypt subjugated Syria in the United Arab Republic.' See Hussein bin Talal, *Mahnati ka-malik*, p. 146.
16. A report of the initial agreement appears in Johnston to FO, 14 February 1958, FO 371.134023/VJ 10393/G, PRO. A full text of the agreement and the AU constitution can be found in Hani Salim Khayr (ed.), *Al-sajl al-tarikhi al-musawwar, 1920–1990* [The Illustrated Historical Record, 1920–1990] (Amman: Al-Eiman Printing Press/Kailani and Scoor, 1990).
17. See Mohammed Ibrahim Faddah, *The Middle East in Transition: a Study in Jordan's Foreign Policy* (London: Asia Publishing House, 1974), p. 176; Abdullah bin al-Hussein, *My Memoirs Completed, 'al-Takmilah'* (London: Longman, 1978); Ilan Pappé, 'Sir Alec Kirkbride and the Making of Greater Transjordan', *Asian and African Studies*, 23 (1989), 43–70; Reeva S. Simon, 'The Hashemite "Conspiracy": Hashemite Unity Attempts, 1921–1958', *International Journal of Middle East Studies*, 5 (1974), 314–27.
18. Middleton to FO, 14 February 1958, FO 371.134382/VY 1015/15, PRO.
19. Minute on 'Nasser's open declaration of war against the Arab Union', 27 February 1958, FO 371.134026/VJ 10393/71, PRO.
20. Tel Aviv to FO, 12 March 1958, FO 371.133876/V 1431/4(B), PRO.
21. Johnston to Rose, 26 March 1958. Al-Madi and Musa discuss the effect Radio Cairo had in Jordan in *Tarikh al-urdunn fi al-qarn al-`ashreen*, p. 661.
22. Johnston to Rose, 26 March 1958, FO 371.133876/V 1431/1, PRO.
23. Mason to Rose, 15 April 1958, FO 371.133876/V 1431/4, PRO.
24. Speech of 11 March 1958 cited in *President Gamal Abdel-Nasser's Speeches and Press Interviews* (Cairo: UAR Information Department, 1958).
25. Dann, *King Hussein and the Challenge of Arab Radicalism*, p. 86. For a discussion of the composition of the CIA station in Amman, see former US diplomat Eric Kocher's *Foreign Intrigue: the Making and Unmaking of a Foreign Service Officer* (Far Hills: New Horizon Press, 1990), pp. 226–8.
26. See Dan Raviv and Yossi Melman, *Behind the Uprising: Israelis, Jordanians and Palestinians* (Westport: Greenwood, 1989), pp. 55–6.

27. Andrew Tully, *CIA: the Inside Story* (New York: Morrow, 1962), p. 74.
28. Wright to DOS, 30 June 1958, DOS 785.00/6-3058, NA.
29. See Douglas Little, 'A Puppet in Search of a Puppeteer?: the United States, King Hussein, and Jordan, 1953–1970', *The International History Review*, 17:3 (August 1995), p. 526.
30. For a discussion of the involvement of al-Rusan and the al-Shar`a brothers, see Johnston to FO, 9 August 1958, PREM 11.2381 and Johnston to FO, 4 October 1958, PREM 11.3028, both PRO.
31. Interview with Sadiq al-Shar`a, 12 April 1993, Amman; interview with Salih al-Shar`a, 19 April 1993, Amman. In his memoirs, Salih al-Shar`a sheds little light on the 1958 crisis and insists that the Baghdad coup was 'unexpected'. See his *Mudhakkarat jundi* [Memories of a Soldier] (Amman: n.p., 1985), p. 108.
32. See Wright to DOS, 11 July 1958 in *Foreign Relations of the United States, 1958–1960: Lebanon and Jordan, Volume XI* (Washington: US Government Printing Office, 1992), p. 298. (FRUS, 1958–1960, Vol. XI.)
33. Johnston to FO, 27 July 1958, PREM 11.2380, PRO.
34. Interview with Sadiq al-Shar`a, Amman, 12 April 1993.
35. Interview with Zaid Nuwairan, Amman, 1 April 1995.
36. Mason to FO, 3 July 1958, FO 371.134067/VJ 1194/5, PRO. Sadiq al-Shar`a insists that this unit was to replace, not supplement, the Iraqi brigade already based in al-Mafraq. Interview with Sadiq al-Shar`a, Amman, 12 April 1993.
37. Salih al-Shar`a writes that he had no idea of his brother's fate for two days. In the end, Sadiq al-Shar`a escaped Baghdad after being beaten by the mobs. See *Mudhakarat jundi*, p. 109.
38. Mason to FO, 14 July 1958, FO 371.134008/VJ 1015/36/G, PRO. Also Dann, *King Hussein and the Challenge of Arab Radicalism*, p. 88; Peter Snow, *Hussein: a Biography* (London: Barrie & Jenkins, 1972) pp. 123–4; and Lunt, *Hussein of Jordan*, pp. 49–50.
39. Most senior army officers supported the attack plan. See Mason to FO, 15 July 1958, PREM 11.2380, PRO.
40. Hussein, *Uneasy Lies the Head*, pp. 63–4. In his Arabic memoirs, he says parliament wanted him to send forces, but wanted to wait until the Iraqi people requested Jordanian assistance. See *Mahnati ka malik*, p. 157.
41. Snow, *Hussein*, p. 124. Syed Ali el-Edroos asserts that Hussein's 'impulsive reaction' to send troops to Iraq was an example of his 'innate personal courage.' See his *The Hashemite Arab Army, 1908–1979: an Appreciation and Analysis of Military Operations* (Amman: The Publishing Committee, 1980), p. 320.
42. Mason to FO, 14 July 1958, VJ1015/36/G, PRO.
43. Wright to DOS, 15 July 1958 in FRUS, 1958–1960, Vol. XI, p. 302.
44. Robert B. Satloff, 'The Jekyll-and-Hyde Origins of the US–Jordanian Strategic Relationship', in David W. Lesch (ed.), *The Middle East and the United States: a Historical and Political Reassessment* (Boulder: Westview, 1996), p. 125.
45. Mason to FO, 14 July 1958, PREM 11.2380, PRO.
46. Mason to FO, 16 July 1958, FO 371.134008/VJ 1015/35(C), PRO.
47. Stewart to FO, 15 July 1958, FO 371.134009/VJ 1015/38(A), PRO.
48. Dann, *King Hussein and the Challenge of Arab Radicalism*, pp. 83–5.
49. Dann, *King Hussein and the Challenge of Arab Radicalism*, p. 84. Britain's role in the crisis is discussed in Lawrence Tal, 'Britain and the Jordan Crisis of 1958', *Middle Eastern Studies*, 31:1 (January 1995), 39–57.

50. Minute from Hayter to Caccia, 28 March 1958, FO 371.134067/VJ 1194/2, PRO.
51. Note by HL Lloyd, Secretary of the Joint Planning Staff, COS Committee, 23 June 1958, DEFE 6/50, PRO.
52. Dann, *King Hussein and the Challenge of Arab Radicalism*, p. 84.
53. 'Rescue and Evacuation of British and Friendly Nationals from Amman', memorandum from COS Committee, 13 June 1958, DEFE 5/84, PRO.
54. Considerations for immediate intervention in Jordan included 'the fact that if the airfield at Amman fell into the insurgents' hands, the opportunity for effective intervention would be lost and King Hussein's will to resist seriously undermined.' Harold Macmillan, *Riding the Storm, 1956–1959* (London: Macmillan, 1971), p. 517.
55. Mason to FO, 16 July 1958, PREM 11.2380, PRO.
56. Mason to FO, 16 July 1958, FO 371.134008/VJ 1015/36(G) and VJ 1015/46(G), PRO.
57. See Minutes from Cabinet meeting at House of Commons, 16 July 1958, CAB 128; Mason to FO, 16 July 1958, PREM 11.2380; Letter from Macmillan to Konrad Adenauer, 17 July 1958, PREM 11.2380, all PRO.
58. See, for example, Wright to DOS, 16 July 1958 in FRUS, 1958–1960, Vol. XI, p. 314.
59. Johnston to FO, 18 July 1958, PREM 11.2380, PRO.
60. Interview with Muhammad Ahmad Salim, 7 April 1995, Irbid. Also, interview with Nayif Muhammad al-Bataynah, 7 April 1995, Irbid.
61. Whitney to DOS, 17 July 1958, DOS 785.00/7-1758, NA.
62. Mason to FO, 17 July 1958, FO 371.134008/VJ 1015/35(D); Mason to FO, 17 July 1958, FO 371.134022/VJ 10389/4, both PRO.
63. Salt to FO, 17 July 1958, FO 371.134345/VR 1222/6(C), PRO.
64. Moshe Zak, 'Israel and Jordan: Strategically Bound', *Israel Affairs*, 3:1 (Autumn 1996), 42.
65. Johnston to Lloyd, 4 December 1958, FO 371.134011/VJ 1015/143, PRO.
66. Johnston to FO, 19 July 1958, PREM 11.2380, PRO.
67. Interview with Yusef Abdel Qadir al-Tell, 7 April 1995, Irbid.
68. Al-Madi and Musa, *Tarikh al-urdunn fi al-qarn al-`ashreen*, p. 691.
69. Johnston to Rose, 23 September 1958, FO 371.134036/VJ 1092/19G, PRO.
70. Stout to FO, 7 August 1958, FO 371.134202/VQ 1015/195; Charles Johnston's conversation with Musa Adel in Johnston to Rose, 28 July 1958, FO 371.134201/VQ 1015/171, both PRO. Also, interview with Sadiq al-Shar`a, Amman, 12 April 1993.
71. Johnston to Rose, 28 July 1958, FO 371.134201/VQ 1015/171, PRO.
72. Quoted in Lunt, *Hussein of Jordan*, p. 47.
73. Interview with Sadiq al-Shar`a, Amman, 12 April 1993.
74. Johnston to FO, 29 July 1958, FO 371.134009/VJ 1015/61, PRO.
75. Johnston to FO, 2 August 1958, FO 371.134009/VJ 1015/66(A), PRO.
76. Two sons of Sharif Sharof were involved in the plot. Sharof was a distant relative of King Hussein. Johnston to FO, 4 August 1958, PREM 11.2380, PRO.
77. Cited in the epigraph to Dann, *King Hussein and the Challenge of Arab Radicalism*.
78. Charles Johnston, *The Brink of Jordan*, p. 107.
79. `Abbas Murad, *Al-daur al-siyassi lil-jaysh al-urdunni, 1921–1973* [The Political Role of the Jordanian Army] (Beirut: Palestine Liberation Organisation Research Center, 1973), p. 101.

80. Periodic Intelligence Report No. 10, 25–28 July 1958, NA. I would like to thank Kirsten Schulze for bringing this document to my attention.
81. Johnston to FO, 27 July 1958, PREM 11.2380, PRO.
82. See Amman to DOS, 24 July 1958, DOS 785.00/7-2358, NA; and Naseer H. Aruri, *Jordan: a Study in Political Development (1921–1965)* (The Hague: Martin Nijhoff, 1972), p. 158. Also, interview with Ali Ibrahim al-Tell, 11 April 1993, Irbid. Murad lists many of the officers arrested in his *Al-daur al-siyassi lil-jaysh al urdunni*, pp. 101–2.
83. Wright to DOS, 21 July 1958 in FRUS, 1958–1960, Vol. XI, p. 362. On 22 July, 17 army officers were compulsorily retired on suspicion of disloyalty. Johnston to FO, 25 July 1958. Johnston to Lloyd, 4 December 1958, FO 371.134011/VJ 1015/143, PRO.
84. Dixon to FO, 22 August 1958. Also, *Middle Eastern Affairs* (October 1958) and al-Madi and Musa, *Tarikh al-urdunn fi al-qarn al-`ashreen*, pp. 693–4.
85. Shattock to FO, 25 October 1958, FO 371.134045/VJ 1091/2250, PRO.
86. The FO decided to play down the news of the appointment of these men as advisors so as not to 'give opportunities for Nasser to claim that we were cheating about our withdrawal'. Minute by Hadow, 28 October 1958, FO 371.133866/V 1196/94, PRO.
87. Johnston to FO, 5 November 1958, FO 371.134008/VJ 1015/131, PRO.
88. Amman to DOS, 2 August 1958, DOS 785.00/8-258, NA.
89. Johnston to FO, 30 October 1958, FO 371.123008/VJ 1015/129, PRO.
90. For details of the incident, see Hussein, *Uneasy Lies the Head*, pp. 179–85; Dann, *King Hussein and the Challenge of Arab Radicalism*, pp. 102–3; Snow, *Hussein*, pp. 130–2; and Lunt, *Hussein of Jordan*, pp. 57–9.
91. Johnston to FO, 10 November 1958, PREM 11.3028, PRO.
92. Johnston to FO, 10 November 1958, PREM 11.3028, PRO.
93. Johnston to FO, 10 November 1958. One British diplomat was quoted during the crisis as saying: 'This is not a country, but a geographical monument to the courage of one young man – Hussein.' See 'Jordan: Where Brave Young King Defied Murder Plots', *US News and World Report*, 1 August 1958, 31–2.
94. Johnston to FO, 23 October 1958, FO 371.133866/V 1196/94; and 10 November 1958, FO 371.133866/V 1196/96, both PRO.
95. Hussein, *Mahnati ka malik*, p. 158. In his radio speech on the seventh anniversary of his accession to the throne on 10 August, Hussein denounced the 1957 and 1958 crises as 'part of the general communist plan for the Middle East and the Arab world in particular.' See Keeley to DOS, 13 August 1958, DOS 785.11/8-1358, NA.
96. Both figures cited in Aruri, *Jordan: a Study in Political Development*, p. 63.

5 Confronting the United Arab Republic

1. Memorandum for the President from John Foster Dulles, 15 January 1959, DOS 785.11/1-1559 CS/G, National Archives (NA), Washington, DC.
2. Lewis Jones, assistant secretary of state, said Jordan 'lacked sex appeal' when the subject of aid was raised in Congressional committees. See Beith to Profumo, 22 October 1959, FO 371.142140/VJ 1121/20, Public Record Office (PRO), London.

3. Johnston to FO, 23 September 1959, FO 371.142198/VJ 1941/12, PRO.
4. Minute by Stevens, 9 April 1959, FO 371.142126/VJ 1052/11, PRO.
5. This tack was a popular one with the Jordanians. For instance, when the US chargé d'affaires drove with Hussein and Samir al-Rifaʾi to an opening ceremony for the East Ghor scheme in the Jordan Valley, he 'was literally sitting between them in the car and got a good hour's concentrated propaganda from both of them on the necessity for the Americans to meet the Jordanian request for financial aid.' See Mason to Hadow, 26 February 1959, FO 371.142140/VJ 1121/13, PRO.
6. See Douglas Little, 'A Puppet in Search of a Puppeteer?: the United States, King Hussein, and Jordan, 1953–1970', *The International History Review*, 17:3 (August 1995), 527.
7. Memorandum of Conversation, Department of State, 24 March 1959, in *Foreign Relations of the United States, 1958–1960: Volume XI, Lebanon and Jordan* (Washington: US Government Printing Office, 1992), p. 693. (Hereafter referred to as FRUS, 1958–1960, Vol. XI.)
8. Memorandum of Conversation, White House, 25 March 1959 in FRUS, 1958–1960, Vol. XI, p. 700.
9. As former diplomat Richard Parker recalls, 'economically unviable' was 'a recurring phrase' to describe Jordan in the 1950s. See his 'The United States and King Hussein', in David W. Lesch (ed.), *The Middle East and the United States: a Historical and Political Reassessment* (Boulder: Westview, 1996), p. 105.
10. See Morris to FO, 29 January 1959, FO 371.142198/VJ 1941/5, PRO.
11. Naseer H. Aruri, *Jordan: a Study in Political Development, 1921–1965* (The Hague: Martinus Nijhoff, 1972), p. 63. As one British official noted: 'Keeping Jordan afloat is an Anglo-American operation which is becoming increasingly unattractive to the United States Government.' See Caccia to FO, 11 December 1959, FO 371.142141/VJ 1121/25B, PRO.
12. See Amman to DOS, 20 September 1958, DOS 785.00/9-2058, NA.
13. See Johnston to FO, 21 March 1959, FO 371.142102/VJ 1015/15, PRO; and Johnston to FO, 8 December 1958, FO 371.134071/VJ 1205/29, PRO. ʿAbbas Murad lists those connected with the al-Sharʿa faction in his *Al-daur al-siyassi lil-jaysh al-urdunni* [The Political Role of the Jordanian Army] (Beirut: Palestine Liberation Organisation Research Center, 1973), p. 103.
14. Wright to DOS, 22 January 1959, DOS 785.13/1-1-2259, NA.
15. Wright to DOS, 17 January 1959, DOS 785.13/1-1759, NA.
16. Interview with Salih al-Sharʿa, 19 April 1993, Amman. Also, Salih al-Sharʿa, *Mudhakarrat jundi* [Memoirs of a Soldier] (Amman, n.p., 1985).
17. Interview with Sadiq al-Sharʿa, 12 April 1993, Amman.
18. Johnston to FO, 30 May 1959, FO 371.142103/VJ 1015/46, PRO.
19. Peter Snow, *Hussein: a Biography* (London: Barrie and Jenkins, 1972), p. 134.
20. Johnston to FO, 15 March 1959, FO 371.142102/VJ 1015/9A, PRO. Strickland reported unease in the army and predicted in February there might be trouble when Hussein left for Washington; see Mason to Hadow, 20 February 1959, FO 371.142102/VJ 1015/8, PRO. Also, interview with Osama al-Sukhin, 19 April 1993, Amman.
21. Minute by Adams, 2 January 1959, FO 371.142156/VJ 1202/1, PRO. Munib al-Madi and Suleiman Musa shed little light on the coup attempt in their *Tarikh al-urdunn fi al-qarn al-ʿashreen* [The History of Jordan in the Twentieth Century] (Amman: n.p. 1959; 2nd edn, Amman: Maktaba al-Muhtasab, 1988), p. 700.

Jamal al-Sha`ir discusses some of the rumours surrounding the case in *Siyassi yatadhakkir* [A Politician Remembers] (London: Riad al-Rayyes, 1987), p. 145.

22. Johnston to FO, 15 March 1959, FO 371.142102/VJ 1015/9, PRO.
23. Mills to DOS, 15 May 1959, DOS 785.13/5-1559, NA.
24. Wright to DOS, 21 April 1959, DOS 785.00/4-2159, NA.
25. Mason to FO, 29 April 1959, FO 371.142156 VJ 1202/2, PRO; also, Mason to Beith, 1 May 1959, FO 371.142156/VJ 1202/3, PRO.
26. See Mason to Hadow, 19 March 1959, FO 371.142102/VJ 1015/16, PRO.
27. Alan Rush, 'Queen Zein of Jordan', *The Independent*, 28 April 1994, 14.
28. Mason to Hadow, 5 March 1959, FO 371.142198/VJ 1941/21, PRO.
29. Interview with Habis al-Majali, 12 April 1993, Amman. Also, Wright to DOS, 4 May 1959, DOS 785.00/5-459, NA; and Mason to Beith, 1 May 1959, FO 371.142156/VJ 1202/3, PRO.
30. Except where noted, this paragraph is based on information from Wright to DOS, 4 May 1959, DOS 785.00/5-459, NA; and Mills to DOS, 15 May 1959, DOS 785.13/5-1559, NA.
31. Johnston to FO, 6 May 1959, FO 371.142103/VJ 1015/32, PRO.
32. Wright to DOS, 29 April 1959, DOS 785.00/4-2959, NA.
33. See Mason to FO, 14 August 1959, FO 371.142104/VJ 1015/60, PRO; and Johnston to FO, 22 May 1959, FO 371.142103/VJ 1015/45, PRO. According to Habis al-Majali's legal advisor, al-Majali refused to grant Sadiq al-Shar'a's requests for cigarettes and food when the latter was in prison. Interview with Osama al-Sukhin, 19 April 1993, Amman.
34. Johnston to FO, 11 May 1959, FO 371.142103/VJ 1015/36, PRO.
35. Johnston to FO, 7 May 1959, FO 371.142103/VJ 1015/33, PRO.
36. Figg to Adams, 11 June 1959, FO 371.142103/VJ 1015/52, PRO.
37. Johnston to FO, 8 May 1959, FO 371.142103/VJ 1015/37, PRO.
38. Johnston to FO, 11 May 1959, FO 371.142103/VJ 1015/36, PRO.
39. Mason to Hadow, 5 March 1959, FO 371.142198/VJ 1941/21, PRO.
40. Johnston to FO, 28 May 1959, FO 371.142200/VJ 1941/68, PRO.
41. See Benjamin Shwadran, 'Husain Between Qasim and Nasir', *Middle Eastern Affairs* (December 1960), 330–45; and J.S. Raleigh, 'The Middle East in 1959 – a Political Survey', *Middle Eastern Affairs* (January 1960), 9. Also, Malik Mufti, 'The United States and Nasserist Pan-Arabism', in David W. Lesch (ed.), *The Middle East and the United States: a Historical and Political Reassessment* (Boulder: Westview, 1996), p. 177.
42. Minute by Beith, 5 January 1960, FO 371.151096/VJ 1193/3, PRO. For the problems in Iraq, see Benjamin Shwadran, 'The Power Struggle in Iraq', *Middle Eastern Affairs* (February 1960), 38–63 and (April 1960), 106–61.
43. Beirut to DOS, 14 May 1959, DOS Lot Files, NA.
44. Comment by Sir Hoyer Millar on Minute by Stevens, 11 May 1959, FO 371.142122/VJ 10393/4, PRO.
45. Johnston to Beith, 16 October 1959, FO 371.142122/VJ 10393/18G, PRO; also, Minute by Beith, 6 January 1960, FO 371.151096/VJ 1193/3, PRO.
46. Minute by Moberly, 16 October 1959, FO 371.142122/VJ 10393/18G, PRO. Brigadier Strickland, however, felt that man-for-man the Jordanians were better trained than their Iraqi counterparts. If the Jordanian army mounted a successful initial engagement, elements of the Iraqi military would probably defect to the Jordanian side. See Minute by Beith, 6 January 1960, FO 371.151096/VJ 1193/3, PRO. Ambassador Johnston believed Jordanian forces

'might well be capable of over-running the Hejaz in the event of chaos in Saudi Arabia.' See Johnston to Beith, 16 February 1960, FO 371.151065/VJ 10325/3, PRO.

47. Interview with Sadiq al-Shar`a, 12 April 1993, Amman.
48. See Johnston to Beith, 29 April 1960, FO 371.151079/VJ 1121/12, PRO.
49. See Memorandum of Conversation, Department of State, 19 November 1959 in FRUS, 1958–1960, Vol. XI, pp. 664–6.
50. See Mason to FO, 5 March 1959, FO 371.142149/VJ 1192/4, PRO.
51. See Mason to Beith, 5 August 1959, FO 371.142136/VJ 1112/10, PRO.
52. Figg to Moberly, 23 October 1959, FO 371.142139/VJ 1115/1, PRO; also, Wright to DOS, 23 January 1959, DOS 785.561/1-2359, NA.
53. See Weir to Rothnie, 12 June 1959, FO 371.142149/VJ 1192/22, PRO.
54. See Minute by Moberly, 18 May 1960, FO 371.151080/VJ 1121/18, PRO.
55. FO to Amman, 20 May 1960, FO 371.151080/VJ 1121/23, PRO.
56. Johnston to Beith, 15 October 1959, FO 371.142175/VJ 1422/1, PRO.
57. See Mason to Rothnie, 26 June 1959, FO 371.142104/VJ 1015/56, PRO.
58. See Johnston to FO, 7 May 1959, FO 371.142103/VJ 1015/33, PRO.
59. For details on al-Fayiz's drought policy, see Mason to Rothnie, 3 July 1959, FO 371.142188/VJ 1701/23, PRO; for more reports of corruption, see Johnston to Stevens, 21 May 1959, FO 371.142196/VJ 1903/3, PRO; Mason to Beith, 7 August 1959, FO 371.142196/VJ 1903/6, PRO; and Johnston to FO, 6 June 1959, FO 371.142103/VJ 1015/47, PRO.
60. Said Aburish claims that Radi Abdullah was framed by King Hussein, who had spent $2 million the CIA had given Jordan to conduct covert operations against Syria. Sam Brewer of the *New York Times* and other journalists doubted the verity of the charges against Radi Abdullah. See Said K. Aburish, *The St. George Hotel Bar* (London: Bloomsbury, 1989), pp. 54–5. Others, however, consider Radi Abdullah a disloyal opportunist who 'prays to the dinar.' Interview with Ma`an Abu Nuwar, 13 May 1996, Amman.
61. Walstrom to DOS, 9 December 1958, DOS 785.00/12-958, NA.
62. See Figg to Moberly, 20 July 1960, FO 371.151117/VJ 1641/1, PRO.
63. For details, see Morris to FO, 30 July 1960, FO 371.151059/VJ 10316/57, PRO; Johnston to FO, 31 March 1959, FO 371.151041/VJ 1015/16, PRO; and Morris to Rothnie, 5 August 1960, FO 371.151059/VJ 10316/61, PRO.
64. See Crowe to FO, 27 June 1960, FO 371.151058/VJ 10316/30, PRO.
65. BBC Monitoring Report, 27 April 1960, FO 371.151058/VJ 10316/32, PRO.
66. Johnston to FO, 29 April 1960, FO 371.151058/VJ 10316/33, PRO.
67. Morris to Beith, 8 July 1960, FO 371.151058/VJ 10316/49, PRO.
68. Both quotes from Hussein bin Talal, *Mahnati ka-malik* [My Job as King] (Amman: The National Press, 1986), p. 167.
69. Johnston to FO, 31 March 1960, FO 371.151041/VJ 1015/15G, PRO.
70. Suleiman Musa notes that 'the incident was the first of its kind in Jordan.' See his *Al-`alam min al-urdunn: safhat min tarikh al-`arab al-hadith* [Prominent Personalities from Jordan: Pages from Modern Arab History] (Amman: Dar al-Sha`ab, 1986), p. 37; also, Johnston to FO, 29 August 1960, FO 371.151044/VJ 1015/47, PRO.
71. See Johnston to FO, 30 August 1960, FO 371.15104/VJ 1015/57, PRO. Eric Kocher, the deputy chief of mission at the US embassy, describes the morning in his *Foreign Intrigue: the Making and Unmaking of a Foreign Service Officer* (Far Hills: New Horizon Press, 1990), pp. 175–9.

72. See Packenham to FO, 30 August 1960, FO 371.151044/VJ 1015/59, PRO.
73. Minute by Beith, 31 August 1960, FO 371.151046/VJ 1015/83, PRO.
74. Johnston to FO, 30 August 1960, FO 371.151044/VJ 1015/56, PRO.
75. Johnston to FO, 31 August 1960, FO 371.151045/VJ 1015/67, PRO.
76. Minute by Moberly on Henniker-Major to Home, 6 January 1961, FO 371.158876/VJ 1015/2, PRO. Some former soldiers believe the al-Majali assassination was the only real coup attempt in Jordan. Interview with Zeid Nuwairan, 1 April 1995, Amman.
77. See Morris to Figg, 11 August 1961, FO 371.157521/EJ 1015/34, PRO. Tribal customs in Jordan generally hold that blood revenge must be taken within 12 months; that the victim should be a prominent member of the other clan; and that a truce, brokered by a third party, ends the blood feud.
78. Johnston to Beith, 28 September 1960, FO 371.151094/VJ 1192/87, PRO.
79. Johnston to FO, 11 September 1960, FO 371.151047/VJ 1015/104, PRO.
80. Johnston to FO, 9 September 1960, FO 371.151046/VJ 1015/90, PRO.
81. See Johnston to FO, 9 September 1960, FO 371.151046/VJ 1015/88, PRO; and Johnston to FO, 12 September 1960, FO 371.151048/VJ 1015/113, PRO. One retired security establishment member, Hikmat Mihayr, says Abdullah Majelli was one of the prime movers behind the invasion plans. Interview with Hikmat Mihayr, 13 April 1993, Amman.
82. See Johnston to FO, 9 September 1960, FO 371.151046/VJ 1015/90, PRO; Johnston to FO, 15 September 1960, FO 371.151049/VJ 1015/130, PRO; and Minute by Beith, 14 September 1960, FO 371.151048/VJ 1015/127, PRO.
83. US official Armin Meyer said 'the Israelis would be certain to occupy part of the West Bank' if Jordan endangered itself by confronting the UAR. See Hood to Stevens, 20 October 1960, FO 371.151063/VJ 10316/142, PRO.
84. Morris to Beith, 3 November 1960, FO 371.151053/VJ 1015/190, PRO.
85. Yossi Melman and Dan Raviv, *Behind the Uprising: Israelis, Jordanians, and Palestinians* (New York: Greenwood, 1989), p. 56; also, Adam Garfinkle, *Israel and Jordan in the Shadow of War: Functional Ties and Futile Diplomacy in a Small Place* (London: Macmillan, 1992), p. 37.
86. Moshe Zak, 'Israel and Jordan: Strategically Bound', *Israel Affairs*, 3:1 (Autumn 1996), 43.
87. Zak, 'Israel and Jordan: Strategically Bound', 43.
88. Edden to FO, 22 September 1960, FO 371.151060/VJ 10316/97, PRO.
89. See Johnston to FO, 12 September 1960, FO 371.151048/VJ 1015/112, PRO.
90. Johnston to FO, 9 September 1960, FO 371.151046/VJ 1015/89, PRO.
91. Kocher, *Foreign Intrigue*, p. 186.
92. See, for example, Kocher to DOS, 18 September 1960, FRUS, 1958–1960, Vol. XI, pp. 740–1. Eric Kocher narrates his efforts to sway Hussein in *Foreign Intrigue*, p. 201.
93. Johnston to FO, 16 September 1960, FO 371.151060/VJ 10316/84G, PRO.
94. Malik Mufti, 'The United States and Nasserist Pan-Arabism', in Lesch, *The Middle East and the United States: a Historical and Political Reassessment*, p. 167.
95. Kocher to DOS, 10 September 1960, in FRUS, 1958–1960, Vol. XI, pp. 738–9.
96. Hussein's speech can be found in Hussein bin Talal, *Uneasy Lies the Head* (London: Heinemann, 1962), pp. 200–7.
97. Details of the meeting can be found in Memorandum of Conversation, 7 October 1960, in FRUS, 1958–1960, Vol. XI, pp. 742–5.

98. Figures from this paragraph are cited in J.S. Raleigh, 'The Middle East in 1960 – a Political Survey', *Middle Eastern Affairs* (February 1961), 80.
99. See Henniker-Major to FO, 2 December 1960, FO 371.151054/VJ 1015/205, PRO.
100. See Musa, *Al-`alam min al-urdunn*, p. 122.
101. This paragraph is based on Henniker-Major to FO, 15 February 1961, FO 371.158877/EJ 103116/13, PRO; Henniker-Major to FO, 5 April 1961, FO 371.157527/EJ 103116/25, PRO; and Henniker-Major to FO, 5 April 1961, FO 371.157527/EJ 103116/23A, PRO.
102. Minute by O'Regan, 14 December 1960, FO 371.151088/VJ 1151/27, PRO.
103. Henniker-Major to FO, 20 December 1960, FO 371.151095/VJ 1192/108, PRO.
104. Henniker-Major to FO, 20 December 1960, FO 371.151095/VJ 1192/109, PRO.
105. Details of the conflict can be found in Henniker-Major to FO, 27 March 1961, FO 371.157555/EJ 1194/4; Henniker-Major to FO, 28 March 1961, FO 371.157555/EJ 1194/5; Henniker-Major to FO, 28 March 1961, FO 371.157555/EJ 1194/6; and Henniker-Major to Hiller, 28 April 1961, FO 371.157555/EJ 1194/14, all PRO. Also, interview with Omar Kayid al-Salim, 16 August 1995, Houston.
106. Message from Hussein to Armed Forces, 27 May 1961, FO 371.157555/EJ 1194/12, PRO.
107. For details, see Minute by Figg, 17 August 1961, FO 371.157552/EJ 1192/41, PRO; and Henniker-Major to Figg, 20 July 1961, FO 371.157551/EJ 1192/31, PRO.
108. This paragraph is based on the British military advisor's report on 'internal dissension within the Jordan Armed Forces' in FO 371.157555, PRO.
109. Henniker-Major to Crawford, 10 March 1961, FO 371.157520/EJ 1015/6, PRO.
110. Henniker-Major to Hiller, 31 August 1961, FO 371.157522/EJ 1015/43, PRO; and Henniker-Major to Figg, 8 September 1961, FO 371.157536/EJ 1072/4, PRO.
111. See Henniker-Major to FO, 31 December 1961, FO 371.164086/EJ 1022/1, PRO; and Henniker-Major to Figg, 8 September 1961, FO 371.157536/EJ 1072/4, PRO.
112. Henniker-Major to FO, 31 December 1961, FO 371.164086/EJ 1022/1, PRO.
113. On this idea, see the Minute by Morris, 19 October 1961, in FO 371.157398, PRO.
114. Minute by Morris, 19 October 1961, in FO 371.157398, PRO.
115. Gerald Sparrow, *Modern Jordan* (London: George Allen and Unwin, 1961), pp. 54–5.
116. Henniker-Major to Home, 28 October 1961, FO 371.157522/EJ 1015/57, PRO. The following account of the elections is based primarily on this dispatch.
117. Henniker-Major to FO, 26 December 1961, FO 371.157532/EJ 1051/4, PRO.
118. Henniker-Major to Hiller, 13 January 1961, FO 371.164081/EJ 1015/4, PRO.

6   From Reforms to Rapprochement

1. See Douglas Little, 'A Puppet in Search of a Puppeteer?: the United States, King Hussein, and Jordan, 1953–1970', *The International History Review*, 17:3 (August 1995), 528–9.

2. See Henniker-Major to FO, 20 January 1962, FO 371.164081/EJ 1015/2 and Henniker-Major to FO, 23 January 1962, FO 371.164081/EJ 1015/6, both Public Record Office (PRO), London. On the reasons for not appointing al-Talhuni or al-Rifa`i, see Henniker-Major to Home, 16 February 1962, FO 371.164082/EJ 1015/28, PRO. Jordanian historian Suleiman Musa notes that, although Wasfi al-Tell was the first Jordanian prime minister who had never been a minister, he had 'served more than twenty years in the military, civil, and diplomatic services.' See Suleiman Musa, *Al-`alam min al-urdunn: safhat min al-tarikh al-`arabi al-hadith* [Prominent Personalities from Jordan: Pages from Modern Arab History] (Amman: Dar al-Sha`ab Press, 1986), p. 122.

3. Uriel Dann, *King Hussein and the Challenge of Arab Radicalism: Jordan, 1955–1967* (New York: Oxford University Press, 1989), p. 120.

4. As Asher Susser writes, al-Tell 'spoke his mind to Husayn in the strongest terms. Indeed, [he] was one of the few, the very few, who would go a long way to impress his views on Husayn, at the risk of displeasing him.' See *On Both Banks of the Jordan: a Political Biography of Wasfi al-Tall* (London: Frank Cass, 1994), p. 37.

5. Parkes to Home, 7 March 1963, FO 371.170265/EJ 1015/40, PRO.

6. See Jamal al-Sha`ir, *Siyassi yatadhakkir* [A Politician Remembers] (London: Riad al-Rayyes, 1987), p. 18.

7. See the *Financial Times*, 22 March 1962. Although many disagreed with al-Tell's policies, nearly every former policymaker and opposition figure interviewed for this study considers him the most significant politician in Jordanian history. Arab nationalist Hamad al-Farhan sums up the views of many when he says, 'Wasfi was a man ahead of his time.' Interview with Hamad al-Farhan, 21 April 1993, Amman.

8. See Henniker-Major to Home, 13 July 1962, FO 371.164083/EJ 1015/57, PRO.

9. See Morris to Hiller, 30 March 1962, FO 371.164083/EJ 1015/43, PRO.

10. Interviews with Salah Abu Zaid, 25 April 1995, Amman; and Tariq Masarweh, 13 May 1996, Amman.

11. Parkes to Home, 7 March 1963, FO 371.170265/EJ 1015/40, PRO.

12. See Susser, *On Both Banks of the Jordan*, p. 17.

13. See Henniker-Major to FO, 6 July 1962, FO 371.164086/EJ 1022/14, PRO.

14. Parkes to Home, 7 March 1963, FO 371.170265/EJ 1015/40, PRO.

15. Parkes to Home, Annual Review for 1962, 9 January 1963, FO 371.170263/EJ 1011/1, PRO.

16. Details on the reorganisation can be found in the report on 'Reorganisation – Jordan Arab Army, September 1962' in FO 371.164122; Morris to Figg, 27 September 1962, FO 371.164122/EJ 1201/62; and Parkes to Figg, 28 December 1962, FO 371.170335/EJ 1641/2, all PRO.

17. See Parkes to Home, 7 March 1963, FO 371.170265/EJ 1015/40, PRO.

18. Information in the following paragraphs is based largely on Parkes to FO, 29 March 1963, FO 371.170266/EJ 1013/63G, PRO; and Parkes to Figg, 28 December 1962, FO 371.170335/EJ 1641/2, PRO.

19. Fawaz A. Gerges, *The Superpowers and the Middle East: Regional and International Politics, 1955–1967* (Boulder: Westview Press, 1994), p. 150. Robin Bidwell describes Yemeni republican leader Colonel Abdullah Sallal as a 'figurehead' leader who 'showed no signs of having any political ideology.' See his obituary of Sallal in *The Independent*, 18 March 1994.

20. On Jordan's initial worries about the Yemen war, see Lewis to DOS, 6 October 1962 in FRUS, 1962–1963, Vol. XVIII, pp. 73–4.
21. Reported in *The Scotsman*, 12 November 1962.
22. Peter Snow, *Hussein: a Biography* (London: Barrie and Jenkins, 1972), p. 152.
23. In particular, Hussein 'still dreamed of marching into Baghdad to restore Hashemite rule there, and he was still trying to persuade the West to give air support to a Jordanian invasion of Iraq.' See Snow, *Hussein*, p. 153.
24. See Laurie A. Brand, *Jordan's Inter-Arab Relations: the Political Economy of Alliance Making* (New York: Columbia University Press, 1994), p. 102.
25. Parkes to Home, Annual Review for 1962, 9 January 1963, FO 371.170263/EJ 1011/1; also, Morris to Figg, 14 December 1962, FO 371.164090/EJ 103125/15, both PRO.
26. See Jerusalem to FO, 20 October 1962, FO 371.164084/EJ 1015/77(A); and Parkes to FO, 18 October 1962, FO 371.164084/EJ 1015/77, both PRO. Also, interview with Kamal al-Sha`ir, 21 April 1995, Amman.
27. Ambassador Parkes said 'there was virtually no corruption and both electorate and candidates were remarkably free.' See Parkes to Home, Annual Review for 1962, 9 January 1963, FO 371.170263/EJ 1011/63, PRO.
28. See Parkes to Home, 30 November 1962, FO 371.164085/EJ 1015/97, PRO.
29. For the background to the Iraqi coup, see the remarks by former Iraqi Prime Minister `Arif `Abd al-Rizaq in *al-Quds al-`Arabi*, 12/13 November 1994, 4.
30. Susser's claim that 'it seems that Husayn did not have complete confidence in the ability of his inexperienced Prime Minister to contend with possible internal unrest' does not make much sense given al-Tell's military background and combat experience. See Susser, *On Both Banks of the Jordan*, p. 67.
31. See Parkes to FO, 29 March 1963, FO 371.170312/EJ 1201/7, PRO. For military opposition to al-Tell, see Maitland to FO, 8 February 1963, FO 371.170265/EJ 1015/22, PRO.
32. See Henderson to FO, 23 March 1963, FO 371.170266/EJ 1015/45, PRO; and Parkes to FO, 29 March 1963, FO 371.170312/EJ 1201/7, PRO.
33. Parkes to FO, 14 March 1963, FO 371.170285/EJ 1072/1, PRO.
34. For a fascinating account of the Cairo tripartite unity negotiations, see Malcolm H. Kerr, *The Arab Cold War: Gamal `Abd al-Nasir and His Rivals, 1958–1970* (Oxford: Oxford University Press, 1971), pp. 44–76.
35. Parkes to Home, 3 May 1963, FO 371.170268/EJ 1015/96, PRO.
36. Parkes to FO, 21 April 1963, FO 371.170267/EJ 1015/77, PRO. Zaid al-Rifa`i says the corruption charges were cooked up by his father's political enemies. Interview with Zaid al-Rifa`i, 21 April 1993, Amman. Members of the al-Rifa`i faction had been accused of corruption in the past. For an example, see Parliamentary Question from Mustafa Khalifa, 17 January 1961, 139/4/3/4, Jordanian National Archives, Amman.
37. Parkes to Butler, Annual Review for 1963, 9 January 1964, FO 371.175645/EJ 1011/1, PRO.
38. Snow, *Hussein*, p. 154.
39. Details of the clashes can be found in Minute by Figg, 1 May 1963, FO 371.170269/EJ 1015/102; Maitland to Figg, 10 May 1963, FO 371.170268/EJ 1015/88; Maitland to Hiller, 29 May 1963, FO 371.170269/EJ 1015/116; and Parkes to Home, 3 May 1963, FO 371.170268/EJ 1015/96, all PRO.

40. One member of the Bani Sakhr who took part in the riots says the initial demonstrations in Irbid were encouraged by Ba`thist school teachers and students who favoured union with nearby Syria. Interview with Omar Kayid al-Salim, 25 August 1995, Houston.
41. See Parkes to Home, 3 May 1963, FO 371.170268/EJ 1015/96, PRO.
42. See Parkes to FO, 24 April 1963, FO 371.170268/EJ 1015/82, PRO.
43. See Memorandum of Telephone Conversation between Ball and McNamara, 27 April 1963 and Memorandum of White House Meeting, 27 April 1963 both in FRUS, 1962–1963, Vol. XVIII, pp. 483–6.
44. See Ball to Tel Aviv, 27 April 1963 and Ball to Cairo, 27 April 1963 in FRUS, 1962–1963, Vol. XVIII, pp. 486–8.
45. Macomber to DOS, 28 April 1963 in FRUS, 1962–1963, Vol. XVIII, p. 493.
46. Minute by Crawford, 24 April 1963, FO 371.170154/EJ 1015/16, PRO. Also, see Israeli intelligence assessments of the crisis in Tel Aviv to FO, 6 May 1963, FO 371.170155/EJ 1015/23, PRO.
47. Memorandum of Conversation with Israeli Representatives, 27 April 1963 in FRUS, 1962–1963, Vol. XVIII, pp. 489–92.
48. Minute by Goodison, 13 March 1963, FO 371.170154/EJ 1015/12, PRO.
49. Washington to FO, 27 April 1963, FO 371.170182/E 1074/1, PRO.
50. New York to FO, 29 April 1963, FO 371.170182/E 1074/5, PRO.
51. See Dann, *King Hussein and Challenge of Arab Radicalism*, p. 133. Israel also had plans for a limited occupation of the West Bank which would involve moving onto the high ground from Jenin in the north through Nablus to Jerusalem. In this way, Israel could 'avoid getting involved with the 900,000 arab [sic] refugees in the Jericho area.' See Israeli military intelligence views in the Israeli Appreciation of pro-Nasser Trends in Jordan, 17 August 1964, FO 371.175650/MA/4/3/64, PRO.
52. The idea of creating 'a theory of administration' emerged after Israel's experience in the Gaza Strip in 1956, when it took some time before an administrative apparatus was set up. See Shabtai Teveth, *The Cursed Blessing: the Story of Israel's Occupation of the West Bank* (London: Weidenfeld and Nicolson, 1970), pp. 10–11.
53. Minute by Goodison, 2 May 1963, FO 371.170182/E 1074/13, PRO.
54. See Minutes of Cabinet Meeting, 2 May 1963, CAB 128/37/CC 28 (63), PRO.
55. Washington considered, but did not favour, using military force to stop an Israeli attack. This was deemed 'a remote possibility.' See Washington to FO, 20 April 1963, FO 371.170182/E 1074/4, PRO. Britain, for its part, would not 'be able to take any action to restrain Israel if it decided to occupy the West Bank.' See Minutes of Cabinet Meeting, 9 May 1963, CAB 128/37/CC 29(63), PRO.
56. See, among others, Yossi Melman and Dan Raviv, *Behind the Uprising: Israelis, Jordanians, and Palestinians* (New York: Greenwood, 1989), p. 71; Moshe Zak, 'Israel and Jordan: Strategically Bound', *Israel Affairs*, 3:1 (Autumn 1996), 44; and Dann, *King Hussein and the Challenge of Arab Radicalism*, p. 133. Adam Garfinkle maintains that the transcripts of Jordanian–Israeli secret talks in Israeli intelligence files provide 500 hours' worth of reading. See Adam Garfinkle, *Israel and Jordan in the Shadow of War: Functional Ties and Futile Diplomacy in a Small Place* (London: Macmillan, 1992).
57. Dann, *King Hussein and the Challenge of Arab Radicalism*, p. 134.

58. Hussein appears to have made the decision himself. Determining which Jordanian policymakers attended the meetings with the Israelis is difficult. The most obvious candidates were those closest to Hussein at the time, a group which included military officers. Few officials, however, are willing to admit they attended the clandestine summits. The Israeli codename for Hussein was *yanuka*, a Hebrew term meaning 'little boy'. See Melman and Raviv, *Behind the Uprising*, p. 89.
59. Patrick Seale, 'Jordan and Egypt are Moving Closer', *The Scotsman*, 11 October 1963.
60. For the 'pro-Egypt' line of thinking in the NSE, see Minute by Stevens, 14 March 1963, FO 371.170284/EJ 1071/2; Parkes to FO, 27 March 1963, FO 371.170266/EJ 1015/40; and Minute by Eastern Department, 20 September 1963, FO 371.170340/EJ 1941/31, all PRO.
61. Parkes to Butler, Annual Review for 1963, 9 January 1964, FO 371.175645/EJ 1011/1, PRO.

7 In Nasser's Grip

1. Steering Brief on Jordan, 29 April 1964, PREM 11.4882, PRO.
2. As one British official put it, Hussein 'has at a price re-established himself as an Arab and an accepted leader among the Arabs.' See Phillips to Walker, Annual Report on Jordan for 1964, 7 January 1965, FO 371.180728/EJ 1011/1, PRO.
3. Remarks by Adnan Abu `Udeh at the 'Politics and the State in Jordan, 1946–1996' conference, 25 June 1997, Institut du Monde Arabe, Paris.
4. Peter Mansfield, *A History of the Middle East* (London: Penguin, 1991), p. 240.
5. Baruch Kimmerling and Joel S. Migdal, *Palestinians: the Making of a People* (New York: The Free Press, 1993), p. 191.
6. See Moshe Shemesh, 'The Founding of the PLO, 1964', *Middle Eastern Studies* (October 1984), 113.
7. Shemesh, 'The Founding of the PLO', pp. 126–7. Hussein himself later conceded that the formation of the PLO marked the genesis of the clash that culminated in September 1970. See his *Mahnati ka-malik* [My Job as King] (Amman: The National Press, 1986), p. 203.
8. Mark Tessler, *A History of the Israeli–Palestinian Conflict* (Bloomington: Indiana University Press, 1994), p. 374.
9. Patrick Seale, *Asad of Syria: the Struggle for the Middle East* (Berkeley: University of California Press, 1988), p. 121.
10. For details on the conference, see Minute on the Palestine Entity by Cradock, 15 June 1964, FO 371.175563/E 1075/50, PRO. For the PLO's pledge to respect the sovereignty of Jordan, see Article 24 of the Palestine National Charter in C.H. Dodd and Mary Sales (eds), *Israel and the Arab World* (London: Routledge and Kegan Paul, 1970), p. 140. Ahmad al-Shuqayri's memories of the period can be found in his *Min al-qima ila al-hazima ma` al-maluk wa al-ru'asa'* [From the Summit to the Defeat with Kings and Presidents] (Beirut: Dar al-`Awdah, 1971).
11. Minute by Sanders on The Palestine Entity, 15 May 1964, in FO 371.175562, PRO.

12. For details on al-Shuqayri and his vision of the PLO, see Phillips to Morris, 3 June 1964, FO 371.175562/E 1075; Minute by Sanders on The Palestine Entity, 15 May 1964, in FO 371.175562; and Minute by Cradock on The Palestine Entity, 15 June 1964, FO 371.175563/E 1075/50, all PRO. Abdullah Schleifer discusses PLO revolutionary ideas in his *The Fall of Jerusalem* (New York: Monthly Review Press, 1972), p. 72.
13. Personal correspondence with Patrick Seale, 25 February 1997.
14. For details, see Jerusalem to Goodison, 28 April 1964, FO 371.175562/E 1075/22, PRO. An assessment of the domestic tensions created by the formation of the PLO can be found in Parkes to Stewart, Jordan's East and West Banks: Will the Twain Ever Meet?, 25 February 1966, FO 371.186548/EJ 1015/8, PRO.
15. Tessler, *A History of the Israeli–Palestinian Conflict*, p. 375.
16. Minute by Cradock on The Palestine Entity, 15 June 1964, FO 371.175563/E 1075/50, PRO.
17. Interview with Moraiwid al-Tell, 4 July 1996, Oxford. As one Jordanian notes, al-Tell 'seldom harboured any inherent anti-Palestinian sentiments *per se*, though probably [he] was dispassionate enough to anticipate the dangers which over-charged Arab radicalism could bring upon Jordan and the Palestinian cause.' See Lu'ayy al-Rimawi's review of Asher Susser's biography of al-Tell: 'Susser's Account of Wasfi al-Tel's Life Lacks Deep Reading of Political Dynamics', *Jordan Times*, 18 January 1995.
18. Interview with Kamal al-Sha`ir, 21 April 1995, Amman.
19. Al-Tell's view of Jordan as the pivotal state in the Palestinian–Israeli dispute was shared by the Western powers. As one Foreign Office brief summarised: 'Jordan is the Arab country most closely affected by the dispute.' See Steering Brief on Jordan, 29 April 1964, PREM 11/4882, PRO. Also, interview with Abdel Ra`uf Abu Rasa', 16 April 1995, Amman.
20. Interview with Tariq Masarweh, 13 May 1996, Amman.
21. Phillips to Butler, Recent Developments in Jordan, 27 August 1964, FO 371.175647/EJ 1015/49, PRO.
22. Parkes to Morris, 6 May 1964, FO 371.175646/E 1015/64, PRO.
23. The *mukhabarat* chief, Muhammad Rasul al-Gaylani, opposed granting amnesty to those who were 'active Nasserites and dangerous.' See Stirling to Sanders, 10 June 1964, FO 371.175646/EJ 1015/27, PRO.
24. This statement and the following account of the summit are based largely on Parkes to Walker, Jordan Moves Towards Non-Alignment, 3 December 1964, FO 371.175647/EJ 1015/65, PRO.
25. Stirling to Goodison, 28 October 1964, FO 371.175647/EJ 1015/60, PRO.
26. Parkes to Walker, Jordan Moves Towards Non-Alignment, 3 December 1963, FO 371.175647/EJ 1015/65, PRO.
27. Kamal Salibi, *The Modern History of Jordan* (London: I.B. Tauris, 1993), p. 214.
28. See Phillips to Morris, 15 July 1964, FO 371.175646/EJ 1015/37, PRO.
29. Phillips to Butler, Recent Developments in Jordan, 27 August 1964, FO 371.175647/EJ 1015/49, PRO.
30. Phillips to Butler, Recent Developments in Jordan, 27 August 1964, FO 371.175647/EJ 1015/49, PRO.
31. Phillips to FO, 26 July 1964, FO 371.175650/EJ 103110/9G, PRO.

32. Phillips to Morris, 15 July 1964, FO 371.175646/EJ 1015/37, PRO.
33. See Asher Susser, *On Both Banks of the Jordan: a Political Biography of Wasfi al-Tall* (London: Frank Cass, 1994), p. 72.
34. See Urwick to Goodison, 9 April 1965, FO 371.180757/EJ 1641/1, PRO.
35. As usual, military leaders were leery of the amnesty and mobilised troops in the Jerusalem area to deal with newly released Communists. See Saunders to Urwick, 13 May 1965, FO 371.180729/1038, PRO.
36. See Muhammad Sa`id al-Mashal, 'Al-tarikh al-awal li-harakat fatah: kayf ta'asasit wa kayf intalaqat?' [The First History of the Fatah Movement: How was it Established and how did it Take Off?], *al-Quds al-`Arabi*, 20 March 1994, 7.
37. For details, see Susser, *On Both Banks of the Jordan*, p. 82.
38. See Fuad Jabber, 'The Palestinian Resistance and Inter-Arab Politics', in William B. Quandt, Fuad Jabber, Ann Mosely Lesch, *The Politics of Palestinian Nationalism* (Berkeley: University of California Press, 1973), p. 164.
39. See Saunders to Urwick, 13 May 1965, FO 371.180729/EJ 1015/20(A), PRO.
40. Quoted in Susser, *On Both Banks of the Jordan*, p. 84.
41. Quoted in Susser, *On Both Banks of the Jordan*, p. 88.
42. See Susser, *On Both Banks of the Jordan*, p. 84.
43. The June 1963 Anglo-American recommendations urged Jordan to 'disband the National Guard by degrees and to replace the active units of this force by new regular infantry units.' See Phayre to Parkes, Annual Despatch on the Jordan Army for 1963, 7 January 1963, FO 371.175673/MA 11090, PRO; Cawston to MOD, Report on Conversation with `Amer Khammash, 17 August 1964, FO 371.175673/MA 11196, PRO.
44. Parkes to Home, 3 July 1963, FO 371.170311/EJ 1195/5, PRO.
45. See the BBC Monitoring Report, 16 September 1965, in FO 371.180652/E 1073/42(c), PRO. As it was, the National Guard based on the West Bank was considered by many to be a potential threat. As Shwadran notes, the Guard 'contained the seeds of possible armed rebellion by the Palestinians against the Jordanian authorities.' Benjamin Shwadran, *Jordan: a State of Tension* (New York: Council on Middle Eastern Affairs Press, 1959), p. 337.
46. Urwick to Goodison, 12 October 1965, FO 371.180733/EJ 1022/10, PRO.
47. See Parkes to FO, 23 October 1965, FO 371.180658/E 10711/5, PRO.
48. Urwick to Goodison, 20 July 1966, FO 371.186549/EJ 1015/44, PRO.
49. Dann, *King Hussein and the Challenge of Arab Radicalism*, p. 151.
50. On Prince Muhammad's views, see Urwick to Goodison, 3 August 1966, FO 371.186549/EJ 1015/51(A), PRO.
51. Some of Khammash's views are summarised in Phayre to MOD, 22 September 1964, FO 371.175677/MA 11196, PRO.
52. See Syed Ali el-Edroos, *The Hashemite Arab Army, 1909–1979: an Analysis of Military Operations* (Amman: The Publishing Committee, 1980), pp. 324–5.
53. Details of the reshuffle can be found in Parkes to FO, 5 May 1965, FO 371.180748/EJ 1201/6, PRO; and Phillips to Morris, 5 January 1965, FO 371.180729/EJ 1015/5/G, PRO.
54. Phayre to MOD, 6 May 1965, FO 371.180748/MA/10101, PRO.
55. Phayre to MOD, 6 May 1965, FO 371.180748/MA/10101, PRO.

8   Jordan's March to War

1. This figure comes from Douglas Little, 'A Puppet in Search of a Puppeteer?': the United States, King Hussein, and Jordan, 1953–1970', *The International History Review*, 17:3 (August 1995), 535. Details on the raid and its aftermath can be found in Adams to FO, 21 November 1966, FO 371.186550/EJ 1015/78; Pullar to FO, 23 November 1966, FO 371.186550/EJ 1015/79; and Adams to FO, 23 November 1966, FO 371.186550/EJ 1015/80, all Public Record Office (PRO), London.

2. For details, see Asher Susser, *On Both Banks of the Jordan: a Political Biography of Wasfi al-Tall* (London: Frank Cass, 1994), pp. 111–12. `Abbas Murad writes that anti-government pamphlets were distributed by members of the Jordanian army – calling themselves the 'Revolutionary Committee of Jordanian Free Officers' – after the al-Sam`u raid. See his *Al-daur al-siyassi lil-jaysh al-urdunni* [The Political Role of the Jordanian Army] (Beirut: Palestine Liberation Organisation Research Center, 1973), p. 120.

3. Eric Rouleau, 'Crisis in Jordan', *The World Today* (February 1967), 65.

4. See Adams to FO, 23 November 1966, FO 371.186550/EJ 1015/80, PRO.

5. See Adams to Morris, 30 November 1966, FO 371.186550/EJ 1015/104; and Urwick to Goodison, 7 December 1966, FO 371.186550/EJ 1015/116, both PRO.

6. Cited in Susser, *On Both Banks of the Jordan*, p. 116.

7. Barbour to Rusk, 14 November 1966, cited in Uriel Dann, *King Hussein and the Challenge of Arab Radicalism: Jordan, 1955–1967* (New York: Oxford University Press, 1989), p. 198, n. 4.

8. Mohammad Ibrahim Faddah, *The Middle East in Transition: a Study of Jordan's Foreign Policy* (Bombay: Asia Publishing House, 1974), p. 87

9. Dann, *King Hussein and Challenge of Arab Radicalism*, p. 155.

10. Little, 'A Puppet in Search of a Puppeteer?', 535. Also, Minute by Morris, 22 December 1966, FO 371.186579/EJ 1193/16, PRO.

11. See Susser, *On Both Banks of the Jordan*, p. 117. A complete listing of the Lower House can be found in *Al-watha`iq al-urdunniyya: majlis al-umma al-urdunni, 1921–1984* [Jordanian Documents: The Jordanian National Assembly, 1921–1984] (Amman: Ministry of Information, 1984), pp. 35–7.

12. P.J. Vatikiotis makes these points in his prescient Epilogue to *Politics and the Military in Jordan: a Study of the Arab Legion, 1921–1957* (London: Frank Cass, 1967), pp. 157–8.

13. Cited in Peter Young, *The Israeli Campaign 1967* (London: William Kimber, 1967), p. 47. As Glubb had noted in the mid-1950s: The 'Arab Legion had never lost a battle and the Syrian army had rarely won one.' Sir John Bagot Glubb, *A Soldier with the Arabs* (London: Houghton and Stodder, 1957), p. 367. Al-Tell's views on the politicised nature of the Arab armies can be found in Wasfi al-Tell, *Kitabat fi al-qadayya al-`arabiyya*, pp. 325–6. Kamal al-Sha`ir argues that the Egyptian military defeat in 1956 should have convinced Jordan beyond a shadow of a doubt that the Arabs had no firm military option against Israel. Interview with Kamal al-Sha`ir, 25 April 1995, Amman.

14. Interview with Kamal al-Sha`ir, 25 April 1995, Amman.

15. Mutawi, 'Jordan in the 1967 War', 193. Al-Tell argued that neither Jordan nor the Arab powers had studied the al-Samu` battle properly. The tactics

Israel employed there, he insisted, would be the same tactics the Jewish state would use in the June war: 'It was an example of the military operation that took place later.' See al-Tell, *Kitabat fi al-qadayya al-`arabiyya*, p. 327.

16. Conversation with Ambassador Adnan Abu `Udeh, 24 June 1997, Paris.
17. Mutawi, 'Jordan in the 1967 War', 193.
18. 'The Least Unreasonable Arab', *Newsweek*, 14 July 1967, 23.
19. See Richard B. Parker, *The Politics of Miscalculation in the Middle East* (Bloomington: Indiana University Press, 1993), pp. 3–20.
20. Quoted in Tim Hewat (ed.), *War File* (London: Cox and Wyman, 1967), p. 62.
21. Interview with Muhammad Ahmad Salim, 7 April 1995, Irbid.
22. Phillips to Walker, Annual Review for 1964, 7 January 1965, FO 371.180738/EJ 1011/1, PRO.
23. Mutawi, 'Jordan in the 1967 War', 234.
24. Snow, *Hussein*, p. 64. Also, Glubb, *A Soldier with the Arabs*, pp. 366–9.
25. National Intelligence Estimate, 23 January 1963 in FRUS, 1962–1963, Vol. XVIII, p. 318.
26. Phayre to Parkes, Annual Despatch on Jordan Arab Army for 1963, 7 January 1964, FO 371.175673/MA/11090, PRO.
27. Minute by McLean on War Between Israel and Jordan, 27 September 1965, in FO 371.180653, PRO.
28. Memorandum from Komer to Bundy, 30 April 1963 in FRUS, 1962–1963, Vol. XVIII, p. 504.
29. Cited in Mutawi, 'Jordan in the 1967 War', 196.
30. Mutawi, 'Jordan in the 1967 War', 193.
31. Snow, *Hussein*, p. 179.
32. See, for example, Cairo to FO, 6 December 1966, FO 371.186554/EJ 103116/10, PRO.
33. Urwick to Goodison, 30 November 1966, FO 371.186550/EJ 1015/106, PRO.
34. Cairo to FO, 6 December 1966, FO 371.186554/EJ 103116/10, PRO.
35. On Nasser's claims to Hussein, see al-Tell, *Kitabat fi al-qadayya al-`arabiyya*, pp. 331–2.
36. Interview with Muhammad Ahmad Salim, 7 April 1995, Irbid. Wasfi al-Tell's description of the war can be found in Vick Vance and Pierre Lauer, *Hussein of Jordan: My 'War' with Israel* (London: Peter Owen, 1969), pp. 125–30.
37. Melman and Raviv, *Behind the Uprising*, p. 79.
38. Golda Meir, *My Life* (London: Wiedenfeld and Nicolson, 1975), pp. 298 and 306, respectively. Israeli General Uzi Narkiss believes that 'Hussein did not really believe the war would break out.' See his *The Liberation of Jerusalem: the Battle of 1967* (London: Valentine, Mitchell, 1983), p. 46. For Israel's relations with Jordan, see the Middle East files for 1967 in PREM 13/1622.
39. Yitzhak Rabin, *The Rabin Memoirs* (London: Wiedenfeld and Nicolson, 1979), pp. 81–2. Jordan's Western Front commander confirms that he passed Odd Bull's warning to higher headquarters. Interview with Muhammad Ahmad Salim, 7 April 1995, Irbid. Also, Hadow to Brown, 6 July 1967, PREM 13/1622/ER2/16.
40. Dann, *King Hussein and the Challenge of Arab Radicalism*, p. 163.
41. Patrick Seale, for one, believes that Jordan had no reason to trust Israel after al-Sam`u. Correspondence with Patrick Seale, 25 February 1997. Michael B. Oren takes the opposite view and argues that Israel did not want war in 1967.

See 'Did Israel want the Six Day War?' (Spring 1999), published on the Azure website on http://www.azure.org.il/7-Oren.html. Oren's interpretation of events will be published in his forthcoming book on the June 1967 war.

42. Snow, *Hussein*, p. 183. On 7 June, Moshe Dayan, defence minister of Israel, replied to Hussein's bombastic statement: 'We have been offering the King an opportunity to cut his losses since Monday morning.' 'So tell him that from now on, I'll talk to him only with the gunsights of our tanks!' Cited in Vance and Lauer, *My 'War' with Israel*, p. 65. After the war started, Israel told British Diplomats that King Hussein could demonstrate his desire to end the fighting by dismissing the Egyptian commander of Jordan's armed forces. See Hadow to Brown, 6 July 1967, PREM 13/1622/ER2/16.

43. Memo by Helms to Rostow, cited in Gerges, *The Superpowers and the Middle East*, p. 215.

44. Mutawi, 'Jordan in the 1967 War', 250. Qassim Muhammad Salih offers little analysis, but provides a concise description of the Jordanian order of battle in his *Al-jaysh al-`arabi al-hashimi wa daurihi fi al-harub al`arabiyya al-isra'iliyya* [The Hashemite Arab Army and its Role in the Arab–Israeli Wars] (Amman: Mudarayya al-Tawjihi, 1988), pp. 51–2.

45. James Lunt, *Hussein of Jordan* (London: Macmillan, 1989), p. 106. Similar views to Lunt's can be found in Hadow to Brown, 6 July 1967, PREM 13/1622/ER2/16 and in the details of the June 1967 fighting in FCO 17/490 and FCO 17/489.

46. Snow, *Hussein*, p. 193.

47. Interview with Tariq Masarweh, 13 May 1996, Amman. For the postwar mood in the Jordanian armed forces, see Tripp to Moore, 20 January 1968, FCO 17/248/J3/21.

48. Lunt, *Hussein of Jordan*, p. 100.

49. Interview with Habis al-Majali, 12 April 1993, Amman; also, interview with Fahd Jureidat, 12 April 1993, Amman.

50. Mutawi, 'Jordan in the 1967 War', 303.

51. Suleiman Musa, 'Harb huzayran 1967: safhat min tarikh al-urdunn al-hadith' [The June 1967 War: Pages from Modern Jordanian History], *al-Ra'i* (13 April 1995), 18.

52. The figures in this and the next paragraph are cited in Mutawi, 'Jordan in the 1967 War', 320–8.

53. Lieutenant-General Muhammad Ishaq Hakuz recalls that Khammash gave a speech at the al-Zarqa officers club in April 1967 in which he proclaimed that Jordan, with Egypt's assistance, could defeat the Israelis. Interview with Muhammad Ishaq Hakuz, 20 April 1995, Amman. Hakuz records his views on the Palestine problem in his *Mudhakarat wa awraq `askari `an al-qadayya al-filastiniyya, 1948–1964* [Memoirs and Papers of a Soldier about the Palestine Problem, 1948–1964] (Amman: Al-Bayt University Press, 1994).

54. See M. Graeme Bannerman, 'Hashimite [sic] Kingdom of Jordan', in David E. Long and Bernard Reich (eds), *The Governments and Politics of the Middle East and North Africa* (Boulder: Westview, 1986), p. 229.

55. See the article, 'The Last Unreasonable Arab', *Time*, 14 July 1967.

56. Neff, *Warriors for Jerusalem*, p. 204.

57. Interview with Kamal al-Sha`ir, 21 April 1995, Amman. Al-Sha`ir supported al-Tell and `Atef al-Majali's opposition to war in 1967 and went as far as requesting a personal audience with the king in May to dissuade him.

58. Interview with Ma`an Abu Nuwar, 14 May 1996, Amman.
59. On Hussein's disenchantment with the UAC, see Amman to FO, 23 November 1966, FO 371.186550/EJ 1015/97; and Amman to FO, 30 November 1966, FO 371.186550/EJ 1015/99. On the king's affirmation of 'Jordan's continued support for the Unified Arab Command', see Amman to FO, 3 December 1966, FO 371.186550/EJ 1015/103, all PRO.
60. Snow, *Hussein*, p. 193 [emphasis in original].
61. *Ibid.*, p. 173.
62. Vatikiotis, *Politics and the Military in Jordan*, p. 162.
63. Gerges, *The Superpowers and the Middle East*, p. 215.
64. Andrew and Leslie Cockburn, *Dangerous Liaison: the Inside Story of the US–Israeli Covert Relationship* (New York: Harper Perennial, 1991), p. 149.
65. Cockburn, *Dangerous Liaison*, p. 151.
66. See al-Tell, *Kitabat fi al-qadayya al-`arabiyya*, p. 333. For Wasfi al-Tell's postwar thinking about how Jordan should transform itself into a 'war society', see the Jordan files in FCO 17/219.
67. See William B. Quandt, *Peace Process: American Diplomacy and the Arab–Israeli Conflict since 1967* (Berkeley: University of California Press, 1993), pp. 25–48.
68. Mutawi, 'Jordan in the 1967 War', 354.
69. Snow, *Hussein*, p. 81.
70. See John Bagot Glubb, *The Changing Scenes of Life: an Autobiography* (London: Quartet Books, 1983), p. 188; also, Trevor Royle, *Glubb Pasha* (London: Abacus, 1993), p. 487.
71. Young, *The Israeli Campaign 1967*, p. 126.
72. Young, *The Israeli Campaign 1967*, p. 126. Journalist Abdullah Schleifer, who was in Jerusalem during the fighting, argues that Jerusalem could have been saved had adequate defence preparations been made. He suggests that Jerusalem's maze of streets, alleyways, and tunnels could 'have provided the cover and confusion to have held off a division for days.' Further, he writes that arming and training the West Bank's population would have made Israel's capture of the territory quite difficult. See Abdullah Schleifer, *The Fall of Jerusalem* (New York: Monthly Review Press, 1972), p. 197.
73. Lunt, *Hussein of Jordan*, p. 24.
74. For an overview of the battle and the 'political mythology' surrounding the event, see W. Andrew Terrill, 'The Political Mythology of the Battle of Karameh', *Middle East Journal*, 55:1 (Winter 2001), 91–111. Also, interview with Zaid al-Rifa`i, 21 April 1993, Amman.
75. See Jamal Halaby, 'Jordan King Says 1967 War a Mistake', *Associated Press*, 5 June 1997.

Select Bibliography

Archives and private papers

Public Record Office, Kew, London

Files consulted for 1955–67:
FO 371   – Political
PREM 11   – Prime Minister's Papers
CAB 128   – Cabinet Office Minutes
CAB 129   – Cabinet Office Memoranda
DEFE 5   – Chiefs of Staff Committee Memoranda
DEFE 6   – Chiefs of Staff Committee/Joint Planning Staff Memoranda
PREM 13   – Prime Minister's Papers
FCO 17   – Political

National Archives, Washington, DC

Files consulted for 1955–67:
RG 59   – Jordan Files
RG 84   – Amman Embassy Records
RG 218   – Joint Chiefs of Staff
RG 330   – Secretary of Defense
Miscellaneous files from the National Security Council and State Department
Office of Intelligence Research

*Jordanian Ministry of Culture and Information, Department of Libraries,
Documentation, and National Archives (*Mudiriya al-maktabat
wa'l-watha'iq al-watiniyya*), Amman*

Files consulted for 1955–67:
143/14   – Jordan Development Board
216/4   – Parliamentary Minutes
225/5   – Parliamentary Questions
230/10   – Jordan Development Board
548/1   – Prime Minister's Directives
592/2   – Public Security
1084/6   – National Guard

The Hashemite Room, University Library, University of Jordan, Amman

Official Gazette (Jarida rasmiyya) [1955–67]
Minutes of Senate/Lower House Meetings [1955–67]

Private Papers Collection, Middle East Centre, St Antony's College, Oxford, England

Patrick Coghill Papers
J.B. Slade-Baker Papers

Room 132, Bodleian Library, University of Oxford

Files consulted for 1955–67:
CAB 128 – Cabinet Office Minutes
CAB 129 – Cabinet Office Memoranda

Other Private Papers

Qarar al-mahkama al-`urfiyya al-`askariyya al-khassa [Decision of the Special Military Court Martial], unpublished document relating to the April 1957 conspiracy, private collection of Mike Doran

Published collections of documents

Jordanian Ministry of Information. *Al-watha'iq al-urdunniyya: al-wazarat al-urdunniyya, 1921–1984* [Jordanian Documents: Jordanian Ministries, 1921–1984]. Amman: Ministry of Information, Directorate of Press and Publications, 1984.
——*Al-watha`iq al-urdunniyya: majlis al-umma al–urdunni, 1921–1984* [Jordanian Documents: The Jordanian National Assembly, 1921–1984]. Amman: Ministry of Information, Directorate of Press and Publications, 1984.
——*Al-majmu`a al-kamila li-khutub jalalat al-malik al-Hussein bin-Talal al-mu`adhim, 1952–1985* [Complete Collection of the speeches of His Majesty King Hussein bin Talal the Great, 1952–1985]. Amman: Ministry of Information, Directorate of Press and Publications, n.d.
Khayr, Hani Salim (ed.), *Al-sajl al-tarikhi al-musawwar, 1920–1990* [The Illustrated Historical Record, 1920–1990]. Amman: Al-Ayman Printing Press, 1990.
United Arab Republic Information Department. *President Gamal Abdel-Nasser's Speeches and Press Interviews.* Cairo: UAR Information Department, 1958.
United States. Department of State. Historical Office. *American Foreign Policy, Current Documents 1958.* Washington: US Government Printing Office, 1962.
——*Foreign Relations of the United States, 1955–1957, Near East: Jordan and Yemen, Volume XIII.* Washington: US Government Printing Office, 1988.
——*Foreign Relations of the United States, 1958–1960: Lebanon and Jordan, Volume XI.* Washington: US Government Printing Office, 1992.
——*Foreign Relations of the United States, 1962–1963: Near East, Volume XVIII.* Washington: US Government Printing Office, 1995.
Zinner, Paul E. (ed.), *Documents on American Foreign Relations 1958.* New York: Council on Foreign Relations, 1959.

Newspapers and periodicals

Various articles, obituaries, and reviews cited from:
Al-Ahram (Cairo)
The Economist (London)

Financial Times (London)
The Guardian (London)
The Independent (London)
Jordan Times (Amman)
Mideast Mirror (Beirut)
Al-Quds al-`Arabi (London)
Al-Ra'i (Amman)
The Scotsman
Washington Post

Theses and dissertations

Mutawi, Samir Abdallah. 'Jordan in the 1967 War.' Doctoral thesis, University of Reading, 1985.
Tal, Lawrence. 'Politics, the Military, and National Security in Jordan, 1955–1967.' Doctoral thesis, University of Oxford, 1997.

Interviews

Major-General Ma`an Abu Nuwar: Head of Public Security Department/Minister, 14 May 1996 (Amman).
Abdel Ra`uf Abu Rasa': Jordanian historian, 16 April 1995 (Amman).
Salah Abu Zaid: Minister of Information/Hashemite Broadcasting Service/ personal advisor to King Hussein, 17 April 1995 (Amman).
Brigadier Nayif Muhammad al-Bataynah: Jordan Arab Army, 7 April 1995 (Irbid).
Hamid al-Farhan: Jordan Development Board/Arab nationalist activist, 20 and 21 April 1993 (Amman).
`Akif al-Fayiz: Minister/tribal leader of the Bani Sakhir confederation, 5 May 1995 (Amman) [Interview conducted by Raad Alkadiri].
Major-General Fahd Jureidat: Jordan Arab Army, 12 April 1993 (Amman).
Lieutenant-General Muhammad Ishaq Hakuz: Jordanian Representative to Mixed Armistice Commission/Jordan Arab Army, 20 April 1995 (Amman).
Major-General James Lunt: Arab Legion officer/author, 17 March 1993 (Oxford).
Mahmud al-Ma`ayta: Free Officer/Ba`thist activist involved in 1957 coup attempt, 15 April 1993 (Amman).
Field Marshall Habis al-Majali: Commander-in-Chief, Jordan Arab Army, 12 April 1993 (Amman).
Tariq Masarwah: Hashemite Broadcasting Service/journalist, 13 May 1996 (Amman).
Brigadier Hikmat Mihayr: Head, Public Security Department, 13 April 1993 (Amman).
Zaid Nuwairan: Corporal, Royal Jordanian Signals Regiment, 1 April 1995 (Amman).
Zaid al-Rifa`i: Prime Minister/Senator/personal advisor to King Hussein, 21 April 1993 (Amman).
Muhammad Sa`ad (pseudonym): Islamic Liberation Party activist, 14 April 1995 (Irbid).
Major-General Muhammad Ahmad Salim: Western Front Commander during June 1967 War, Jordan Arab Army, 7 April 1995 (Irbid).

Omar Kayid al-Salim: Ba`thist student activist involved in 1963 Tripartite Unity riots, 16 August 1995 (Houston).
Kamal al-Sha`ir: Minister/Senator/Ba`thist activist, 21 April 1995 (Amman).
Major-General Sadiq al-Shar`a: Chief of Staff, Jordan Arab Army, 12 April 1993 (Amman).
Major-General Salih al-Shar`a: Jordan Arab Army, 19 April 1993 (Amman).
Abdel Rahman Shuqayr: National Front leader, 20 April 1993 (Amman).
Brigadier Osama al-Sukhin: Legal Counsel, Jordan Arab Army, 19 April 1993 (Amman).
Ali Ibrahim al-Tell: Lieutenant, Royal Jordanian Artillery, 11 April 1993 (Irbid).
Moraiwid al-Tell: Private Secretary to King Hussein, 6 April 1993 (Amman) and 4 July 1996 (Oxford).
Yusef `Abdel Qadir al-Tell: Finance Manager, Ministry of Foreign Affairs, 7 April 1995 (Irbid).

Arabic and English memoirs

Abdullah, bin al-Hussein. *My Memoirs Completed, 'al-Takmilah.'* London: Longman, 1978.
Abu Nuwar, Ali. *Hayn talashat al-`arab: mudhakarat fi al-siyassa al-`arabiyya (1948–1964)* [When the Arabs Decline: Memoirs of Arab Politics (1948–1964)]. London: Dar al-Saqi, 1990.
Abu Shahut, Shahir Yusef. *Al-jaysh wa al-siyassa fi al-urdunn: dhikriyat `an harakat al-dubat al-urdunniyeen al-ahrar* [Army and Politics in Jordan: Memories of the Jordanian Free Officers Movement]. N.P.: al-Qabas Publishing, 1985.
Burns, E.L.M. *Between Arab and Israeli*. London: George G. Harrap, 1962.
Dayan, Moshe. *The Diary of the Sinai Campaign 1956*. London: Sphere, 1967.
Eden, Anthony. *Full Circle*. London: Cassell, 1960.
El-Sadat, Anwar. *In Search of Identity: an Autobiography*. London: Fontana, 1978.
Eveland, Wilbur Crane. *Ropes of Sand: America's Failure in the Middle East*. London: Norton, 1980.
Glubb, John Bagot. *A Soldier with the Arabs*. London: Hodder and Stoughton, 1957.
— *The Changing Scenes of Life: an Autobiography*. London: Quartet Books, 1983.
Hakuz, Muhammad Ishaq. *Mudhakarat wa awraq `askari `an al-qadaya al-filastiniyya, 1948–1964* [Memoirs and Papers of a Soldier about the Palestine Problem, 1948–1964]. Amman: Al-Bayt University Press, 1994.
Heikal, Mohamed H. *Cutting the Lion's Tail: Suez Through Egyptian Eyes*. London: Andre Deutsch, 1986.
Hussein, bin Talal. *Uneasy Lies the Head*. London: Heinemann, 1962.
— *Mahnati ka-malik* [My Job as King]. Amman: The National Press, 1986.
Johnston, Charles. *The Brink of Jordan*. London: Hamish Hamilton, 1972.
Jum`a, Sa`ad, *Al-mu'amarah wa ma`araka al-masir* [The Conspiracy and the Battle of Destiny]. Beirut: Dar al-Katab al-Arabi, 1968.
Kocher, Eric. *Foreign Intrigue: the Making and Unmaking of a Foreign Service Officer*. Far Hills: New Horizon Press, 1990.
Macmillan, Harold. *Riding the Storm, 1956–1959*. London: Macmillan, 1971.
Al-Majali, Hazza`. *Mudhakkarati* [My Memoirs]. Beirut: Dar al-`ilm lil-Malayeen Press, 1960.

Meir, Golda. *My Life*. London: Wiedenfeld and Nicolson, 1975.
Narkiss, Uzi. *The Liberation of Jerusalem: the Battle of 1967*. London: Valentine, Mitchell, 1983.
Nutting, Anthony. *No End of a Lesson: the Story of Suez*. London: Constable, 1967.
Parsons, Anthony. *They Say the Lion: Britain's Legacy to the Arabs*. London: Jonathan Cape, 1986.
Rabin, Yitzhak. *The Rabin Memoirs*. London: Wiedenfeld and Nicolson, 1979.
Al-Sha`ir, Jamal. *Siyassi yatadhakkir* [A Politician Remembers]. London: Riyad al-Rayyes, 1987.
Al-Shar`a, Salih. *Mudhakkarat jundi* [Memories of a Soldier]. Amman: n.p., 1985.
Al-Shuqayri, Ahmad. *Min al-qima ila al-hazima ma` al-maluk wa al-ru`sa`* [From the Summit to the Defeat with Kings and Presidents]. Beirut: Dar al-`Awdah, 1971.

Books and articles

Arabic

Al-`Abidi, 'Awni Jadu`a. *Hizb al-tahrir al-islami* [Islamic Liberation Party]. Amman: Dar al-Liwa' Press, 1993.
Aboudia, Sa`ad. *`Amaliyat ittikhadh al-qarar fi-siyassat al-urdunn al-kharijiyya* [The Foreign Policy Decisionmaking Process in Jordan]. Amman: n.p., 1983.
Daghur, Ahmad. *Aghwar al-urdunn* [The Jordan Valley]. Amman: Dar Rashd, 1988.
Al-Kilani, Musa Zeid. *Al-harakat al-islamiyya fi al-urdunn* [The Islamic Movements in Jordan]. Amman: Dar al-Bashir, 1990.
Al-Madi, Munib and Suleiman Musa. *Tarikh al-urdunn fi al-qarn al-`ashreen* [The History of Jordan in the Twentieth Century]. Amman: n.p., 1959; 2nd ed., Amman: Maktaba al-Muhtasab, 1988.
M`arouf, Iskander. *Al-urdunn al-jadid wa al-ittihad al-`arabi* [New Jordan and the Arab Union]. Baghdad: The New Iraq Press, 1958.
Al-Mashal, Muhammad Sa`id. 'Al-tarikh al-awal li-harakat fatah: kayf ta'asasit wa kayf intalaqat?' [The First History of the Fatah Movement: How was it Established and how did it Take Off?]. *Al-Quds al-`Arabi* (20 March 1994): 7.
Murad, `Abbas. *Al-daur al-siyassi lil-jaysh al-urdunni, 1921–1973* [The Political Role of the Jordanian Army, 1921–1973]. Beirut: Palestine Liberation Organisation Research Center, 1973.
Musa, Suleiman. *Al-`alam min al-urdunn: safhat min tarikh al-`arab al-hadith* [Prominent Personalities from Jordan: Pages from Modern Arab History]. Amman: Dar al-Sha`ab, 1986.
Musa, Suleiman, 'Harb huzayran 1967: safhat min tarikh al-urdunn al-hadith' [The June 1967 War: Pages from Modern Jordanian History]. *al-Ra`i* (13 April 1995): 18.
Salih, Muhammad. *Al-jaysh al-`arabi al-hashimi wa daurihi fi al-harub al`arabiyya al-isra'iliyya* [The Hashemite Arab Army and its Role in the Arab–Israeli Wars]. Amman: Mudarayya al-Tawjihi, 1988.
Al-Tell, Wasfi. *Kitabat fi al-qadayya al-`arabiyya* [Writings on the Arab Problem]. Amman: Dar al-Liwa`, 1980.

English

Abidi, Aqil Hyder Hasan. *Jordan: a Political Study, 1948–1957*. London: Asia Publishing House, 1965.

Abu Jaber, Kamel S. 'The Jordanian Parliament', in *Man, State and Society in the Contemporary Middle East*, ed. Jacob M. Landau, pp. 91–121. London: Pall Mall Press, 1972.

Aburish, Said K. *The St. George Hotel Bar*. London: Bloomsbury, 1989.

Anderson, Lisa. 'Absolutism and the Resilience of Monarchy in the Middle East', *Political Science Quarterly* 106 (1991): 1–15.

Amin, S.H. *Middle East Legal Systems*. Glasgow: Royston Limited, 1985.

Aruri, Nasser H. *Jordan: a Study in Political Development (1921–1965)*. The Hague: Martinus Nijhoff, 1972.

Bannerman, M. Graeme. 'Hashimite [sic] Kingdom of Jordan', in *The Governments and Politics of the Middle East and North Africa*, eds David E. Long and Bernard Reich, pp. 220–39. Boulder: Westview, 1986.

Be`eri, Eliezer. *Army Officers in Arab Politics and Society*. London: Praeger, 1970.

Bloch, Jonathan and Patrick Fitzgerald. *British Intelligence and Covert Action: Africa, Middle East and Europe Since 1945*. Junction: London, 1983.

Brand, Laurie A. *Jordan's Inter-Arab Relations: the Political Economy of Alliance Making*. New York: Columbia University Press, 1994.

Brynen, Rex. 'Economic Crisis and Post-Rentier Democratization in the Arab World: the Case of Jordan', *Canadian Journal of Political Science* 25 (March 1992): 69–97.

Childers, Erskine B. *The Road to Suez: a Study of Western–Arab Relations*. London: MacGibbon and Kee, 1962.

Cockburn, Andrew and Leslie. *Dangerous Liaison: the Inside Story of the US–Israeli Covert Relationship*. New York: Harper Perennial, 1991.

Cooley, John K. *Green March, Black September: the Story of the Palestinian Arabs*. London: Frank Cass, 1973.

Copeland, Miles. *The Game of Nations: the Amorality of Power Politics*. London: Weidenfeld and Nicolson, 1969.

— *The Game Player*. London: Aurum, 1989.

Cordesman, Anthony H. *After the Storm: the Changing Military Balance in the Middle East*. Boulder: Westview Press, 1993.

Crystal, Jill. 'Authoritarianism and its Adversaries in the Arab World', *World Politics* 46 (January 1994): 262–89.

Dann, Uriel. 'Regime and Opposition in Jordan since 1949', in *Society and Political Structure in the Arab World*, ed. Menachem Milson, pp. 145–81. New York: Humanities Press, 1973.

— 'The Foreign Office, the Baghdad Pact and Jordan', *Asian and African Studies* 21 (1987): 247–62.

— *King Hussein and the Challenge of Arab Radicalism: Jordan, 1955–1967*. New York: Oxford University Press, 1989.

Dessouki, Ali E. Hillal and Karen Aboul Kheir. 'The Politics of Vulnerability and Survival: the Foreign Policy of Jordan', in *The Foreign Policies of Arab States: the Challenge of Change*, eds Bahgat Korany and Ali E. Hillal Dessouki, pp. 216–35. Boulder: Westview, 1991.

Dodd, C.H. and Mary Sales (eds), *Israel and the Arab World*. London: Routledge and Kegan Paul, 1970.

Dupuy, Trevor N. *Elusive Victory: the Arab–Israeli Wars, 1967–1974*. London: MacDonald and Jance, 1978.

El-Edroos, Syed Ali. *The Hashemite Arab Army, 1908–1979: an Appreciation and Analysis of Military Operations.* Amman: The Publishing Committee, 1980.

Faddah, Mohammad Ibrahim. *The Middle East in Transition: a Study of Jordan's Foreign Policy.* Bombay: Asia Publishing House, 1974.

Fischbach, Michael R. 'The Implications of Jordanian Land Policy for the West Bank', *Middle East Journal* 48 (Summer 1994): 492–509.

Gabriel, Richard A. and Alan Scott MacDougall. 'Jordan', in *Fighting Armies: Antagonists in the Middle East, a Combat Assessment,* ed. Richard A. Gabriel, pp. 27–40. Westport: Greenwood, 1983.

Garfinkle, Adam M. 'Jordan and Arab Polarization', *Current History* (January 1982): 24–8.

—*Israel and Jordan in the Shadow of War: Functional Ties and Futile Diplomacy in a Small Place.* London: Macmillan, 1992.

Gerber, Haim. *The Social Origins of the Modern Middle East.* London: Mansell Publishing, Limited, 1987.

Gerges, Fawaz A. *The Superpowers and the Middle East: Regional and International Politics, 1955–1967.* Boulder: Westview Press, 1994.

Glubb, John Bagot. 'Violence on the Jordan-Israel Border', *Foreign Affairs* 32 (July 1954): 552–62.

Golan, Galia. *Soviet Policies in the Middle East: From World War II to Gorbachev.* Cambridge: Cambridge University Press, 1990.

Haas, Marius. *Husseins Königreich* [Hussein's Kingdom]. Munich: Tuduv Buch, 1975.

Harris, George L. *Jordan: Its People, Its Society, Its Culture.* New York: Grove Press, 1958.

Hewat, Tim (ed.), *War File.* London: Cox and Wyman, 1967.

Howard, Harry N. 'Jordan in Turmoil', *Current History* (January 1972): 14–19.

Howard, Michael and Robert Hunter. 'The Six Day War', in *Comparative Defense Policy,* eds Frank B. Horton, III, Anthony C. Rogerson, and Edward C. Warner, III, pp. 550–65. Baltimore: The Johns Hopkins University Press, 1974.

Huntington, Samuel P. *Political Order in Changing Societies.* New Haven: Yale University Press, 1968.

Hurewitz, J.C. *Middle East Politics: the Military Dimension.* Boulder: Westview Press, 1982.

Jabber, Fuad. 'The Palestinian Resistance and Inter-Arab Politics', in *The Politics of Palestinian Nationalism.* William B. Quandt, Fuad Jabber, and Ann Mosely Lesch, pp. 157–216. Berkeley: University of California Press, 1973.

Kanovsky, E. *The Economy of Jordan: the Implications of Peace in the Middle East.* Tel Aviv: University Publishing Projects, 1976.

Kennedy, Gavin. *The Military in the Third World.* London: Gerald Duckworth, 1974.

Kerr, Malcolm. *The Arab Cold War: Gamal `Abd al-Nasir and his Rivals, 1958–1970.* London: Oxford University Press, 1971.

Khader, Bichara and Adnan Badran. *The Economic Development of Jordan.* London: Croom Helm, 1987.

Kimmerling, Baruch and Joel S. Migdal. *Palestinians: the Making of a People.* New York: The Free Press, 1993.

Kyle, Keith. *Suez.* London: Weidenfeld and Nicolson, 1991.

Little, Douglas. 'A Puppet in Search of a Puppeteer?: the United States, King Hussein, and Jordan, 1953–1970', *The International History Review* 17 (August 1995): 505–41.

Lunt, James. *Hussein of Jordan: a Political Biography*. London: Macmillan, 1989.

Mansfield, Peter. *Nasser*. London: Methuen, 1969.

— *A History of the Middle East*. London: Penguin, 1991.

Mazur, Michael P. *Economic Growth and Development in Jordan*. London: Croom Helm, 1979.

Migdal, Joel S. 'Dispersal and Annexation: Jordanian Rule', in *Palestinian Society and Politics*, ed. Joel S. Migdal, pp. 34–43. Princeton: Princeton University Press, 1979.

Milward, Alan S. *War, Economy and Society, 1939–1945*. London: Penguin, 1977.

Monroe, Elizabeth. *Britain's Moment in the Middle East, 1914–1956*. London: Chatto and Windus, 1963.

Morris, Benny. *Israel's Border Wars, 1949–1956*. Oxford: Clarendon Press, 1993.

Morris, James. *The Hashemite Kings*. London: Faber and Faber, 1959.

Mosely, Leonard. *Dulles: a Biography of Allen and John Foster Dulles and their Family Networks*. New York: The Dial Press, 1978.

Mufti, Malik. 'The United States and Nasserist Pan-Arabism', in *The Middle East and the United States: a Historical and Political Reassessment*, ed. David W. Lesch, pp. 167–86. Boulder: Westview, 1996.

Mutawi, Samir. *Jordan in the 1967 War*. Cambridge: Cambridge University Press, 1987.

Nevo, Joseph. 'Is there a Jordanian Entity?' *The Jerusalem Quarterly* 16 (Summer 1980): 98–110.

Oren, Michael B. 'A Winter of Discontent: Britain's Crisis in Jordan, December 1955–March 1956', *International Journal of Middle Eastern Studies* 22 (1990): 171–84.

— 'Nuri al-Sa`id and the Question of Arab–Israel Peace, 1953–1957', *Asian and African Studies* 24 (October 1990): 267–82.

— 'Did Israel want the Six Day War?' (Spring 1999), published on the Azure web-site on http://www.azure.org.il/7-Oren.html

Pappé, Ilan. 'Sir Alec Kirkbride and the Making of Greater Transjordan', *Asian and African Studies* 23 (1989): 43–70.

Parker, Richard B. *The Politics of Miscalculation in the Middle East*. Bloomington: Indiana University Press, 1993.

— 'The United States and King Hussein', in *The Middle East and the United States: a Historical and Political Reassessment*, ed. David W. Lesch, pp. 103–16. Boulder: Westview, 1996.

Plascov, Avi. *The Palestinian Refugees in Jordan, 1948–1957*. London: Frank Cass, 1981.

Podeh, Elie. 'The Struggle over Arab Hegemony after the Suez Crisis', *Middle Eastern Studies* 29 (January 1993): 91–110.

Raad, Zeid. 'A Nightmare Avoided: Jordan and Suez 1956', *Israel Affairs* 1 (Winter 1994): 288–308.

Raleigh, J.S. 'The Middle East in 1959 – a Political Survey', *Middle Eastern Affairs* (January 1960): 3–20.

— 'The Middle East in 1960 – a Political Survey', *Middle Eastern Affairs* (February 1961): 34–81.

Raviv, Dan and Yossi Melman. *Behind the Uprising: Israelis, Jordanians and Palestinians*. Westport: Greenwood, 1989.

Reguer, Sara. 'Controversial Waters: Exploitation of the Jordan River', *Middle Eastern Studies* 29 (January 1993): 121–53.

Rouleau, Eric. 'Crisis in Jordan', *The World Today* (February 1967): 60–4.

Royle, Trevor. *Glubb Pasha*. London: Abacus, 1993.

Salibi, Kamal. *The Modern History of Jordan*. London: I.B. Tauris, 1993.

Salloukh, Bassel F. 'State Strength, Permeability, and Foreign Policy Behavior: Jordan in Theoretical Perspective', *Arab Studies Quarterly* 18 (Spring 1996): 39–65.

Satloff, Robert B. *From Abdullah to Hussein: Jordan in Transition*. New York: Oxford University Press, 1994.

——'The Jekyll-and-Hyde Origins of the US–Jordanian Strategic Relationship', in *The Middle East and the United States: a Historical and Political Reassessment*, ed. David W. Lesch, pp. 117–30. Boulder: Westview, 1996.

Saunders, Richard M. 'Military Force in the Foreign Policy of the Eisenhower Presidency', *Political Science Quarterly* 100 (Spring 1985): 97–116.

Schleifer, Abdullah. *The Fall of Jerusalem*. New York: Monthly Review Press, 1972.

Schmidt, Dana Adams. *Armageddon in the Middle East*. New York: The John Day Company, 1974.

Seale, Patrick. *The Struggle for Syria: a study of Post-War Arab Politics, 1945–1958*. London: I.B. Tauris, 1986.

——*Asad of Syria: the Struggle for the Middle East*. Berkeley: University of California Press, 1988.

Shemesh, Moshe. 'The Founding of the PLO, 1964', *Middle Eastern Studies* (October 1984): 105–40.

Shlaim, Avi. *The Politics of Partition: King Abdullah, the Zionists and Palestine, 1921–1951*. Oxford: Oxford University Press, 1990.

Shwadran, Benjamin. *Jordan: a State of Tension*. New York: Council for Middle Eastern Affairs Press, 1959.

——'The Power Struggle in Iraq', *Middle Eastern Affairs* (February 1960): 38–63.

——'Husain Between Qasim and Nasir', *Middle Eastern Affairs* (December 1960): 330–45.

Simon, Reeva S. 'The Hashemite "Conspiracy": Hashemite Unity Attempts, 1921–1958', *International Journal of Middle East Studies* 5 (1974): 314–27.

Snow, Peter. *Hussein: a Biography*. London: Barrie and Jenkins, 1972.

Sparrow, Gerald. *Modern Jordan*. London: George Allen and Unwin, 1961.

Springborg, Robert. 'Patterns of Association in the Egyptian Political Elite', in *Political Elites in the Middle East*, ed. George Lenczowski, pp. 83–107. Washington, DC: American Enterprise Institute, 1975.

Susser, Asher. *On Both Banks of the Jordan: a Political Biography of Wasfi al-Tall*. London: Frank Cass, 1994.

Tal, Lawrence. 'On the Banks of the Stormy Jordan: the Coming Middle East Water Crisis', *Contemporary Review* 260 (April 1992): 169–74.

——'Is Jordan Doomed?' *Foreign Affairs* 72:5 (November/December 1993): 45–58.

——'Britain and the Jordan Crisis of 1958', *Middle Eastern Studies* 31 (January 1995): 39–57.

——'Dealing with Radical Islam: the Case of Jordan', *Survival* 37 (Autumn 1995): 139–56.

Tal, Lawrence. 'Jordan', in *The Cold War in the Middle East*, eds Yezid Sayigh and Avi Shlaim, pp. 102–24. Oxford: Oxford University Press, 1997.

Terrill, W. Andrew. 'The Political Mythology of the Battle of Karameh', *Middle East Journal* 55:1 (Winter 2001): 91–111.

Tessler, Mark. *A History of the Israeli–Palestinian Conflict*. Bloomington: Indiana University Press, 1994.

Teveth, Shabtai. *The Cursed Blessing: the Story of Israel's Occupation of the West Bank*. London: Weidenfeld and Nicolson, 1970.

Tully, Andrew. *CIA: the Inside Story*. New York: Morrow, 1962.

Vance, Vick and Pierre Lauer. *Hussein of Jordan: My 'War' with Israel*. London: Peter Owen, 1969.

Vatikiotis, P.J. *Politics and the Military in Jordan: a Study of the Arab Legion, 1921–1957*. London: Frank Cass, 1967.

Wilson, Mary C. *King Abdullah, Britain and the making of Jordan*. Cambridge: Cambridge University Press, 1987.

— 'King Abdullah and Palestine', *British Society of Middle Eastern Studies Bulletin* 14 (1987): 37–41.

Yorke, Valerie. *Domestic Politics and Regional Security, Jordan, Syria, and Israel: the End of an Era?* Aldershot: Gower for IISS, 1988.

Young, Peter. *The Israeli Campaign 1967*. London: William Kimber, 1967.

Zak, Moshe. 'Israel and Jordan: Strategically Bound', *Israel Affairs* 3 (Autumn 1996): 39–60.

Index

Abdel Illah, Iraqi Crown Prince, 55, 62–3
Abdullah, Radi, 31
Abdullah I, King, 3, 8, 12, 14–15, 73, 99
Abdullah II, King, xii, xiv, 130
Abul Huda, Tawfiq, 22, 29, 131
Abu Nuwar, Ali, 28, 44–9, 102–3, 131
Abu Nuwar, Ma`an, 31, 44, 46, 49, 121
Abu `Udeh, Adnan, 99, 112
Abu Zaid, Salah, 89, 131
`Amer, General Abdel Hakim, 35, 37, 102–3, 119, 121
Arab Union (AU), 55–7
Arab summits,
    first summit, 97, 98
    second summit, 103
    third summit, 106
Arafat, Yasser, 105

Baghdad Pact, 20–1
Ben-Gurion, David, 61–2, 79, 95, 96

Churchill, Colonial Secretary Winston, 2

Dayan, Moshe, 35, 36
Dulles, Secretary of State John Foster, 34, 36, 40, 42, 49, 51, 61

economic development, 4–5, 87, 92
Eden, Prime Minister Anthony, 29–30
Eisenhower, President Dwight D., 49–51, 66, 67–9, 79, 80
Eisenhower Doctrine, 41, 43, 45, 60
elections, parliamentary
    1954 polls, 24
    1956 polls, 38–9
    1961 polls, 85–6
    1962 polls, 92–3
Eshkol, Levi, 111

Faisal II, Iraqi King, 55–6
al-Fatah movement, 104–5

al-Fayiz, `Akif, 15, 48, 76, 83, 93, 131–2
foreign aid to Jordan, 3–4, 27, 41, 50, 53, 67–9, 75
Free Officers
    origins, 26
    factions, 31–4

Glubb, John Bagot, 21–2, 26–30, 116, 123, 132

al-Haditha, Mashour, 9, 120
Hashim, Ibrahim, 24–5, 34, 52, 62, 132
Hashemite Broadcasting Service, 13, 52, 56, 89, 102
Helms, Richard, 119
Hussein, Sherif, 94, 101
Hussein bin Talal
    leadership of, 11–13, 64–5, 98, 108, 117, 124, 127–30, 132
    relations with military, 17, 28
    relations with Nasser, 6, 73, 81, 91, 113–15, 122
    relations with Israel, 6, 96, 110, 118–19
    sacking of Glubb, 27
    views on PLO, 106
    views on USSR, 5, 40, 68
al-Hiyari, Ali, 31, 44–5, 104

intelligence services (Jordanian), 49, 91, 104
Iraqi revolution, 58–60
Islamic Liberation Party, 7, 38, 54

Johnson, President Lyndon, 110–11, 116, 122–3
Jordan, Hashemite Kingdom of
    literature on, xi–xiii, 1
    relations with Soviet Union, 5, 41
    relations with Israel, xiii, 6, 62, 78–9, 95–6, 118–19
    resource scarcity in, 2, 4–5
    state-building in, 2–3

DATE DUE